Labour relations in Eastern
Europe

SOCIAL ANALYSIS
A Series in the Social Sciences
Edited by Richard Scase,
University of Kent

Beyond Class Images: Explorations in the Structure of Social Consciousness
Howard H. Davies

Fundamental Concepts and the Sociological Enterprise
C. C. Harris

Urban Planning in a Capitalist Society
Gwyneth Kirk

The State in Western Europe
Edited by Richard Scase

Autonomy and Control at the Workplace: Contexts for Job Redesign
Edited by John E. Kelly and Chris W. Clegg

The Entrepreneurial Middle Class
Richard Scase and Robert Goffee

Capitalism, the State and Industrial Relations: The Case of Britain
Dominic Strinati

Alcohol, Youth and the State
Nicholas Dorn

The Evolution of Industrial Systems
Timothy Leggatt

Sociological Interpretations of Education
David Blackledge and Barry Hunt

Sociological Approaches to Health and Medicine
Myfanwy Morgan, Michael Calnan and Nick Manning

School Organisation: A Sociological Perspective
William Tyler

Entrepreneurship in Europe
Edited by Robert Goffee and Richard Scase

The Theory and Philosophy of Organizations: Critical Issues and New Perspectives
Edited by John Hassard and Denis Pym

Small Business and Society
David Goss

Deciphering the Enterprise Culture
Roger Burrows

Labour relations in Eastern Europe

Organisational design and dynamics

Krastyu Petkov

and

John E. M. Thirkell

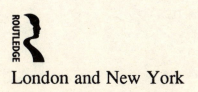

London and New York

First published in 1991
by Routledge
11 New Fetter Lane, London EC4P 4EE

Simultaneously published in the USA and Canada
by Routledg.·
a division of Routledge, Chapman and Hall. Inc.
29 West 35th Street, New York, NY 10001

Laserprinted from authors' disks by LaserScript Limited, Mitcham, Surrey
Printed and bound in Great Britain by
Biddles Ltd, Guildford and King's Lynn

British Library Cataloguing in Publication Data

Thirkell, John E. M.
  Labour relations in Eastern Europe: organisational design
  and dynamics. – (Social analysis).
  1. Eastern Europe. Industrial relations
  I. Title II. Petkov, K. III. Series
  331.0947

  ISBN 0-415-00159-5

Library of Congress Cataloging-in-Publication Data

Has been applied for

For Dragomir Beloev, Dimitrina Dimitrova, Grigor Gradev, Plamen Kerelski and Elena Tseneva – members of the research collective who became self-managing researchers

Contents

List of figures   ix

List of tables   xi

Preface   xiii

Acknowledgements   xvii

Glossary   xix

1   Introduction   1

2   The development of the Soviet model and its transfer to Bulgaria   14

3   Strategy formulation in Bulgaria, 1978–1988   40

4   Case studies and fieldwork in Bulgarian enterprises – research methodology   61

5   Redesigning structures to establish the labour collective   72

6   Counterplanning and worker proposals – designed pressure from below   88

7   Distribution – wage funds, wage interests and pressures from below   103

8   Agreements and the engagement of interests   123

9   Elections – interests, representation and conflicts   132

10   The labour collective, the labour community and self-management – the emergence of organic mechanisms   146

11 Organisational design, the labour process and labour
    relations   160
12 Alternative models of enterprise management – a historical
    and comparative analysis   172

13 Conclusions   202

    Postscript: Redesign of the second structure   211
    Bibliography   223
    Index   230

Figures

P.1 Theorising   xv

1.1 The process of strategy formulation   9

2.1 Enterprise and department forums   35

2.2 The department hierarchy   36

3.1 Traditional model of labour relations   49

3.2 New model of labour relations   49

5.1 Redesign of intermediate level   82

7.1 Distribution of income and profit (industrial enterprises)   106

7.2 Calculation and distribution of profit and income   110

12.1 Models of strategy formulation   200

Tables

3.1 Concepts and the redesign of structures and mechanisms   44

5.1 The diffusion of brigade organisation   77

6.1 Sequence and timing of changes in mechanisms   89

7.1 Calculation of individual earnings in brigade 'A' according to the co-efficient of labour participation   113

7.2 Wage rates (in leva) for different categories of workers   115

7.3 Changes in funds   118

Preface

In 1983 John Thirkell spent six weeks at the Georgi Dimitrov Trade Union Research Institute in Sofia, Bulgaria, under the British Council's Cultural Exchange Scheme. The main aim was to research the brigade system of work organisation, which at that time had rarely been discussed in western academic literature, but a secondary aim was to see if some of the concepts developed for the study of British industrial relations and used in *Strategies Issues and Events in Industrial Relations* (Jackson-Cox *et. al.* 1987) could be applied to a different industrial relations system. The results were published as an article 'Brigade Organisation and Industrial Relations Strategy in Bulgaria 1978–83' (Thirkell 1985). This visit was important for two reasons. First, it showed that in Bulgaria it was possible for an academic from the west to be given research access to interview key industrial informants of a kind that is often difficult to secure in the west and at a time when this was not possible in most socialist countries. Second and more importantly, it was clear from the research in 1983 that Bulgaria was undertaking a major process of strategic change in both economic organisation and labour relations which would continue to develop through the 1980s and which merited extended study. John Thirkell realised that the only practicable way of undertaking the extensive fieldwork that such a project entailed was on a collaborative basis. In November 1984 he therefore asked Krastyu Petkov, who, at the time, was Director of the Georgi Dimitrov Institute, to consider whether the project could be undertaken in collaboration with the Institute. One reason why Professor Petkov in particular was approached was that he had published books on the sociology of the labour collective and on the sociology of work (Petkov and Kolev 1982; Petkov 1985). The topics discussed in the latter work included 'socialist labour relations', 'the division of labour', 'alienated labour', and the 'labour collective as a labour community'. In the spring of 1985 Krastyu Petkov was able to ensure that the project was included in the Institute's research programme and to allocate a team of research assistants to conduct the greater part of the fieldwork.

At the start of the project the authors agreed that the book should focus on the processes of organisational change and their significance for labour relations. This implied a study of both the sequence and conditions under which organisations were restructured and of the changes that derived from restructuring. Subsequently it was decided that organisational design (explained in the Introduction) should be used as the principal paradigm. The initial dialogue between the authors about the concept and content of the book and the type of presentation and analysis they wished to undertake led them to decide on three general principles for the project. The first was to adopt a historical perspective on the grounds that this was necessary in order to show what had and had not changed in organisations and organisational processes. The second was the choice of the extended case study method, which had been used for the British factories studied for *Strategies, Issues and Events*, as the most effective method of providing indications of the qualitative changes in organisational processes which were to be the principal focus of the fieldwork. The third was to undertake a comparative analysis of the sequence and content of the organisational changes in Bulgaria with the sequence and content of changes in some other socialist countries – the premiss was that the significance of organisational changes in one country becomes clearer when they are compared with those in other countries. Thus the Soviet model has historically had a major influence on the models developed in other countries; more recently there have been significant differences between, for example, the Bulgarian and the Hungarian models, and the comparison between them illustrates what is common and what is distinctive.

The authors agreed at the start of the project that to achieve a unity of conception and a unity between conception and execution the book would have to be an integrated product and not an aggregation of chapters separately conceived and written. This meant that the detailed planning, development and writing of each chapter had to be based on extensive dialogue between them. In the autumn of 1986 a synopsis of the book with detailed outlines of each chapter was drawn up. Although there have been some changes in order and content, this synopsis has provided both the basis of the book and the focus of the fieldwork and other research conducted since then.

The western and Soviet–Bulgarian social science traditions from which the authors come differ significantly in their approach to theorising, in their vocabularies of concepts and in their methods of empirical research. Thus theorising in the Soviet–Bulgarian tradition is mainly developed deductively from general concepts of society, while the western tradition is more empiricist. Sociological research in the former tradition has been dominated by surveys based on questionnaires while the western practice of fieldwork, observation and the use of case studies has rarely been practised. It was, however, an implicit hope from the beginning of the project that it would be possible to draw on concepts from both traditions and to achieve a synthesis in which both authors could freely associate and mutually develop their ideas and approach.

Theorising in the social sciences, other than that which is developed deductively, is most frequently based on evidence which has already been collected and published, for example as statistical or survey data. Where, however, data of this kind is not available, there are two general approaches to the relationship between theorising and the collection of empirical evidence. One approach is to collect evidence in order to test a theory which has already been developed. The opposite approach, sometimes characterised as 'ethnographic', is to enter and observe a situation and then to theorise about what has been observed. The authors adopted an approach which was intermediate between these two approaches. They considered that it was necessary to have an initial set of concepts related to the level of theorising at which they intended to work but which did not constitute a fully testable theory. The concepts as initially defined would be applied to the evidence and then if necessary redefined or discarded. On occasions, study of the evidence would suggest the need for an additional concept or concepts. Theorising would thus develop as an interactive process as the empirical evidence was collected. Schematically theorising in this form can be represented as a cyclical process in the following way, as shown in Figure P.1.

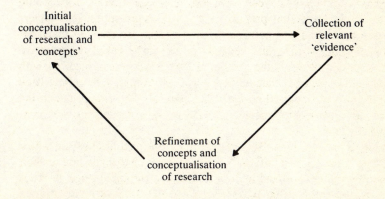

Figure P.1 Theorising

The theoretical approach adopted has been a multidisciplinary one drawing particularly on organisation theory, the sociology of work and on labour relations.

Since the completion of the fieldwork there have been political revolutions in Bulgaria and other socialist countries which herald major changes in economic organisation and in labour relations. The post-revolutionary changes in labour relations in Bulgaria up to the beginning of July 1990 are analysed in the postscript, which compares them with what has happened in Hungary and Czechoslovakia. The history of organisational design shows that redesign necessarily starts from what is already there (or has been there at some time in the past). Certain structures and mechanisms continue to function while others are redesigned or re-introduced. It is the view of both authors that the content of this book will facilitate the understanding of further developments in labour relations as they unfold in both Bulgaria and other countries in Eastern Europe. In addition, it is the view of John Thirkell that the processes of organisational design in Bulgaria from 1978 to 1988 which form the core of the book were so radical and innovative in conception, coherence and implementation that they will continue to merit the attention of students of organisational design and labour relations.

Acknowledgements

The successful completion of a collaborative project by two authors based in different and quite distant countries, would not have been possible without the support of several organisations and many individuals. The Central Council of the Bulgarian Trade Unions funded the fieldwork in Bulgarian enterprises. Support from the British Council under the Academic Links Scheme was especially important in funding Krastyu Petkov's stay at the University of Kent, where many of the discussions essential for the planning of the research and the development of the book took place, at a time when it was difficult to secure support of this kind from other institutions. The Nuffield Foundation made a valued contribution to the costs of preparing the book for publication and to some of John Thirkell's travel costs.

Numerous individuals have contributed in different ways to the completion of this project. Most of them were members of the Georgi Dimitrov Trade Union Research Institute at the Central Council of the Bulgarian Trade Unions or of the Faculty of Social Sciences at the University of Kent. Members of both institutions responded readily to requests for help and provided rapid answers to questions which would have taken a long time to research. We wish to record our thanks to Stoyan Andreev, Iordan Bozhilov, Richard Sakwa and to Richard Scase who, as editor, made many important suggestions for improving the presentation of the text. In addition we wish to acknowledge the contribution of Grigor Gradev to the theory of organisational mechanisms, and to the series of spirited dialogues with David Reason, which both challenged and encouraged us. Outside these institutions John McQueeney commented creatively on drafts of several chapters, Len Dawson, who facilitated the first meeting between the two authors, continued to assist in maintaining communications and Stoyan Kamburov made contributions based on his reading of the penultimate draft.

Part of the material in Chapter 9 was originally published as an article,

'Managerial Elections in Bulgaria: Interests, Conflicts and Representation', in *Labour and Society* vol. 13, no. 3, July 1988 and is reproduced with the permission of the International Institute for Labour Studies.

Krastyu Petkov   John E.M. Thirkell
Sofia   Canterbury

Glossary

aktiv (R, B) Activists from operational and party/trade union structures mobilised to resolve issues (see pp. 166–7).

basic organisation of associated labour (BOAL) (Y) The primary unit in which workers manage production. In practice the design criteria, especially the accounting one, meant that the BOAL was often equivalent to the department or shop.

dvoika (R, B) Two (as compared with *troika* q.v., three).

edinonachalie (R, B) One-man management and responsibility, especially in contrast with management by a collective or board (see pp. 23–4).

khozain (R) Equivalent of *stopanin* (B).

khozraschet (R) A complex Soviet accounting and managerial concept explained in note on pp. 38–9.

majstor (R, B) Foreman, chargehand. The lowest level of the management hierarchy.

nachalnik (R, B) Superintendent, manager or head of shop/department or of shift.

nomenklatura (R, B) Schedule of posts requiring party approval and of approved persons (see p. 133).

obednenie (R, B) Group of enterprises combined in unit for management.

operativka (R, B) Group of senior managers and position holders convened by director to solve operational problems.

stopanin (B) Manager, person who actually runs an organisation but not necessarily the owner (see pp. 47–8).

stopanska smetka (B) Equivalent of *khozraschet*.

subbotnik (R, B) Voluntary work carried out on Saturday or rest day.

tsekh (R, B) Shop, department, internal subdivision of enterprise; the unit responsible for a finished or semi-finished product.

troika (R, B) Three. The top position holders of the enterprise, director, party secretary and trade union president.

udarnichestvo (R) Shock work, undertaken by skilled workers to complete work quickly.

uravnilovka (R, B) Wage equalisation/levelling.

VGMK *(vállalati gazdasági munkaközösség* (H) Enterprise work partnership. In practice internal sub-contracting to achieve plan targets at higher pay.

B – Bulgarian   R – Russian   H – Hungarian   Y – Yugoslav

1   Introduction

The main purpose of this introduction is to explain and illustrate the three conceptions of labour relations, of organisational design and of organisational dynamics.

SOCIALIST LABOUR RELATIONS

Labour (or industrial) relations is well established in western social science both as a field of academic research and as a subject taught on courses in institutions of higher education. (The concepts, however, have often been derived from other disciplines in the social sciences such as economics, and sociology.) In socialist countries, on the other hand, labour relations has traditionally been regarded mainly as an aspect of legal studies. The concept of labour is, of course, central to Marxism but the predominance given to the concept of production relations in Marxist theory has traditionally excluded the concept of labour relations or assigned it a secondary place. However, historically 'labour relations' preceded production relations in Marx's thought. In his manuscript on 'alienated labour' in 1844 he discussed the relation of the worker to the product of labour and the relation of labour to the act of production, that is, to the worker's activity (Marx 1975: 325–7). Later, his analysis at the level of political economy and the development of capitalist society concentrated on production relations and their predominance in political and economic terms. Although he and Engels discussed many concrete topics using, particularly, examples from English industrial experience, Marx's main concern was with the analysis of the relations between workers, owners and the state and he did not seek to develop the concepts of labour relations and the labour process.

   In socialist countries, lawyers have long been concerned with the theory and practice of the relationship of the individual worker to the employing enterprise, as an aspect of 'individual legal labour relations' (Trocsanyi 1986). However, this usage in labour law is derived from the concept of production relations and not from labour relations as such. Apart from legal theory, the general tendency has been to regard labour relations as an element or aspect of production relations which derive essentially from the ownership of the means of production, that is, whether property is privately or publicly owned. However, in the course of economic and social development, categories other than that of production relations have come to be recognised in socialist theorising about the relations between enterprises and their employees. Thus the concept of economic relations gained currency in the context of proposals for economic reform in the 1960s, while in the 1970s mechanisms to promote worker participation in management were associated with the emergence of a category of managerial relations which dealt with the relations between managers and 'participating workers'. However, in the 1980s, recognition of the importance of the human factor especially in relation to economic performance and motivation became widespread. This, for example, was the main theme of Zaslavskaya's article on the human factor and the development of economic and social management (Zaslavskaya 1986: 61–73). In these conditions a conception of labour relations wider than that of the legal relationship of the individual worker with the employing enterprise is becoming recognised. This wider conception has been associated with the growing significance of sociology as a key social science discipline. At an abstract theoretical level the conception of socialist labour relations outlined below was set out in Krastyu Petkov's *The sociology of work* (1985: 43–97). In that work, however, there was no attempt to explain the operation of labour relations, which is the principal aim of this book.

In Bulgaria the decisive political step for the recognition of labour relations was the party conference of November 1982. The main document, *A new conception of labour and labour relations* (Zhivkov 1982), took labour relations as a central concept for strategy formulation (see Chapter 3) and this has encouraged theoretical discussion and clarification of the nature of labour relations and its connection with production relations. The reasons for this interest in labour relations in the 1980s and 1990s in the fields of sociology, political science and economic and social management are related to the structural changes made in the labour process, especially the brigade organisation of work, and the concept of direct democracy which was embodied in its design, and the development of the idea of the labour collective. This became associated with a conception of collective labour relations as distinct from individual labour relations.

Socialist labour relations are to be distinguished from both the western conception of industrial relations and the Marxist conception of production relations in terms of three aspects: the subjects (that is, the parties), the contents and the structural levels at which they operate. In terms of subjects/parties they are relations between four parties: workers, the enterprise, the labour collective and the trade union. The western approach to labour relations has concentrated on the three parties which are generally recognised in western societies, that is, the worker, the employer and the trade union, and, of course, beyond them the state. The concept of the labour collective, which has been recognised in several socialist societies including Yugoslavia, the Soviet Union, Bulgaria and Czechoslovakia, has no direct equivalent in western societies. In Yugoslavia, in Bulgaria (until a political decision was made in January 1989 to establish the 'firm' as the generic type of industrial organisation) and in the Soviet Union, the labour collective has been recognised as a party in labour relations. This recognition has been associated with particular concepts of self-management in these countries which are only of limited occurrence in western societies usually in connection with some types of co-operative. Where the concept of the labour collective has been developed, it has involved a change in the worker's status from that of 'hired labour'. (The traditional concept in socialist countries was that the worker is both a co-owner of public property and 'hired labour' of the state.) The concept of the labour collective leads to one of 'collective labour relations' (explained in Chapter 3) in which the labour collective is a party to agreements and decision making. This differs from that in western societies where collective labour relations are usually connected with the relations between employers and trade unions.

The issues in labour relations derive from the labour process or in connection with it. In this sense labour relations are relations deriving from the division of labour, the organisation of work, the content and specification of jobs, and remuneration. The concept of the division of labour, which was central to Marx's analysis of labour and society, is used here in relation to the detailed division of labour within the enterprise as distinct from the division of labour in society as a whole. However, within the enterprise the division of labour is evident both horizontally in the relations between workers in different occupations at the workplace and vertically in the relations between the managers and the managed. The organisation of work is seen as involving both the forms, whether collective – group or team – or individual, and the basis on which the work is directed in terms of authority and consent. Thus a team working with an elected supervisor is a different form of work organisation from one in which the supervisor is appointed by management and there will be differences in the labour process in the two forms. In terms of organisational levels, socialist labour law has been mainly concerned with labour within the enterprise, but labour relations are seen as extending beyond the level of the enterprise and operating at regional, sectoral and national levels. Finally, the connection between labour relations and the ownership of property is seen as being of central significance. Traditionally, socialist theorising regards state ownership of the means of production as the fundamental basis on which both production and labour relations are established. Now new forms of property relations as alternatives to state ownership are being widely recognised as necessary for economic and societal development. New forms such as co-operatives, family and group ownership or joint ventures with foreign firms have direct consequences for labour relations.

Although this conception of the scope of socialist labour relations differs in some respects from western conceptions of labour relations, it nevertheless links to a whole series of topics which have been central concerns of western social scientists studying western organisations. These include the nature and structure of effective organisations, the relations between ownership – public or private – and the exercise of control over and within organisations; the place of hierarchy and the sources of authority in organisations; and the rights of employees and the representation of their interests as employees. All these topics have been relevant to the development of socialist societies since 1917, though many of the structures and mechanisms which have been created for industrial organisation reflect the different basis of political organisation and different models of societal and economic development. Since the late 1970s issues connected with all aspects of socialist labour relations have emerged strongly in Bulgaria and an explanation of them constitutes the core of this book. However, the same issues have emerged in other socialist societies and in most of them are gaining increasing importance.

LABOUR RELATIONS AND THE LABOUR PROCESS

The publication of Braverman's (1974) *Labour and monopoly capitalism* initiated a major debate about both the nature of the labour process under capitalism and the validity of his analysis. One of the consequences of Braverman's work and the ensuing debate was that the concept of the labour process became established as an integrating concept in western academic discourse (at least in England and the United States) for the discussion of topics related to the organisation of work. Braverman argued that 'the central place in the first volume of Marx's *Capital* is occupied by the labour process as it takes place under the control of Capital' (Braverman 1974: 8). Marx was concerned with the questions of ownership, control and the appropriation of surplus value deriving from capitalist ownership and the alienation of the worker. The concept of the division of labour, however, was central to his analysis and it was on this aspect that Braverman concentrated his attention. His thesis was that:

> It . . . becomes essential for the capitalist that control over the labour process pass from the hands of the worker into his own. This transition presents itself in history as the progressive alienation of the process of production from the worker; to the capitalist it presents itself as the problem of management.
>
> (Braverman 1974: 58)

Braverman argued that the dynamics of monopoly capitalism led to a labour process characterised by the degradation of work through deskilling and the fragmentation of tasks, that is to an extension of the division of labour. This process of fragmentation and deskilling was evident in non-manual as well as manual work. Analytically, the central result was that in the intensified division of labour, conception was separated from execution and this intensified the alienation of the worker from his work. The alienation of the worker thus derived from the nature of the labour process as well as from property and ownership relations.

However, the conception of the labour process used here is wider than the concentration on the design of jobs and tasks at the point of production, which was the focus of Braverman's book. Although the division of labour at the base is recognised as being of fundamental importance for labour relations, the nature of the division of labour between top and base is equally seen as a fundamental aspect of labour relations. Thus the division of labour between top and base may be one in which conception is confined to the top and execution is imposed on the base, or it may be one in which the interests of the base are recognised and represented in the process of conception. In discussing the hierarchical division of labour and function between top and base the approach adopted by Burawoy in *The politics of production* (1985) is used and extended. Writing from within a labour-process perspective, Burawoy used a core–periphery polarity to analyse aspects of hierarchy and control.

ORGANISATIONAL DESIGN – STRATEGY, STRUCTURES AND MECHANISMS

In this book, organisational design is used as the principal paradigm.[1] This is derived from the approach developed by the American theorists Lawrence and Lorsch (1967, 1969, 1970), Thompson (1967), and Galbraith (1977). Galbraith argues that 'every organisation is designed' and defines the subject in the following way:

Organization design is conceived to be a decision process to bring about a coherence between the goals or purposes for which an organization exists, the patterns of the division of labour and interunit coordination and the people who will do the work.

(Galbraith 1977: 11)

The main reason for using organisational design as the principal paradigm was that it seemed especially appropriate to the process of national restructuring that began in 1978 in Bulgaria because there was a conscious strategy at the political level for organisational development by redesigning the internal structures and mechanisms of enterprises. As will be explained in Chapter 3, this process was associated with the official recognition of new concepts particularly that of the labour collective as *stopanin*, and with substantial changes in organisational structures. A further reason was that the concepts associated with this paradigm were appropriate to the concern with the nature of managerial and trade union strategies which had been a theme of *Strategies, issues and events*. Galbraith recognised that organisational design is directly connected with organisational strategy and the 'choice of strategy'. The concept of strategy used in this book is one developed from that in *Strategies, issues and events*, where 'the development of strategy' is seen as:

generally comprising two processes: strategy formulation followed by structuring. Strategy formulation is the process of identifying strategic issues; that is issues believed to be amenable to structural resolution. Structuring, at its simplest is the process of creating developing or changing institutions.

(Jackson-Cox *et al*. 1987: 57)

An example drawn from British industrial relations may clarify the distinction between strategy formulation and structuring. In the 1970s the recognition of trade unions for all or a particular section of the workforce was a strategic issue for many employers. Strategy formulation was the process by which an employer recognised and sought to define this issue. Structuring was the process by which the recognition of a trade union was put into effect, that is to say, the categories of employees for whom the trade union was recognised, the forums for negotiation and consultation and the range of issues for which it was recognised. In the 1980s, on the other hand, withdrawal or limitation of recognition was formulated as a strategy by some employers, and events such as mergers were used to make such structural changes. Strategy is therefore seen as being about the design of enterprise structures, including managerial hierarchies and the forums where decisions are made, and the internal divisions such as departments and work groups which constitute units of organisational structure. Thus, as explained in Chapter 3, in Bulgaria the party conference decided in 1978 that the new type of brigade should become the generic structure for the organisation of work throughout industry. The party conference in deciding on structural change took the final step in this stage of strategy formulation but it was, of course, preceded by a process in which, first, the issue of work organisation was identified as a strategic one and, second, support for the strategy was mobilised. One aspect of structures is what Giddens (1979: 69) has termed the 'duality of structures' – structures both 'enable and constrain'. This means that while the redesign of structures is intended to facilitate the resolution of some issues, it may both constrain the resolution of others and facilitate the emergence of new issues. Similarly, the redesign of structures may have consequences unintended or unforeseen by the designers – for example, the coalescence of the self-management and trade union structures discussed in Chapter 12.

The concept of mechanism, not developed in *Strategies, issues and events*, is used here as an integral feature of organisational design and strategy. It is a concept widely used in the Soviet Union and Eastern Europe, but mainly in the context of discussion of economic mechanisms. Mechanism has sometimes been used in western organisation theory. Thus Galbraith and Nathanson discuss various 'mechanisms of integration' for overcoming the problems of co-ordination in large organisations (1978: 63–75). The operation of mechanisms in organisations has several aspects. In this book the core function of mechanisms is that they are seen as making, or as designed to make, structures work. This means that they contribute to the dynamics of structures (the conception of dynamics is further elaborated below). Thus in centrally planned economies the mechanisms of planning and control are designed to make enterprises work according to national criteria. Within Bulgarian enterprises the mechanism for the distribution of earnings in brigades provides the dynamics for the monthly meeting of the brigade assembly (structure) and so makes it work. Mechanisms also provide the dynamics of the relations between levels of structure. Thus agreements between management at the top of the enterprise and brigades at the base were designed to shape the process of interaction between these two levels of structure (see Chapter 8).

A key distinction made here is between mechanistic and organic mechanisms. The basis for this distinction lies in the origin of the mechanism. Mechanistic mechanisms are imposed on organisations, or units of organisation, from outside or from above. In centrally directed socialist countries, mechanistic mechanisms are mainly those which are designed centrally and imposed by normative regulation through the state and other agencies. Organic mechanisms are those which are created autonomously within enterprises either by workers at the base or at the top by management, the party or the trade union. Often organic mechanisms are a response to the operation of imposed mechanisms. Examples of organic mechanisms are the creation of the counterplanning mechanism at the Karl Marx factory in Leningrad in 1930, discussed in Chapter 2, and the mechanism developed by the brigade to deal with an alcoholic worker and other forms, discussed particularly in Chapter 10. All mechanisms are activated in relation to issues and are designed to shape and resolve them.

When relationships between levels of structure are involved, a structure may itself operate as a mechanism. Thus the Production Meeting or Conference (structure) long established in enterprises in socialist countries, operated as a mechanism linking the base with higher levels. Equally, the redesign of a structure may itself operate as a mechanism, for example, when the strategic issue is seen as that of altering the relationship between levels of structure. Thus in the process of strategy formulation in Bulgaria the new-type brigade (structure) was used as a mechanism for altering the relationship between the top of the enterprise, where general management is located, and the base, where the majority of employees work. Within an organisation mechanisms may operate in different directions. They may operate vertically between levels of structure, that is exercising pressure upwards from the base to the top or downwards from the top to the base. They may also operate laterally. The direction in which they operate is an indicator of the balance of power within and between units of structure. Thus the mechanism for the distribution of earnings within a brigade, which had been decided by the party conference in 1978, may operate in the direction of wage equalisation or it may operate in another direction to protect the earnings of older more highly skilled workers relative to those of younger workers with lower formal skills. Similarly, an agreement between a brigade and management may operate as a mechanism for pressure from the base to the top or in the reverse direction. Changes in the direction in which mechanisms operate indicate shifts in the balance of power. The duality of structures was discussed above; the duality of mechanisms lies in the directions in which they may operate.

Normative regulation is the aspect of organisational design concerned with the process of implementing strategic change. In socialist countries normative regulation is used as a general concept to categorise the legal and other normative regulations and directives which set out criteria and standards to be followed in organisations. A central issue in strategy formulation at the national level is how far the regulations should specify the standards for the internal structures of enterprises and the mechanisms in detail, and the degree of autonomy that enterprises or other structures should have in designing mechanisms and establishing internal regulation.

The process of organisational design in socialist industry is shown in Figure 1.1.

Strategy formulation
Process of identifying structural
issues and associated mechanisms
and securing their recognition

**Redesign of structures and mechanisms
imposed through normative regulation**

The enterprise
Operation of imposed mechanisms
leads to creation of some organic
mechanisms and, occasionally,
organic organisational structures

Strategy formulation
Identification of new structural
issues and mechanisms

Figure 1.1 **The process of strategy formulation**

In relation to the concepts of organisational design and labour relations as developed in the present book, the labour process is seen as a product of a process of organisational design so that any redesign of structures and mechanisms may lead to changes in the labour process and labour relations.

Organisational design and organisational dynamics

A fundamental question in organisational design is the basis of organisational dynamics. Organisational dynamics are generated by the pressures which activate the organisation and the people who work in it. There are two main sources of pressure – pressure deriving from the environment in which the organisation operates and pressure from within the organisation itself. In principle there are two main types of external pressure. The first, traditionally dominant in centrally planned socialist economies, is hierarchical pressure from the centre operating through the mechanisms of authority and planning. The second is pressure from the market operating through the mechanisms of supply and demand. In reality pressures of both kinds may be present and provide the driving force. Both types of pressure have implications for organisational design at the level of the enterprise. Thus, as explained in Chapter 2, the structures and mechanisms of the Soviet enterprises of the 1930s were designed to comply with the external dynamic of the centrally planned command economy. In the same way the structures and mechanisms of capitalist corporations partly depend on the nature and pressures of the product markets in which they operate. Thus Chandler (1962) in his seminal work on the structure of American corporations argued that the adoption of divisionalised internal structures was a key to the long-term survival and growth of successful corporations.

In any economic system external pressures from the environment will be transmitted internally from top to base, though the intensity of these pressures will vary widely. However, internal pressures may also be a source of dynamics within the enterprise. Thus internal accounting systems may be designed in such a way as to promote competition between different units and thus to generate some lateral pressures. Other pressures may not be the result of conscious design but derive from perceived inequalities in distribution or from the defence of relativities. Internal pressures, especially those at the base can be seen as arising from the protection of interests or what Hethy (1989: 107) terms 'the assertion of interests'. The concept of interests has long been an integral part of socialist theorising on society. Major changes in politics and society have generally been associated with some redefinition of the configuration of interests in society and this has been the case in Bulgaria since the 1980s. Here interests are discussed in relation to the level of the enterprise and to organisational design. Interests are seen as deriving in the first place from practice, that is, from the processes of action and interaction in which people in organisations are involved. As Harris puts it:

> Those engaging in a practice may be said to have an interest in the existence of states of affairs which constitute favourable circumstances of engagement in that practice ... all interests are relative to the practices from which they derive. ... However ... while practices generate interests, interests generate practices. ... The concept of interest is therefore a concept which links 'practice' with both 'resources' and 'circumstances'.
>
> (Harris 1980: 60–2)

Thus a primary work group in an enterprise is engaged in a practice, that is, a work-derived activity and this provides a basis of interests. However, the significance of interests in relation to the action of a primary work group is contingent upon the organisational design, that is, on the structures and mechanisms. Thus the design of the brigade organisation (discussed in Chapter 5) as an economic and accounting unit with mechanisms of internal distribution and elections of brigade leader and brigade council, constituted it as a stronger unit of interests than less formally structured primary work groups. As such, its potential for 'the assertion of interests' is greater.

Kyuranov (1980: 10–18) has characterised the organisation of work in the process of production as 'the organisation of interests'. In the paradigm of organisational design the 'organisation of interests' extends to the whole of the organisation. The essence of organisational design is the creation of units of organisational structure – for example, enterprise, department, brigade – and the mechanisms to make them work. Such units of structure become integrated as units of practice and interests. The extent of integration depends on the mechanisms: mechanisms can be created to engage the interests of members of a unit or indeed to disengage and separate those interests. Thus the mechanisms of individual norms and payment which were predominant in the 1950s and 1960s in Bulgaria functioned to separate the interests of workers and make the individual the key unit; the brigade form of organisation, on the other hand, included mechanisms to engage collective interests. However, as explained in Chapters 3 and 5, the design process of establishing the labour collective as *stopanin* provided a basis in normative regulation for the legitimation of the interests of the collective which had been absent earlier.

This approach gives primacy to interests over the psychological needs of workers and other participants in the activities of enterprises: 'social–organisational relations are less affected by needs than by interests and interests are the main motivating factor in industrial organisation' (Mako 1978: 30). Interests are, therefore, a driving force in labour relations, a source of pressure expressed through mechanisms, and consequently a source of the internal dynamics of the enterprise as an organisation.

History and the study of organisational design

The organisation of this book as a whole, and of most of the individual chapters, is historical in the sense that it seeks to show and explain the processes of organisational design as the result of actions taken in specific historical contexts. Throughout the book the presentation is organised around models – a model is defined as a specific set of structures and mechanisms. Models are discussed mainly in relation to the organisation of the economy and labour relations: for example, 'the centralised model', the 'intermediate model' and 'the emerging self-management model' are used as categories in Chapters 6 to 9 to focus the discussion. However, models of societal development are also discussed in some chapters. Thus the period of the New Economic Policy (NEP) in the Soviet Union from 1921 to 1928 is considered as a particular model of societal development associated with a specific model of economic organisation and labour relations. At its simplest, the comparison of models facilitates explanation and understanding of what is common and what is different, of what is new and what has previously been established.

However, there are other reasons for adopting a historical and developmental approach to organisational design. One is the concern with the creation of prototypes, that is, with the first appearance of structures or mechanisms in response to specific conditions which were later adopted centrally and diffused on a wide scale. The maintenance of such structures or mechanisms over time or their transfer into different contexts is an indication of their significance while their disappearance or atrophy is an indication of real change. Thus, as explained in Chapter 2, *subbotniks* emerged in the Soviet Union in 1920 as an organic mechanism. *Subbotniks* were workers who volunteered to work on Saturdays without pay to solve the industrial and community problems of War Communism. In 1989 it was still possible on some Saturdays in Sofia to see citizens engaged in voluntary community, though not industrial, tasks. Thus the mechanism has been maintained as a movement but transferred to a different social setting. On the other hand, the brigade as a collective structure of work organisation was significant in the Soviet Union in 1928–31. It was then replaced but re-emerged in the Soviet Union and Bulgaria in the late 1970s. Another reason is that a fundamental issue in organisational design relates to the relationship between changes in structures and changes in mechanisms. It is possible to introduce a new mechanism into an existing structure, or to redesign a structure without altering its mechanisms. This leads to the issue of the effectiveness and coherence of the design. In so far as design is intended to modify patterns of human behaviour, there is the possibility that old patterns will persist in new structures if the design is inadequate. Another issue which is related to the historical approach is that of design sequence. It is rarely possible to design a complete organisation on the drawing board and to establish it as a complete set of structures and mechanisms. In practice, the design process is usually concerned with the modification or adaptation of existing models. The sequence in which the redesign of structures and mechanisms takes place has significant consequences for the whole process. Thus, as argued in Chapter 12, the redesign of the socialist enterprise can, in principle, start at the top, in the middle or at the base, and the choice of starting point influences the later stages and may indeed close off some options. The sequence of redesign of structures and mechanisms in Bulgaria in 1978–88, which forms the core of the book, is argued to have been of great significance. The final value of the historical approach is that it facilitates the inductive development of a theory of organisational design. In this sense the approach is analogous with that adopted by Chandler (1977) in his study of the American business enterprise. Chandler used a historical study of the development and changes in the structures of the enterprise to formulate a series of propositions to explain the initial appearance of the modern business enterprise and its continuing growth (Chandler 1977: 6–12).

THE STRUCTURE OF THE BOOK

The structure of the book is in three main parts. The first part, which is Chapter 2, on the Soviet model and its transfer to Bulgaria, explains the development of successive models of Soviet labour relations from 1917 to the 1930s and the transfer of the Soviet model to Bulgaria after the war. In this chapter the unit of analysis is the enterprise. The second part, Chapters 3–11, is devoted to Bulgaria. Chapter 3 deals with the processes of strategy formulation at the national level, principally for the period 1978–88. Chapter 4 explains the approach to the fieldwork in Bulgarian enterprises and introduces the concepts of incidents, episodes and events. Chapter 5 discusses the redesign of organisational structures. Chapters 6 to 10 are concerned with the mechanisms which make structures work. Chapters 6 to 9 describe the set of mechanistic mechanisms which were imposed from above. Chapter 10 deals with the organic mechanisms which emerged in enterprises as complementary or counter-mechanisms mainly in response to the imposed mechanisms. Chapter 11 is devoted to changes in the labour process deriving from redesign. For Chapters 5 to 11 the unit of analysis is the labour collective. For Chapter 12, which analyses, on a historical and comparative basis, the process of redesign in different socialist countries, the unit of analysis is again the enterprise.

NOTE

1   M. Masterman (1970) discusses Kuhn's uses of 'paradigm'. She suggests that there is a usage in which 'the paradigm is something which can function when the theory is not there', and another usage in which 'a paradigm is an artefact which can be used as a puzzle-solving device', that is, as supplying tools. Here the usage of paradigm draws on both of these but they are used to develop theories about organisational design.

2 The development of the Soviet model and its transfer to Bulgaria

This chapter derives from the recognition of the fact that most of the concepts, structures and mechanisms to be found in the operation of the Bulgarian economy and its enterprises in the 1970s originated in the Soviet Union in the 1920s and 1930s. It was, therefore, seen as desirable to set the creation of these structures and mechanisms in the historical context in which they originated. The central unit of analysis is the enterprise and the dynamics of its operation as an organisation, especially as it affected labour relations. The main focus is on the 1930s model which was established with the centrally planned economy and the administrative command system of management and then transferred to Bulgaria and to other countries of Eastern Europe in the late 1940s and early 1950s (also in part to China (1953–5). The aim is to explain the historical design process in which the structures and mechanisms of this model were created. Of particular interest is the process by which mechanisms were created as prototypes in response to particular conditions but survived in different conditions or were recreated at a later period. Some of the mechanisms of the 1930s model, such as socialist emulation, had their origins in the earlier stages of Soviet development, while others such as the factory councils (structure) of the post-revolutionary period, which were rejected in the 1920s, were to re-emerge in the design of alternatives to the Soviet model as explained in Chapter 12. The 1930s enterprise can be conceptualised as a 'two subject/ two structure model', that is, as a model with two main internal hierarchical structures: the structure of operational management designed for the organisation of the processes of production; and the socio-political structure composed of the party, trade union and Komsomol which generally operated parallel to the internal levels of the operational structure. (The two subjects were management and the social political organisations.) This two-structure model is in contrast with the three-structure model in which there is a Council which includes representatives of the workers at the top of the enterprise and some form of workers' assembly at the base. (In this model there is a third subject.)

In presenting the historical material the aim is to relate it to a series of themes which are considered to be of particular significance for the approach adopted in this book. These themes relate to: first, the externally generated dynamics of the enterprise deriving from its relationship with external structures (higher units in the hierarchy of organisation) and the associated mechanisms; and, second, the internal structures of the enterprise and the mechanisms providing the dynamics of the relationship between structures at the top of the enterprise (line management, the party and the trade union) and the base (where the majority of the workers were employed) and within the base itself (especially the organisation of the labour process and the mechanisms of distribution). At a more general level these themes are related to consideration of the relationship between models of labour relations and economic organisation and between models of societal development. Models of labour relations and of economic organisation are necessarily interlinked and interdependent, but in the process of strategy formulation at the political level a central question is the sequence in which redesign takes place in the creation of a model – whether changes in economic organisation are seen to require conscious redesign of labour-relations mechanisms and how far the economic and labour-relations issues are consciously integrated or separated. These questions are considered in relation to the three models of societal development which emerged in the Soviet Union: War Communism, NEP and the administrative command model with centralised planning that was established in the 1930s. (The term 'administrative system' was introduced by the Soviet academic and commentator Gavrila Popov to characterise the Stalinist model for the management and operation of society. It is widely used in academic and political literature. In politics Gorbachev and other leaders of *perestroika* use the term 'administrative-command system'.)

THE REVOLUTION AND WAR COMMUNISM 1917–1921

The seizure of power in 1917 and the subsequent period of military, political and economic crisis inevitably shaped the Bolshevik approach to the issues of economic organisation and management, and in this period the design of structures and mechanisms was necessarily influenced by the necessity of solving immediate problems. However, there was a continuing attempt, in strategy formulation at the political level, to relate such solutions to broader theoretical concepts and in this way to relate them to models of societal development. The absence of existing models of socialist industrial organisation and the lack of any elaborated theory meant that these were essentially open questions. Consequently, groups within the Bolshevik Party or outside it were able to develop different and competing concepts about, for example, the position of trade unions and the system of payment and to rally around them in the political forums. In the immediate aftermath of the revolution, the central economic issue for the Bolsheviks was to define a strategic model for the process of establishing control over the economy and the sectors of industry in private ownership. In the period after the February Revolution factory committees with worker representatives had been created autonomously in many industrial enterprises and the Bolsheviks had supported this as a movement. The political importance attached to this by the Bolsheviks is shown by Lenin's preparation of draft regulations on workers' control on 26 October as one of the first tasks after the seizure of power. A revised draft was issued as a decree on November 14 (Lenin 1967: 80). Lenin was concerned to ensure that factory committees should operate as part of a general concept of 'workers' control'. This was:

> to be a sort of dual control of employers and workers over industry, a condominium in which the workers were to train themselves for future management and in which they were progressively to widen the sphere of their responsibility . . . 'workers' control' . . . provided the framework for the struggle between capitalists and workers in a transition period, at the end of which the former were to be expropriated.
>
> (Deutscher 1950: 14)

The movement for workers' control assumed a momentum which created a problem for the Bolsheviks as workers took over factories from their owners in that it threatened to introduce a concept of workers' ownership which ran counter to their concept of state ownership and centralised control (Kaplan 1969: 127). Kaplan quotes Lozovsky, the trade union leader, in the *Trade Union Herald* of 5 January 1918: ' "Workers' control" . . . does not mean the immediate socialization of the factories and shops, and much less the transfer of enterprises into the hands of individual groups' and comments that 'Over and over again speeches and articles by both the Bolsheviks and Mensheviks emphasise the fact that workers' control is not equivalent to group ownership and that group ownership is not equivalent to socialism.' At the same time the Bolsheviks sought to establish trade union supervision over the factory committees, which became 'incorporated in the unions' (Deutscher 1950: 18) and then to establish control over the trade unions themselves.

The organisation of the economy through state bodies was an early priority for the Bolsheviks, and the Supreme Council of National Economy

(Vesenkha) was created as early as December 1917 to guide and co-ordinate the organisation of the economy, and in June 1918 a decree on the nationalisation of factories was issued. Up to that time expropriation had occurred piecemeal through the initiative of workers in specific localities as a manifestation of workers' control. By August 1918 participation in management by elected factory committees or workers' control commissions was widespread (Malle 1985: 103) and these committees were often linked externally to the local soviets. As early as the spring of 1918 Lenin had put forward the concept of *edinonachalie* as an alternative to these forms of collective management although in nationalised enterprises appointed directors were balanced by an elected economic and administrative council with representatives of both internal interests (workers, engineers and staff) and external interests (trade unions, soviets etc.). The strategic issue of the structure of enterprise management continued to be contested. At the 9th Party Congress in 1920 the general principle of *edinonachalie* rather than collective management was endorsed. However the issue of form and structure was again contested at the 10th Congress in 1921, where the central issue was the position of the trade unions in relation to the state and the enterprise. The Workers' Opposition argued (drawing on point 5 of the 1919 Party programme) that there should be 'the concentration of industrial management in the hands of the Trade Unions' and that the management of the economy should be transferred to an All-Russian Congress of Producers; while the Trotsky–Bukharin motion argued equally for the gradual transfer of economic administration to the trade unions, which would become part of the state apparatus and be responsible for the process and discipline of production. Lenin's successful position was that the trade unions should not be part of the state organisation. However, as Deutscher (1950: 58) comments: 'in practice Trotsky's formula came to govern the position of the trade unions in later years, in the period of the planned economy. . . . In theory, however, Lenin's formula, unrevised, was to remain in force'.

The debates about enterprise structure took place in the context of the experience of War Communism, in which the abolition of market relationships, the practice of requisitioning by the state, and the militarisation of labour were aspects of the response to the crisis situation. The process of mobilisation of labour saw the emergence of prototypes of organisation and movements – in particular shock work, brigades and the *subbotniks* who undertook unpaid Saturday labour originally on the Moscow–Kazan railway in May 1919. Shock work (*udarnichestvo*), like the *subbotniks*, was usually led by politically active workers who undertook special tasks at the request of party or state. Such work was often episodic, but might also be on a regular basis. Shock workers sometimes formed shock brigades (Nosach 1976: 76), but there were also other workers in brigades. According to Deutscher (1954: 495): 'It was Trotsky who first systematically applied military terms, symbols and metaphors to civilian economic matters'; and it is logical to suppose that the creator of labour armies should have been associated with the transfer of the term brigade to a unit of work organisation. However, it should be noted that as early as June 1918 Stalin telegraphed Lenin to 'provide Shliapnikov with construction engineers, capable workers and locomotive brigades' (*Voprosi istorii* 1988: 91) which shows that the term was established on the railways by that date even though it may not have been diffused elsewhere until later, possibly as a result of Trotsky's experience as transport commissar.

Recent theoretical writing in the Soviet Union interprets War Communism as deriving from a Marxist conception of socialism as a classless, non-commodity society with public distribution of the means of consumption (Butenko 1987). In the process of strategy formulation in relation to the organisation of the economy in conditions of continuous crisis the guiding principle for the Bolsheviks was to secure control of the economy by the state under party control. This necessitated the foundation of the administrative command system and the nationalisation of industry. In one sense, however, the economic model had to be imposed on a partially established model of socialist labour relations that had emerged with workers' control and the factory committees. By 1921 the predominance of a model of the enterprise with two vertical structures, that is, an operational structure working on the principle of *edinochalie* and the parallel structure of party and trade union rather than the three structures that were implicit in the factory committee model had been established. However, recent reports suggest that in the textile industry the three-structure model survived till the late 1920s, and it is an indication of the original significance of this model that in the Soviet Union the trade union committee is still designated the factory committee, so that it takes its title from the structure that it replaced. The general sequence of the design process in this period was 'workers' control, state control, party control' (Malle 1985: 89) with the trade union achieving a place as an institution concerned with the organisation of labour and a measure of control over labour relations. In this period, in contrast to the NEP period which followed, there is evidence of mobilisation from the base, initially through the movement for workers' control and subsequently through shock work.

THE NEW ECONOMIC POLICY, 1921–1928

Although NEP was occasioned by economic crisis and especially the shortage of food, which led to reappraisal of the relationship between the state and the peasantry, its significance as a model of economic and societal development was at the centre of political debates in the 1920s. More recently, in the context of *perestroika*, the interpretation of the model which has been established in Soviet historiography since the 1930s has been subject to reappraisal. This has been associated with greater emphasis on Lenin's opinion that NEP would operate for 'a long time' rather than his earlier presentation of it as a 'temporary retreat'. Such approaches emphasise Bukharin's view of a gradual transition to socialism and Lenin's last works, especially that on co-operatives, which saw this form of property and organisation as appropriate for parts of all sectors of production and distribution and not for agriculture alone. (The leasing in 1921–2 of state enterprises controlled by Vesenkha is seen as a precedent for the revival of this form of property for industry and services in the 1980s.) Cohen (1988: 61) sees Bukharin as advocating an evolutionary policy that would allow the rural majority and private enterprise to flourish and 'root itself in socialism' through market relations. This approach sees NEP as a model of societal development in which there is a social order of civilised co-operators and co-operative socialism prefigures socialist society (*Pravda* 1988).

The essence of NEP was the restoration of a significant degree of market relations for the state sector of industry as well as for agriculture. As a result the mechanism of *khozraschet*[1] was elaborated in 1921 and applied to the trusts which controlled groups of enterprises. (Under War Communism most enterprises had no funds of their own and costs were met from the state budget.) *Khozraschet* meant that the trusts were to operate on the principle of profitability ('control by the rouble') and to buy materials and sell products at prices fixed by contracts, except where they were fixed by the state. (In 1929 the level of *khozraschet* was taken down to that of the enterprise – the history of socialist economic organisation indicates that changes in economic mechanisms are usually associated with changes in the structural level at which *khozraschet* is intended to apply and such changes generally have consequences for labour relations.) The design dynamic of NEP was to encourage entrepreneurial management (managerial bonuses based on results were introduced and there were competitions for the 'Best Director'), and this logic had consequences for the position of the trade unions and for labour relations. Top management were thus to be paid at least in part for the overall results of work, but workers were paid for work done.

Although the trade union was to promote production and productivity, it was specifically instructed not to directly intervene in the administration of enterprises. It was recognised that NEP created some conflicts of interests between workers and management and that defence of worker interests was a trade union responsibility. The Labour Code of 1922 provided for the right of the trade union to negotiate on terms and conditions of workers and this was implemented through the mechanism of collective agreements negotiated with management at the level of the trust or in some cases at industry level. These agreements included wages, which under NEP were not so tightly controlled by the plan as they later became under the centralised model. Accompanying agreements was the procedure for arbitration through the Assessment and Conflict Commission (RKK), set up by the Labour Code, which adjudicated on disputes arising from the interpretation of the collective agreement. A new internal structure, which in the Soviet Union continues till the present, was the Production Conference. The prototype seems to have been created autonomously in a Moscow textile factory in 1921. The director addressed the workforce on the production situation. Workers criticised some deficiencies in the organisation of production and put forward their proposals for improving it (Petrochenko and Kuzhetsova 1974: 64). The prototype was diffused on a wide scale during 1923, and in 1924 was endorsed at the political level by a resolution of the Party Conference. Its function was to discuss and resolve production problems. Conferences were to be attended 'by representatives of the economic organs and of the trade unions and also workers both Party and non-party' (Bettelheim 1978: 217). It thus combined representatives of both the operational and the social–political structures with workers from the base and so functioned as a mechanism for integrating structures both horizontally and vertically, but unlike the factory committee it did not operate at the top of the enterprise. Bettelheim (1978: 218) refers to the successive calls at the political level to make it a more effective mechanism for participation, and this suggests that from the design standpoint at that time it was inadequately linked to other mechanisms.

NEP also saw the development of strategy on a fundamental aspect of labour relations – the norming of tasks ('norming': the setting of quotas for individuals or groups of workers). Lenin's condemnation of Taylorism before the Revolution and his endorsement of it in 'The Immediate Tasks of Soviet Government' is well known. He recognised, however, the duality of Taylorism as 'a combination of the refined brutality of bourgeois exploitation and a number of the greatest scientific achievements'. Alexei Gastev, founder of the Central Labour Institute, became a leading exponent of Taylor's ideas albeit in the context of a vision of a new proletarian culture in which 'Machines from being managed will become managers' and a new type of 'mechanised collectivism' would dominate working-class psychology (Bailes 1977: 378). This vision was contested by others. Thus Bogdanov envisaged a '"proletarian collective" . . . distinguished and defined by a special organisational bond, known as comradely co-operation' (Bailes 1977: 380). Gastev's approach was especially opposed by Kerzhentsev's 'Group of Communists', who argued for a broader approach than the use of the stopwatch to determine norms. Kerzhentsev wanted improved productivity based on a mass movement organised in cells at the base and criticised Gastev's strategy as a top-down one involving plant management, experts and selected workers who would be 'aristocrats of the working class, priests of scientific management' (Bailes 1977: 390). In 1924 Gastev's position and that of his Central Labour Institute triumphed at the All-Union Conference on Scientific Management. However, although this consolidated the basis of the movement for the Scientific Organisation of Work (NOT) during the NEP, the institutional resources for its widespread implementation were lacking at this period.

The creation of the NEP can be seen as an example of strategy formulation in which an economic model was designed first and a labour-relations model was then designed and adapted to suit the logic of the economic model. (It is of interest to note that alternative models of enterprise organisation and of labour relations, were debated at this time. Thus in 1926 the Central Committee considered a proposal for the trade unions to organise the workers as a producers' collective in a way which both looked back to the debates of 1921 and forward to the approach adopted in Bulgaria in the 1980s (*Literaturnaya gazeta 1988*).) Although participation was desired through production conferences, it does not seem that 'pressure or control from below' was a significant feature of the model. In contrast to War Communism and centralised planning, this was a model without significant campaigns and movements. The most important aspect of labour relations under the NEP was that there was space for open negotiations in which conflicts of interests were recognised. This space was partly implicit in the model and partly due to the absence, or lesser significance, of mechanisms such as those of norm determination and the tariff scales which later became more prominent.

THE CENTRALLY PLANNED ECONOMY AND THE CONSOLIDATION OF THE ADMINISTRATIVE COMMAND SYSTEM – THE 1930s MODEL

The decision in 1929 to create the first Five-Year Plan marks a turning point in the development of Soviet society as well as in the redesign of the structures and mechanisms for the running of the economy as a whole and within individual enterprises. The essence of societal development lay in accelerated industrialisation, especially in heavy industry, the transformation of peasants into industrial workers and the industrialisation of agriculture through collectivisation.

The concept of centralised planning which was to achieve this involved an increase in the activities of the state and in the activities of the party as an organisation. As Carr and Davies put it:

> Planning in the conception formulated in the late 1920s involved the fundamental reshaping of the economy; through planning, resources would be directed towards the fuel and power industries and iron and steel in order to transform the Soviet Union as rapidly as possible into a self-sufficient economy based on advanced technology.
>
> (Carr and Davies 1969: 788)

In the philosophy of central planning the direction in which the planning mechanisms were to operate was clearly articulated:

> the state is becoming the real master of its industry. Therefore it is only the state economic agencies which can construct the industrial plan; the industrial plan must be constructed not from below but from above.
>
> (Carr and Davies 1969: 825)

Soviet theorists at this period contrasted the new approach with that which operated hitherto in the Soviet Union and in capitalist countries. Thus in 1927 Strumilin wrote that 'not prediction but targets . . . are the central focus of any plan' and in the same year Kuibyshev contrasted Soviet with American planning: 'We can construct plans based not only on foreseeing what will happen but also on a definite will to achieve specific tasks and purposes' (Carr and Davies 1969: 729). Stalin was later to express this most succinctly: 'Our plans are not forecasts but instructions.'

The expansion of state structures and mechanisms for the control of the planned economy involved a new stage in the application of the principle of democratic centralism. Democratic centralism had been established in the party since 1903 and in the political system after the Revolution. Now it was applied to the management and operation of industry. Democratic centralism is about the relationship between the 'centre' and the 'base' and the mechanisms which link the two and provide the dynamics of the relationship. Granick explains how the centralist aspect applied to the organisation of industry:

> 1. The structure of administration of industry is built on the basis of strict subordination of lower to higher organs. Officials are commonly appointed by their immediate superiors or by those not very far above. Directives of higher organs are obligatory for all bodies under them.

Each organ supervises the activities of those below it, and checks on their execution of its orders.

2. Individual industrial units have obligatory planned tasks, the sum of which comprises the plan of the organ immediately in charge of these units.

3. In general, the method is followed of one-man authority and responsibility for each economic unit. However, in higher organs which combine the work of many branches of the economy, group decision and responsibility – through collegia – is the governing system.

(Granick 1954: 12)

Democratic centralism requires the associated mechanisms of normative regulations to give detailed instructions or guidelines on enterprise structures and procedures.

In September 1929 the party passed a special resolution on *edinonachalie* a concept directly derived from that of democratic centralism. The event which triggered party concern over managerial effectiveness was the Shakty trial in 1928 of engineering specialists alleged to have engaged in 'wrecking activities'. The leadership defined the situation as one in which 'Red Directors' had to assert real control over the technical specialists and the redefinition of *edinonachalie*, stressing the accountability of directors, was a mechanism for securing this. The accountability of enterprise directors was increased by the efforts, associated with centralised planning, to make the enterprise rather than higher bodies the main structural level for *khozraschet* accounting. However, *edinonachalie* is a more complex concept that the literal translation of 'one-man management' suggests. In practice it came to mean especially accountability for operational decisions and for the implementation of the tasks specified in the plan. It also has to be related to the position of the party organisation. With the establishment of centralised planning came the expansion of party structures directly concerned with economic questions and plan fulfilment, partly paralleling the state structures of ministries and their subordinate structures. Consequently both the enterprise director and the party secretary were accountable for the plan and the director was expected to consult the party organisation on issues with 'policy' implications, as distinct from those which were routine or purely operational. The elaboration of *edinonachalie* in the context of centralised planning was accompanied by redefinition of the place of the trade union from what it had been under the NEP. Following the removal of Tomsky and other trade union leaders in April 1929, it was decided that the trade unions should concentrate on production rather than the representative function. (In the process of industrialisation in the 1930s trade unions took a leading place in the recruitment and relocation of workers.) Thus at the top of the enterprise the *troika* became rather a *dvoika* with the leading positions taken by the management and the party.

However, *edinonachalie* as an expression of democratic centralism was intended to combine a democratic as well as a centralist element. 'The party leaders never identified it with despotic power. Nor did they intend to oppose it to workers' control. *Edinonachalie* meant institutionalised, accountable one-man management with workers' control incorporated' (Kuromiya 1984: 185). Consequently, with centralised planning there was a conscious strategy of encouraging mobilisation and pressure from the base of the enterprise, primarily with the aim of increasing production and ensuring the fulfilment or overfulfilment of plan targets, but also as a mechanism for exercising some control over the top of the enterprise. The control function was focused on the officially encouraged right of the workers to criticise managerial failures in relation to plan fulfilment especially through the mechanism of production meetings and worker control commissions. Mobilisation of the base to increase plan fulfilment came through sponsorship of socialist emulation as a movement.

Initially the main agency for mobilisation of socialist emulation was the Komsomol, which in the early 1920s had developed a strong emphasis on military training and were more prominent in the Red Army and Navy than in industry. However, Stalin 'chose the Komsomol to set the wheels in motion for the First Five-Year Plan' (Baum 1987: 23). In 1927 the Komsomol had taken the lead in organising 'shock work' and shock brigades of young workers. Then in January 1929 Lenin's 1918 article 'How to Organise Competition' (Lenin 1967: 85–94) was published for the first time as the starting point for campaigns of mass emulation, that is, of mobilisation from the base, and the Komsomol began to extend the organisation of these campaigns. They took the form of 'production challenges' issued by shock brigades to workers in other shops of the same enterprise or to different factories. 'Such challenges included the lowering of production costs, improving quality, combating absenteeism and raising output' (Siegelbaum 1982: 48–67). However, despite the importance of the Komsomol in the initial phase, a distinctive feature of the period 1928–31 was the wider involvement of manual worker activists who took the initiative in socialist emulation and were usually members of primary party cells. The party's strategy at this period was based on the recognition that the active participation of these volunteers was essential for achieving the goals of the Five-Year Plan. In Leningrad and Moscow and probably in other industrial centres the number of manual worker party members increased substantially, as did the number and activity of the primary party cells in factories.

In the shock brigades payment was usually to the individual according to his work, but the idea of payment from a 'common pot' emerged as a mechanism for securing shared responsibility for a finished product and securer earnings. In a Moscow electrical factory the Komsomol organised a production commune (*Znanie-sila* 1982) and in 1931 a Gosplan survey showed that 10.5 per cent of workers were in production collectives or production communes and they were especially common in engineering and textiles. Distinctive features of these organisations were their high productivity, their internal distribution and equalisation of earnings and leaders whose selection and appointment owed more to the collective than to the managerial hierarchy (Siegelbaum 1986: 65–94).

> Typically, collectives pooled wages among workers of the same skill grade or divided them on the basis of different grades (rather than individual performance); communes consisted of workers who shared their wages on an equal basis or according to family need, irrespective of skill levels or output. Both types of organization elected their own leaders . . . drew up their own statutes, introduced rationalization measures, rotated jobs among their members, and imposed fines on those who violated the statutes.
>
> (Siegelbaum 1988. 46–7)

The organisational dynamics of collective mobilisation at the base by activists is illustrated by two cases from Leningrad. The first shows the origin of the mechanism of counterplanning.

> The originators of the industrial–financial counterplan were the workers in the Karl Marx factory at Leningrad. The matter began with a discussion of the production programme of the factory, which according to the instructions of the party and the government had to be taken up with each workbench and with each worker. Thus when the industrial–financial plan was being thoroughly considered, the workers stated that on the basis of their own production experience the control figures which had been given to the workers and the brigades could be increased. The shock brigade of the fourth workshop showed that it was quite possible to utilize 42 machines for other work; the brigade of the cast iron foundry suggested that the quota of the shop be increased from 11,000 to 15,000 tons of castings; the toolmakers proved that their shop could double the output of tools. The result was that the programme of the current year could be increased by 120 per cent thanks to the suggestions of the workers. Comrade Ojogin a member of the shock brigade in the factory wrote to the V. K. K. (Temporary Control Com-

mission): Three months ago I produced 50 cylinders a day; now I make about 100. The former cost of production was 13 kopeks a cylinder and now is 8 kopeks. In the industrial–financial counterplan I pledge myself to increase production by an additional 40 to 50 cylinders and reduce the cost by 30 per cent.

(Solokov 1931: 19–20)

This account shows clearly the design sequence of the creation of the counterplan as an organic mechanism at the base in response to the central decision that the imposed planning mechanism should be taken down from the level of the shop to the level of the brigade and the workbench – the change in levels thus influenced labour relations. It also shows the leading role of the shock brigade in identifying and mobilising worker proposals for increasing production and reducing costs and the conception of the counterplan as a pledge to overfulfil plan targets. The next stage in the design sequence was that the prototype from the Karl Marx factory was taken up at the national level and used to create a movement sponsored from above which was widely diffused in industry and which was developed as a theory by Kuibyshev. As a movement mobilised from the top by the party and trade union organisations it had something of an imposed character. However, the political leadership regarded worker involvement at the base as essential and the party secretary of a Leningrad factory who had submitted a counterplan which had not been discussed by the workers had to appear before Ordzhonikidze who was in charge of Heavy Industry.

The second case shows a response to the central decision that the mechanism of *khozraschet* should be taken down below the level of the enterprise to that of the shop and the brigade and illustrates how a change in the level and nature of economic organisation leads to a change in labour relations. Brigade leader Nikolayev's (1932) account shows how he created a *khozraschet* brigade in the machine-casting shop of the Baltic shipyard in Leningrad. He explains that his action was prompted by a report in *Trud* of the initiative of brigade leader Kapkov at the Lenin works in establishing a *khozraschet* brigade. He decided to investigate the possibility of introducing these methods in his own brigade and discussed them with his shop manager and fellow workers. The essence of the concept was that 'We decided to buy from the shop all the necessary material for the work of our brigade and to sell the products of the brigade's work to the same shop at a fixed price' (Nikolayev 1932: 6). (At the Congress of the Bulgarian Trade Unions in 1987 a brigade leader speaking from the floor argued that the same concept of the brigade buying materials from the stores and selling its product to the enterprise should be adopted in Bulgaria. This is an example of the kind of approach which can emerge at the base when the mechanism of *khozraschet* is applied at the level of the brigade.) Nikolayev elaborated his concept in the following terms:

> The brigade working on these methods will keep exact account of how much it spends and how much it produces for the state. So it will always know how profitable its work is and what benefit it brings to the state. The workers must economise on materials; they must use them rationally and make the most of every screw and nail. Khozraschet methods will revise the productivity of labour – as soon as the work slacks off, or production falls or the cost of production increases or the quality of the product deteriorates, the brigade will notice it immediately: there will be a shortage of money. Therefore khozraschet in the brigade will increase our responsibility. The money we economise will go for the construction of new plants and factories and new machines and tractor stations.
>
> (Nikolayev 1932: 7)

Nikolayev describes how he discussed the idea with brigade members and when they accepted it an agreement based on the month's tasks was signed with the shop head – this was done monthly for each plan period. Nikolayev defined his initiative as 'a new stage of socialist competition and shop brigade work'. This definition by an organisational designer is interesting because it shows the need to legitimate a prototype by linking it to the established concept of socialist competition. As explained in Chapter 5, the management at Metals who pioneered radical redesign in the 1980s judged it necessary to legitimate their strategy by defining it as movement for socialist emulation. Nikolayev is explicit that the party and trade union organisations did not welcome his initiative from the base:

> The party and trade union organisation co-operated poorly. Although the Party Committee took us under its patronage it did not pay us much attention. . . . Since there were no party members in our brigade we asked them to give us Comrade Alexeyev to conduct the political work but instead we were given someone else whom the brigade refused to accept because of his rudeness to the workers.
>
> (Nikolayev 1932: 10)

Nikolayev is equally open about the criticism and scepticism of the workers and leaders of other brigades in the shop, an experience which, as explained in Chapter 5, was shared by brigade leader Miloushev in the 1970s.

Adoption of *khozraschet* required the reorganisation of tasks in the brigade and an accounting system to record materials used and the results. This led to substantial savings in costs and increases in earnings and the method was then transferred to other brigades. However, Nikolayev's problems were not yet over: in the next planning period the planning department increased the targets for his brigade to such an extent that the workers regarded them as impossible. The experiment was threatened and the situation was only saved by extending the action field and invoking the help of the Leningrad District Trade Union Soviet and *Trud* who sent in an economist to vet the planning department's calculations and revise the brigade's targets. Political endorsement of *khozraschet* brigades was given by the All Union Committee of the trade union and then as with counterplanning they were mobilised as a movement.

The essence of the agreement signed each month between Nikolayev as brigade leader and the departmental manager was a specification of the planned targets which the brigade would set out to achieve as their responsibility and the obligation of the manager to ensure supply of the materials needed. The brigade's earnings would depend on the extent to which they met the targets but their earnings would be protected if the manager failed to ensure the necessary supplies. Nikolayev is explicit that the agreement put pressure on management as well as on the brigade and claimed that it made management 'more careful about providing the shop and the brigade with supplies on time' (Nikolayev 1932: 16). In essence this was the type of internal agreement between brigades and management which was developed fifty years later in Bulgaria after 1982. A further extension of this mechanism was an emulation agreement which Nikolayev's brigade made with Kapkov's brigade in the Lenin factory: each brigade committed itself to achieve targets in such matters as cost saving and reduction of absenteeism.

From the standpoint of theory, these collective forms of work organisation have a significance as examples of embryonic 'third structures' emerging at the base of enterprises in the sense that collective decisions were made within the units. It was noted that the elected bodies took over functions from the management, the trade union and even the party organisation and 'as a result the *troika* dissolved' (*Znanie-sila* 1982). Although there was no general assembly of the workforce or council at the top of the enterprise, the presence of these collectives can be seen as an emerging form of self-management. (This interpretation has recently been presented in 'The Lessons of Self-Management' (*Znanie-sila* 1982).) However, such prototypes of structures and mechanisms which were to be recreated in the late 1970s and 1980s were seen by the political leadership as contrary to the goals of rapid industrialisation and improved productivity they had identified in the 1930s. The apparatus for the implementation of norm setting for the individual worker rather than the work-group according to the Taylorist principles elaborated by the institutions for the

Scientific Organisation of Work was now in place. The individual 'progressive' piecework system became the dominant mechanism and widened, as it was designed to do, the earnings differentials between workers. The tariff scales setting out the grades and rates for all jobs were established for each industrial branch. Internal distribution of earnings by brigades was incompatible with these mechanisms and in the same way elections of brigade leaders was seen as contrary to the stronger *edinonachalie* of the hierarchy of operational management. In 1934 the Party Congress replaced the principle of functional management by which specialist management were responsible for different aspects of worker activity and gave full responsibility to the hierarchy of line management. (Functional management was derived from Taylor's principle of functional foremanship, a feature of Taylorism which was rarely adopted in the west, so that in this respect at least, Taylor's influence was greater in the Soviet Union.)

Recognition of the feats of individual workers as opposed to groups began with the creation of the status of 'Hero of Labour' in 1929. Its intensive development came with the Izotov and Stakhanovite movements which took their names from the individual workers who initiated the methods which other workers were encouraged to imitate. In 1932, in the Donbass, the miner Izotov greatly exceeded the production norms and was subsequently involved in the transfer of his techniques to other workers. However, his fame was eclipsed by Stakhanov in 1935 when he hewed 102 tons in a shift at the Irmino mine. This was fourteen times the shift norm and his earnings increased almost tenfold. Stakhanov had been chosen for the record-breaking shift by the mine's party organiser, who had ensured that good conditions and supplies would be provided. An essential factor in his achievement, however, was the redesign of the task: the standard method was for the miner both to cut the coal with his pick and to set the timber for support, but Stakhanov extended the division of labour and only cut coal while two timberers looked after the supports. This reorganisation of tasks between direct and supporting workers was to become a regular feature of record breaking in other industries as Stakhanov's feat was taken up by the political leadership and mobilised as a movement with the aim of following Stakhanov's example. This division of labour, however, cannot be seen as a manifestation of Taylorism. As Siegelbaum points out: 'The latter turned on a clear distinction between managers' conceptualization of work tasks and workers' execution of them; the thrust of Stakhanovism was to abolish the distinction between these two functions' (Siegelbaum 1988: 12). Generally, Stakhanovism emphasised the achievements of workers as individuals rather than as members of a collective with shared responsibility (although Stakhanovite brigades were created in some industries). As such, it strengthened a trend which was to persist, until the 1980s in which leading workers were given the status of 'frontranker' on the basis of their individual performances. In terms of organisational relations between top and base within enterprises, there was a duality in the dynamics deriving from Stakhanovism: from the standpoint of the political leadership at the national level, Stakhanovites were seen as a mechanism for the mobilisation of pressure from below on top management to achieve improvements in performance; on the other hand there was differentiation between Stakhanovites and other workers at the base in the rewards they received and in the creation of the conditions that were often necessary for their achievements. Stakhanovites often became a 'core' of leading workers participating in production *aktivs*, on special commissions and other forums designed to link top and base.

THE SOVIET MODEL

The emergence and mobilisation of Stakhanovites provided the last major internal component of what was to become the 'classical' Soviet model, a 'universal' model for industrialising societies which after the war was transferred to other socialist countries. Although there were many changes in the details of its structures and mechanisms over the next forty years, its core structures and dynamics remained essentialy unchanged and any innovations in organisational design were variations on earlier prototypes. The economic reforms initiated in the 1960s altered economic mechanisms and relations with external structures, but did not significantly alter internal dynamics. In the process of strategy formulation at the political level and the subsequent shifts in the design of structures and mechanisms for the centralised model, there are significant differences between the initial model of 1929 and the modified model of the latter part of the First Five-Year Plan and the Second Five-Year Plan. Essentially, these differences turn on the significance of collective labour relations in the initial model and their replacement by individual labour relations in the latter. This was accomplished through the individual piecework system, but was also associated with the conscious strengthening of hierarchy in the operational structure. It is, however, important to note that, in the process of strategy formulation for the centralised model, the redesign of labour relations centring on socialist emulation was identified in 1929 concurrently with the new planning model.

At a more general level a number of comments can be made about the processes of organisational design and strategy formulation that emerged as distinctive features of the process in the Soviet Union. First, the three main models – War Communism, NEP and the 1930s model – were at the same time models of societal development and models of economic organisation and labour relations. The economic and labour relations model was fundamental to the societal model. Second, in terms of strategy formulation in War Communism and the 1930s model, the institution of the models of economic organisation and the models of labour relations can be seen as integrated in conception and in structures and mechanisms. The 1930s model can, in particular, be seen as the product of the synoptic model of strategy formulation which is discussed in Chapters 3 and 12. The NEP model was initially an economic model to which the structures and mechanisms of labour relations were adapted. In this model, in theory and to some extent in practice, the trade unions were separated from management in the enterprise, whereas in the other models they were integrated. Third, a distinguishing feature of socialist organisational design was the organic creation of prototypes of structures and mechanisms at the base which subsequently became centrally supported as movements. The examples discussed in this chapter are the *subbotniks*, production conferences, counterplanning, *khozraschet* brigades and Stakhanovism. Their appearance can be seen as a response by activists at the base to needs articulated by the political leadership with which activists could identify. The absence of such organic contributions to organisational design in the NEP model suggests that its design dynamics were significantly different. The maintenance or subsequent re-emergence of such structures and mechanisms obviously depended on central support. However, it also relates to the significance of history in the development of socialist societies. On the one side political and societal strategy has always been orientated to the future – the construction of socialism and the eventual transition to communism. On the other side, the past has been used as a reference point to legitimate changes in models. Thus the reassessment of the NEP has been a significant feature of the current debate in the Soviet Union on the future development of socialist society. More specifically, the adoption of the concept of self-management has led to renewed interest in the precedent of the factory council of the immediate post-Revolution period.

THE TRANSFER OF THE SOVIET MODEL AND ITS ESTABLISHMENT IN BULGARIA

From the standpoint of economic planning and enterprise organisation, the process of transition lasted from 1944 to about 1951. Bulgaria was liberated by the Soviet army in September 1944, but until 1947 was ruled by a coalition of political parties organised within the Fatherland Front. It has generally been assumed that the goal of the Communist Party was to

establish the Soviet political model and the Soviet model of industrialisation based on state ownership and central planning. However, recent
research has suggested that Dimitrov argued, unsuccessfully, for a political
model based on the concept of a people's democracy and not that of the
dictatorship of the proletariat (Boev *et al.* forthcoming). Whether this
would have affected the model of economic organisation and labour
relations is unclear. A specialist in the organisation of work who was
familiar with the early 1950s considered that the Soviet model was the only
one available. Although the mines and railways were already under state
control, the manufacturing sector, made up mainly of small enterprises,
generally remained in private ownership until nationalisation in December
1947, when about 6,000 enterprises were taken over by workers led by
party cadres. (Over 90 per cent of the enterprises had less than 50
employees and the average size was 23.) Party strategy for control over
industry drew on Lenin's concept of workers' control as applied in the
Soviet Union in 1917–1921, combined with state controls regulating prices
and production (Petrov 1975: 69). The structure for implementing workers'
control in enterprise was the factory council established initially in 1944 by
the Fatherland Front and later on by the trade union workers. Supervision
over production in the capitalist enterprises served a dual purpose: (1) it
was an instrument for increasing production, for raising its quality and for
bringing down the prices; and (2) it helped train the cadres who later took
over the management of the nationalised industries. Factory councils were
also important at this period in Czechoslovakia and in Poland: workers'
councils, dominated by Communists and Socialists took power from the
collapsing Nazi authorities in places of work and initiated attempts to
revive the shattered economy.

At the base of Bulgarian enterprises in the period 1944–9, there was the
beginning of the socialist emulation movement, consciously modelled on
Soviet prototypes with shock brigades and frontrankers (Petrov 1987:
18–19). As early as September 1944 Stakhanov was cited as a model to be
followed in Bulgaria. Petrov (1975: 68) argues that during this period, when
private industry continued under state guidance and control, 'the Party built
its economic policy on the basis of Lenin's principles laid down in the New
Economic Policy' introduced in Soviet Russia. The main mechanism in
labour relations at this period was the collective agreement which derived
from the pre-war Bulgarian regulation of 1936. In June 1945 a general
collective labour agreement was signed by the General Workers Trade
Union and the General Confederation of Bulgarian Industry which
represented the private employers, though at this period such agreements
were not signed at enterprise level. Thus the transitional period in Bulgaria
was characterised by the adoption of concepts and the transfer of structures

and mechanisms derived from different stages of the Soviet model – factory councils, shock brigades and shock workers from 1917 to 1921, collective agreements from the NEP and Stakhanovism from the second half of the 1930s, as well as from pre-war Bulgaria.

Central planning began with the Two Year Plan of 1947–9, and was followed by the Five-Year Plan in 1950. Wage regulation in the transitional period was based on three wage blocks corresponding to the skill categories traditional in Bulgarian industry, but in 1952 were replaced by tariff scales on the Soviet model: the tariffs drawn up for each industrial branch set up the structure of grades for manual and non-manual workers and these were accompanied by the Soviet mechanisms of piecework and norming. In 1951 the Bulgarian Labour Code was enacted. This remained in force, though with important changes, until 1986. It set out general standards on the right and duty to work, the length of the working day, holidays, and health and safety as well as procedures for resolving disputes.

Although in structure and content the Code was influenced by the Labour Code of the Russian Federal Republic, it also drew on provisions from the Bulgarian Regulations on Collective Agreements of 1936 and on provisions from international labour law. In the same year (1951) a decree disbanded the *troika* of party secretary, director and trade union president. This was intended to strengthen the *edinonachalie* of the director at the expense of the socio-political organisations. Thus by 1951 the transfer to Bulgaria of the Soviet model was in all essentials complete, and throughout the 1950s the Bulgarian enterprise operated with the same mechanisms as in the Soviet Union. (The brigades of Communist labour, a specific form of socialist emulation, introduced in the late 1950s were a direct transfer from the Soviet Union.)

Starting in 1964 proposals for economic reform began to be implemented in Bulgaria. They were essentially for a degree of economic decentralisation, a reduction in the number of plan indices, and an attempt at using indices of profit as well as those of physical output for assessing enterprise performance. The redesign of planning mechanisms was followed in 1968 by the reorganisation of structures above the enterprise with the creation of the DSO (Drzhavni Stopanski Obedinenie: State Economic Corporation) as a level between enterprises and ministries with responsibility for the economic management of a group of enterprises. (Similar patterns of creating 'corporations' occurred in other socialist countries at this period.) Although a new structure, the production committee was established at the top of the enterprise and its functions were essentially consultative and advisory. The 1960s redesign was essentially an economic one unaccompanied by any significant changes in the structures and mechanisms of labour relations. The organisation of work, the system of payment and relations between top and base of the enterprise remained essentially the same.

However, at a theoretical level the case for more radical redesign had been put by Miloshevski. He argued that 'the present combination of the democratic principle and the principle of *edinonachalie* does not provide the best possible conditions for convincing the workers that the enterprise is their own'. The conditions were now appropriate for creating an institution in enterprises for worker participation in the making of decisions on 'production, the organisation of work, wages and the distribution of profits and to have a say in the appointment of the enterprise director' (Miloshevski 1963: 88).

Conclusions: the dynamics of the centralised model

The dynamics of the enterprise under the administrative command system of economic management derived essentially from the pressures generated by the planning mechanisms of imposed plan targets (and from the frequent revision or alteration of those targets). Consequently all significant internal issues and decision processes were linked to the planning cycles and processes. Internally these pressures were transmitted from top to base mainly through the first (operational) structure, but also by movements and campaigns mobilised through the second structure (the party and trade union). The general direction of the mechanisms was downward, although movements and campaigns, and especially the mechanism of counter-planning were intended to generate some internal pressure from below. Spontaneous, as opposed to stimulated, pressure from the base was limited to pressures on the wage fund and other mechanisms of distribution described in Chapter 7. Accountability in this system was almost entirely upwards and the design was to establish a chain of command and the accountability of individuals through the principle of *edinonachalie*; accountability to the base was confined to the provision of information on plan fulfilment and given the strength of upward accountability was necessarily only on a consultative basis. In terms of organisational theory the subjects were management and the trade union, and this expressed the theory of interests in which plan fulfilment was in the interests of society to which the interests of the enterprise as both an economic and social unit were essentially subordinate. Vertically, the centralised model was characterised by a long series of levels both externally (state planning committee, ministry, corporation, enterprise) and internally (enterprise, department, section); thus there was a great distance between top and base.

As an aid to the understanding of the internal dynamics of the enterprise in the centralised model, Figures 2.1 and 2.2 show the organisational

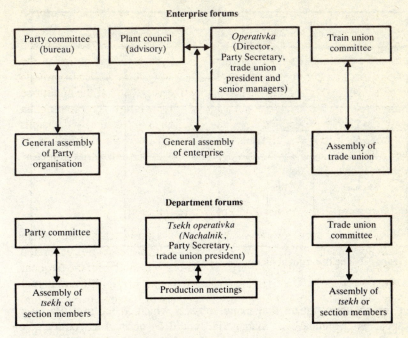

Figure 2.1 Enterprise and department forums

structure of the enterprise and its principal level and unit of internal structure, the department (in Bulgarian the *tsekh*, sometimes translated as 'shop') which was frequently the unit responsible for the production of a final product or a complete technological cycle. Figure 2.1 shows the forums at which decisions were made and issues mobilised at the levels of the enterprise and of the department. Figure 2.2 shows the hierarchy within the department.

At the top of the enterprise the director, party secretary and trade union president operated as a *troika* and as an *operativka* (a working group for considering operational problems). The relative authority of director and party secretary would depend in practice on the individuals, but both were accountable for the fulfilment of plan targets – the director to the next level of the state hierarchy (usually the DSO) and the party secretary to the district party committee. The primary role of the party in the enterprise was always officially defined as political and ideological. This meant the education of party members in a Marxist–Leninist approach and in the understanding of party policy. However, the close linkage of party and state structures and the involvement of the party organisation in the management

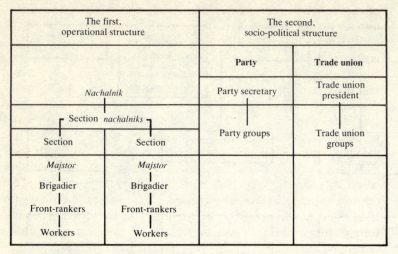

The first, operational structure		The second, socio-political structure	
		Party	**Trade union**
Nachalnik		Party secretary	Trade union president
Section *nachalniks*		Party groups	Trade union groups
Section	Section		
Majstor	*Majstor*		
Brigadier	Brigadier		
Front-rankers	Front-rankers		
Workers	Workers		

Figure 2.2 The department hierarchy

of the economy meant that many subjects which to the outsider might appear as 'technical' or 'managerial' could be defined as 'political' or 'ideological'. Thus improving the quality of production was the subject of a national party conference in 1984 and as such was therefore in the domain of politics and ideology. (In 1983 John Thirkell met a district trade union official who worked in the ideological department. He was surprised to learn that the content of his work was concerned with the collection and dissemination of information on standards of quality control, as these were then in the domain of ideology.) Its accountability for the plan meant that the enterprise party organisation was necessarily concerned with operational issues in so far as they were significant in relation to the plan, as well as with strategic issues related to the development of the enterprise. This made necessary its participation in the *operativka* and its role in convening the *aktiv*. The party organisation was responsible for ensuring the implementation of specific party instructions. Its other main area of activity was the development of reserve cadres, and the assessment and selection of individuals for supervisory, managerial positions, and for party and trade union positions within the enterprise (discussed in Chapter 9).

Under the centralised model the trade unions were regarded primarily as representing the interests of the working class as a whole and only secondarily as representing the interests of their members in different industrial sectors and enterprises. The trade union organisation was responsible for both production and protection and for social welfare, especially housing and holidays. The production function was carried out through the mechanisms of socialist emulation and of production meetings which were organised by the trade union and intended to solve operational problems and improve plan results; the protective function was based on ensuring adherence to the standards set out in the Labour Code and other normative regulations (workers could appeal to the trade union if they felt that standards were being breached or that work norms were incorrectly assessed). Beyond this, and the mechanisms of counterplanning and worker proposals discussed in Chapter 6, there were no recognised mechanisms for the regular articulation of interests at the base and their mobilisation.

Within the *tsekh* hierarchical authority lay with the *nachalnik* whose power lay in his control over the allocation of work (distribution of better- or worse-paying jobs) and bonuses. Below him came the *majstor* the lowest level of the managerial hierarchy – experienced as workers but with few formal qualifications – and the brigadier, in effect, a chargehand. Generally, workers were paid on individual piece-rates and slotted into grades on the national tariff scales – payment was thus entirely according to work done. Within the sections, frontrankers who had won their status in socialist emulation were top of the earnings hierarchy. They would be expected to play an active part in production meetings and might be drawn into special *aktivs* as a core (see Chapter 11) convened by top management and specialists to solve particular problems. A specialist noted that there was sometimes 'silent pressure' from frontrankers or other individual 'core' workers but rarely any collective pressure. Forums such as the production meetings were convened from above and not on the initiative of workers at the base. However, at production meetings management would give reports on their work and performance in relation to the plan and this could be used by workers as an opportunity to express criticisms of managerial performance. At a more abstract level of analysis the administrative command model can be seen as embodying, through its structures and mechanisms, an individual rather than a collective model of labour relations. This was also related to the theory of interests as expressed in the ideological formulations of that period: although the personal interests of the individual worker were recognised (for example, in the provisions of the Labour Code), the collective interests of workers at the base were assumed to mainly coincide with the general interests of the working class in society and the latter were defined by the party through its strategies for societal development. The administrative command model can also be seen as one in which space and autonomy at the base was very limited so that the range of choices was mainly restricted to coping with day-to-day operational problems within a centrally determined system of rewards.

NOTE

1 As explained in the text the concept of *khozraschet* was introduced by Lenin
   with the introduction of the New Economic Policy. It is a concept which
   continues to be used in the context of changes in the organisation of the
   economy and of the redesign of internal planning and accounting mechanisms.
   The Bulgarian equivalent is *stopanska smetka*. Although sometimes translated
   as 'profit and loss accounting' or literally as 'economic accounting' it is worth
   noting Baykov's comment (1950: 116) that: 'There is no adequate English
   equivalent of the Soviet expression *khozraschet*. The notion implies that cost
   accounting is applied to definite quantitative and qualitative tasks prescribed by
   the plan as well as to financial results.' Nove (1977: 28) quotes the definition
   given by Tyagay (1956: 393) 'the carrying out of state-determined tasks with
   the maximum economy of resources, the covering of money expenses of enterprises by their own money revenues, the ensuring of profitability of enterprises'.
   Nove explains:

   > this means that a normally functioning enterprise will cover its operating
   > expenses out of income derived from the sale of goods and services to other
   > enterprises or (in the case of retail establishments) to the population.
   > Similarly, it will pay for its material inputs to supplying enterprises, all at
   > prices determined by the planning authorities; it pays amortization
   > (depreciation) charges, also at rates determined from above. Working capital
   > is in part provided by short-term credits obtained from the State Bank; these
   > too are planned, and bear a low rate of interest. Wages paid to workers and
   > employees are likewise based on officially laid down scales. Note that in this
   > model what is done is laid down in the plan, and the object of *khozraschet* is
   > to encourage the carrying out of instructions with due economy and
   > efficiency.

   (Nove 1977: 28)

   In socialist accounting terminology a basic distinction is made between 'full'
   and 'partial' *khozraschet*. Taking account of the qualifications and definitions
   given above, in terms of western accounting usage, it may be helpful to refer to
   the distinction between 'cost' and 'profit' centres. In a cost centre costs are
   calculated and compared with a budget but there is no calculation of the centre's
   revenue or income. For a profit centre, however, a calculation of revenue is
   made and the profit or loss is the difference between costs and revenue. Essentially, partial *khozraschet* refers to a cost centre, with comparison between
   planned (budgeted) costs and planned physical outputs, and full *khozraschet* to
   a profit centre with comparison between costs and revenue. When prices are
   centrally determined, as has been the general practice in socialist economies,
   plan fulfilment has been seen as more important than profitability.
     One of the central, and recurring, issues in socialist economies has been the
   level of the unit of structure to which full *khozraschet* should be applied –
   should it be the trust as under NEP or the enterprise as from 1929? Equally,
   there is the issue of *khozraschet*, or at least partial *khozraschet*, within internal
   units of the enterprise – full *khozraschet* requires the fixing of a transfer price to
   determine the unit's income. The case of Nikolayev's *khozraschet* brigade
   illustrates internal *khozraschet*. It is clear that his approach led to accounting for
   costs within the brigade; although he spoke of selling its products to the

enterprise for a price, it appears that in practice the emphasis was on planned physical output targets. In the 1980s in Bulgaria the aim of getting brigades to operate on *stopanska smetka* was implemented in different degrees. In the majority of cases costs were calculated for the brigade and these were set against physical production targets. However, the calculation of costs was often difficult especially in sequential production processes, although in a few enterprises computerisation made this possible. In many enterprises an attempt was made to draw up an account comparing brigade costs with the 'income' from its production though this was calculated on prices established administratively by the enterprise or a higher formation.

3 Strategy formulation in Bulgaria, 1978–1988

At the beginning of the 1980s a process of radical redesign of labour relations was initiated in Bulgaria and elaborated in the party conception of labour relations (Zhivkov 1984). This process had two distinctive features: (1) the changes covered all aspects of labour relations whereas previous reforms had been partial in scope; and (2) parallel with its implementation a new approach to the management of the economy was being introduced. The redesign of labour relations and economic management was followed by the elaboration of a comprehensive conception for the self-management of society and the reconstruction of its political superstructure, which was adopted at the July 1987 Plenum of the CC of BCP (Zhivkov 1987c). This sequence of change, as will be explained, can be seen as a characteristic of the *perestroika* model in Bulgaria and a starting point for comparison with the strategies adopted in a number of other socialist countries.

The general aim of this chapter is to analyse the process of strategy formulation at national level in Bulgaria for the restructuring of labour relations. At its simplest, strategy formulation is defined as the process of identifying strategic issues, that is, issues which are thought to require and be amenable to redesign of structures (Jackson-Cox *et al*. 1987: 57). This definition leaves open the question of how issues come to be identified and recognized, and the process by which the issue is linked to specific changes in structures and/or mechanisms. Similarly, when more than one strategic issue has been identified, there is the question of the sequence in which restructuring is to be carried out. A further question relates to the place of concepts in the process of identifying and defining strategic issues. Thus an organisational problem may be identified and this may lead to recognition that a concept is needed. If an appropriate concept is found, then the nature and definition of the concept itself may come to shape the nature of the solution reached in the process of strategy formulation.

Some western political scientists (Bertsch 1978: 133–4; Holmes 1986: 246–7; Cocks 1976: 157) have suggested that there are two general models of the policy process – the incremental and the synoptic – and have argued that there is greater scope for the synoptic model in centralised socialist states than in pluralist western societies, where the incremental model is more common. Of the latter model Holmes (1986: 246) writes:

> Policies are made in an ad hoc manner, as a response to a particular problem or pressure group. There is no clear end-goal, and the nature of the political and economic system is such that it would not be possible to integrate policies fully even if this were desired.

In the 'synoptic teleological' model on the other hand 'decisions are not made in a random way . . . but rather in a planned way. . . . Synoptic means comprehensive, while Teleological means, in this context, geared to some distant goal'. In this book somewhat different definitions of the two models are used. In the incremental model, strategic issues are identified singly, redesign is implemented in practice and this leads to the identification of the next strategic issue, or alternatively to the suspension of strategy formulation in the specific field because there is no recognition of further strategic issues. In the synoptic model, a series of strategic issues are identified and a sequence of implementation through structures and mechanisms is elaborated. Strategy formulation of this kind depends on being able to conceptualise the relationships between the sequence of strategic issues and the emergence of issues at each stage of redesign. This requires a primary concept from which secondary concepts (or a set of concepts) can be derived. Examples of such primary concepts are 'enterprise', 'firm', 'community' and 'labour collective'. In this model the successive implementation of each stage of redesign only influences the timing and form of the succeeding stage, because the strategic issue for each stage has already been identified and recognised.

STRATEGY FORMULATION IN THE 1970s

The process of strategy formulation in the 1980s has to be set in the context of the 1970s. As explained in Chapter 2, the redesign of structures initiated in the 1960s was confined to structures above the enterprise, the internal structures of which remained essentially unchanged. During the 1970s official policy statements consistently identified a series of issues related to the improvement of the economy and the radical improvement of living standards, but did not specify any changes in enterprise structure. The internal dynamics of enterprises still conformed substantially to those generated by the administrative command model of economic management despite the introduction of the counterplanning mechanisms (see Chapter 6). In terms of strategy formulation at national level, therefore, the period up to 1978 can be characterised as one in which a number of strategic issues related to the improvement of the economy were identified, but no definition related to the design or redesign of management or labour relations structures was forthcoming. By the end of the 1970s, however, the reduction in the rates of economic growth created pressures for the reassessment of approaches to economic management. During the 1970s, although most workers were paid individually, it became increasingly recognised that the results of individual work were becoming more dependent on the work of the enterprise as a whole, so that the link between the earnings of the worker and the overall results of work became weaker. Recognition of this trend lay behind the decision of the National Party Conference of April 1978 to create a new-type brigade as the generic structure of work organisation in all sectors of employment. The Report Note (Zhivkov 1977) to the Politburo published in August 1977 to set the agenda for the party conference was entitled 'For the Improvement of the Planned Management of the Economy and Socialist Organisation of Work'. However, the Report of the Conference Decisions reversed the title of the Report Note placing 'Socialist Organisation of Work' first (Zhivkov 1982), indicating a significant shift in the identification of strategic issues and their priority. The significance of the conference in terms of strategy formulation was, first, that it identified the socialist organisation of work as a strategic issue to be resolved in the context of other long-term economic and societal changes, and, second, that it defined the new-type brigade as the structural unit which was to be the starting-point for the redesign of the enterprise. This was an innovative approach to organisational design in that its starting-point was the base of the enterprise. Theoretically, there are three levels at which the redesign of enterprise structures can start: at the top, in the middle, or at the base. The starting-point necessarily influences subsequent redesign by precluding certain options. In the 1960s, as explained in Chapter 2, there had been a minor redesign at the top with the creation of the Plant Council but other changes in economic organisation were at levels above the enterprise.

Changes in the organisation of work, and the pressures for an increasing emphasis on the enterprise as an economic unit, would necessarily have had consequences for labour relations. But such changes could have been those derived from, and been dependent on, changes in economic organisation, rather than from a conscious strategy of developing a new model of labour relations. This, however, was the purpose of *A new conception of labour and labour relations in socialist Bulgaria* (Zhivkov 1982) approved by the national party conference in November 1982. This raises the question of the process by which labour relations came to be recognised as a primary rather than a secondary field for national strategy. The process can be seen as one in which an internal dynamic for the redesign of economic mechanisms was developing at the same time as external events in Poland raised the strategic issue of the future role of trade unions in socialist societies. The dynamic for economic reform was shifting from the DSO (the corporation) towards the enterprise as the main unit of economic organisation and this was seen as requiring a redefinition of relations between top and base within the enterprise. Thus in a speech on the new economic approach in January 1980 President Zhivkov foresaw workers exercising pressure on managers if the practical results of their work did not yield economic results and suggested that workers should have the right to give an opinion on the appointment of their managers (Zhivkov 1984). The Party Congress in March–April 1981 appointed P. Dyulgerov President of the Trade Unions and a candidate member of the Politburo, a status not enjoyed by his predecessor. At the Trade Union Congress in April 1982 the trade unions were given a new function as 'organiser of the labour collective' and 'guarantor' of the New Economic Mechanism. These changes enhancing the place and responsibility of the trade unions in strategy formulation, were in part a response to events in Poland and provided the basis for the elaboration of the New Conception of Labour and Labour Relations presented to the party conference in November.

STRATEGY FORMULATION: CHOICE AND ELABORATION OF CONCEPTS

In the synoptic model of strategy formulation the choice and elaboration of primary concepts and the recognition of their interrelationship is the critical element in the process. In Bulgaria, the primary concepts, the elaboration and linkage of which made possible the synoptic model of strategy formulation, were those of the labour collective and of *stopanin*. At the political level the linkage of the two concepts was made in President Zhivkov's report to the Party Congress in April 1981, which stated that 'the labour collective should become the *stopanin* of socialist property' (Zhivkov 1981a). The elaboration of these linked primary concepts led to a redefinition of the relationships between individual workers and the enterprise, and between the enterprise and the state, and consequently to the redesign of enterprise structures and mechanisms. This choice of the labour collective as the primary concept led not only to the redesign of enterprises, but also precluded the development of a model of labour relations based upon 'enterprise' as the primary concept. Table 3.1 is intended to show the sequence of the elaboration of concepts and their relationship to the redesign of structures and mechanisms as explained in the remainder of this chapter.

Table 3.1 Concepts and the redesign of structures and mechanisms

Event	Concept	Structure
Party Conference 1978	Collective forms of work organisation	Brigades
Party Congress 1981	Labour collective as *stropanin*	Enterprise as unit (level) of redesign
Party Conference 1982	Labour collective as subject and social unit	Enterprise as two-level structure with third vertical structure
	Primary and main collective	Brigade as self-managing unit
Labour Code 1986		(Incorporates these structural changes)
Party Conference 1987	Labour collective as self-managing community	
National Assembly Declarations and Economic Regulation 1988	Labour collective as economic subject	Agreements on transfer of property

The conception of the labour collective is derived from the classic Marxist concept of associated labour. Marx wrote that the social organisation of the new (communist) society would be an 'association of free producers' (Marx and Engels 1973; Marx 1981: vol. 3, ch. 48). The theory of associated labour has not been elaborated in detail, but in the spirit of Marx's logic. It can be argued that it relates to the direct integration of individuals into labour associations. 'Direct' means that the association itself is a production unit. However, to be integrated as 'free producers', these individuals should have an equal economic status –that is, they should have the same status in relation to the means of production.

Implementation of Marx's conception of associated labour has not been a strategic aim in socialist countries (with the exception of Yugoslavia, as explained in Chapter 12). Instead it has generally been assumed that the concept relates to the second stage in the development of socialism – the transition to a communist society. This interpretation has influenced approaches to the potential of the labour collective as a basis for organisation of workers in production. The first attempt to define the concept of a 'labour collective' was made by Makarenko. Based on the experience in the Soviet Union of the labour colonies created in the 1930s and the labour communes of the 1920s, he defined the labour collective as 'a group of working people united by a common goal. Acting in common, organised and having management organs, with defined discipline and responsibility' (Makarenko 1986: 13). The emphasis in this definition is on the organisational characteristics – the collective is integrated by the common goal and not by the interests of its members. This reflects the traditional theory of collectivism which sees the common goal as identical with the interests of society and deriving from it. Subsequently, the concept of the labour collective did not have a significant place in the further development of organisational theory. Although the concept was used in pedagogy and more recently in social psychology and sociology, the collective has not been seen as an object of investigation in political economy or economic theory. The view dominant in managerial practice was that the labour collective was related only to the human factor, that is, with only one of the elements of the labour process. This relegated it to a secondary role in organisational innovation – the worker was always expected to adapt to changes in organisational structure and other changes introduced from above.

In the centralised model of economic management the labour collective was given a role in the mechanisms for mobilisation from bottom to top in the movements for emulation. As such the concept of 'labour collective' or 'production collective' was regularly used in Bulgaria from the 1950s (especially in political or similar statements), as a term broadly equivalent to the 'workforce' of a unit of production such as an enterprise. The first serious attempts to reconceptualise views of the labour collective and develop a special theory date from the late 1970s when Shkaratan made the analytical distinction between the labour collective and the enterprise. Hitherto, collective and enterprise had not been separated in theorising and the distinction he made facilitated the separation between the collective as a social entity and the enterprise as an economic organisation (Shkaratan 1978: 8–29). In Bulgaria the impetus for theorising came first from the extensive empirical investigations carried out in industry during this period, and second from the reassessment of the conception of the state as the unique and supreme owner. Until the early 1980s sociological research in industrial enterprises in Bulgaria and the work of the plant sociologists (of whom there were 400 in 1987) was generally related to the labour collective and only in a few cases to the enterprise as a complete system (Mikhailov 1978). Researches into the problems of social planning and participation in management were very important for the elaboration of the sociological conception of the labour collective. The common element of these topics is that they presuppose the active involvement not of individual workers or groups of workers, but of the entire collective. Social planning deals with the collective needs for housing, transport, a safe working environment and holidays etc. These needs are categorised according to their significance and this necessarily implies a common collective stand. For social planning, special social passports are issued (with data about the social, demographic, educational and professional structure of the labour collective), and this leads to the recognition of the workers of an enterprise as a social entity. The position that the collective is a social entity was also derived from studies of the system of participation in management (on a consultative basis), which became popular during this period. The main forums of participation were the general assembly of workers and the production committee (plant council during the 1970s). The general assembly was used as a mechanism for reaching an opinion acceptable to the collective as a whole, while the plant council was elected to represent its interests. Logic and analysis therefore led to the conclusion that the labour collective differs both from the institution (the enterprise) and from the sum of the individual workers.

THE LABOUR COLLECTIVE

Under the centralised model, it is clear that the labour collective had a secondary role, and was not a party in labour relations. The concept 'labour collective' was not used in labour or economic regulations before 1982 and any attempt to connect the labour collective with the functions of management and not of a full owner, were subjected to the criticism that this was a deviation which would lead to 'group' property (Butenko 1982: 16–29). In these circumstances the view of the labour collective current in political economy was that the collective is a social entity of producers which does not have real economic power to administer property (Yanchev 1984: 30). In management theory, the collective was viewed a managed sub-system, along with the technical and economic sub-systems which were also an object of management (*Sotsiologicheski problemi* 1983: 3–32). In sociology the dominant view was that the labour collective was a social (human) entity, linked by the activity of work (Kyuranov 1982). Legal interpretations of the labour collective from the early 1980s universally assumed that the collective was an aggregation of individual labour relations. The conventional legal logic followed the line that the enterprise is a corporate body, which uses the means of production granted by the state and establishes legal relations with each worker, and since the worker has legally established his relations with the enterprise, he becomes by virtue of this a member of the labour collective (Tadjer 1983: 20). In summary, therefore, until the beginning of the 1980s, the labour collective was excluded from the management of both economic and labour relations.

It was assumed to be a party only in management relations (as a managed sub-system) and in social (personal) relations (as a human entity).

The concept of *stopanin* and the labour collective as *stopanin*

The elaboration of the conception of the labour collective as *stopanin* requires more attention. The term *stopanin* in its economic, social and political sense has no direct equivalent in English – the nearest are 'manager', 'supervisor', 'administrator'. (*Khozain*, which is the Russian equivalent of *stopanin*, is translated as 'owner' (Russky yazik 1987). Although the term *stopanin* has been used in political discourse for a long time, its usage did not originally imply a substantially new concept. The document for the 'Plenum of the CC of BCP' in May 1963, which was the basis for the strategy of economic reform, noted that the collective should become *stopanin* of the enterprise (Zhivkov 1975: 407), but neither *stopanin* nor 'labour collective' was clearly defined at the time. It appears that at this juncture the workers in the collective of the enterprise were still viewed as representatives of the working class, that is, in the context of socio-political and not economic relations. The concept of *stopanin* next emerged with an essentially new and wider definition in the documents prepared for the 12th Party Congress in 1981, where *stopanin* was linked to ownership. The report to the congress stressed that while the state is authorised by the people to be the owner of socialist property, the labour collective should be its *stopanin* (Zhivkov 1981b: 39). This was the first time in a political context that two parties, the state and the labour collective, were mentioned in relation to the management of socialist property. At the political level the labour collective as *stopanin* now existed as a primary concept and was therefore capable of elaboration and development in relation to other concepts at this level. In the subsequent debates in the academic literature, attention was concentrated on how the functions of the two parties were to be defined, and how an economic mechanism consistent with this new conception should be elaborated. Thus the crucial question of the economic status of the state and of the labour collective remained unresolved and in the background, though logically it should have preceded the question of functions. This could not be done until the established view of the economic status of the individual had been reassessed.

Interpretation of the conception of *stopanin* requires an explanation of the concepts of socialist property, the role of the state, the individual worker, the enterprise and the labour collective in the centralised model. As explained in Chapter 2, nationalisation of the industrial means of production was implemented in 1947. In political economy the interpretation of this is that the socialisation of the means of production establishes all-people's (state) property – 'state' is in brackets because it was assumed that ownership was all-people's in content and state in form. This implied that the people as a whole had to exercise their ownership rights, but this was clearly impossible. The theoretical answer was that the people authorised the state to manage their property, and therefore delegated their ownership rights to the state, which took over the functions of management. It was postulated that the individual worker, as a member of the people, was also a co-owner, although as a citizen the worker had already delegated his rights of managing property to the state. The worker's relations with the owner were regulated through the mechanism of central distribution of a part of the national income (the public consumption funds), and the political mechanisms for control over the administrative apparatus (elections, referendums etc.). In reality the worker only became linked to the means of production when he started work in an enterprise. He offered his labour power as his personal property, receiving wages as 'hired labour' in return for his work. This merging of labour power with the means of production shaped the system of labour relations in the enterprise, which were essentially individualised in that norms, bonuses and qualifications were set individually. The legal bases of labour relations with regard to appointment and dismissal, discipline and social insurance were equally individual. Given this complete individualisation of labour relations, alternatives to the development of relations between the worker and the labour collective only existed informally in psychological terms, or were mobilised externally, through political and moral mechanisms for promoting a collective consciousness. The interests of the state and the individual meet and are integrated in the enterprise, which is the employer of the worker and is the lowest unit in the network of institutions established for the management of state property and its utilisation in the production process. As explained in Chapter 2, the traditional model of the socialist enterprise was a two-structure hierarchical one of pyramidal form, with the director at the top and the mass of workers at the base in which the director managed property on behalf of the state and was accountable to it.

Redesign of labour relations meant that the existing concept of the labour collective had to be reassessed in terms of both labour and managerial relations. Theoretical work in the area of labour relations accompanied the drafting of the new Labour Code (1982–6) while in the area of managerial relations it continued throughout the period in which the Regulation on Economic Activity, which came into force in 1987, was being drafted. The essential change in labour relations lay in the development of the concept of 'collective labour relations'. This implies that as a social entity, the collective is a party in these relations, directly expressing its interests without mediation by the enterprise or the trade unions. The collective's partners can be the enterprise, the individual worker or the trade union committee. Thus the traditional triangle of parties in labour relations ('enterprise–workers–trade union committee') is transformed into a quadrangle ('labour collective–enterprise–worker–trade union committee'). From the worker's standpoint, the logic of this model leads to the formation of three categories of relations: (1) between the worker and the enterprise; (2) between the worker and the collective; (3) between the worker and the trade union. This change in the system and structure of relations is shown in Figures 3.1 and 3.2. In these figures a distinction is made between the top and the base of the enterprise both because it is of real importance and because the Labour Code distinguished between the primary and the main collective.

		State ◄————————► Trade union	
Enterprise	Top	Director	Trade union
	Base	Employee of enterprise	Member of trade union

Figure 3.1 Traditional model of labour relations

Theoretically and normatively the Bulgarian Communist Party has not been a subject of labour relations though in reality it intervenes in labour relations. The convention is that the Party does not solve labour relations problems directly but may operate to influence them through economic management or the trade union.

		State ◄————————————► Trade union		
Enterprise	Top	Director	Main collective	Trade union
	Base	Employee of enterprise	Member of primary collective	Member of trade union

Figure 3.2 New model of labour relations

These figures show the subjects of relations and the links between them. However, the question of object is very important, that is, the ground for the rise of relations in which their content is revealed. Figure 3.2 gives a general idea of this aspect of the new model. It indicates the most important aspects of labour relations with the exception of specific material responsibility and control over labour legislation. (The nature of the change may become clearer if it is recalled that in the traditional model of labour relations, the labour collective was not included as a party but, even under the collective agreement, was represented by the trade union committee.) Conversely, under the new model, the collective is the main party in nearly all relations in the categories of both individual and collective labour relations.

THE REDESIGN OF STRUCTURES AND MECHANISMS

To establish the labour collective, the creation of a new structure was needed to transform the traditional model of the socialist enterprise from a model with two vertical structures into a model with three vertical structures. The new structure was designed to become the central one. This meant that it was not sufficient simply to create space for its operation in the organisation, but that the internal structural levels of the enterprise should be redesigned. The significant change here was the conceptual distinction made between the 'primary' and 'main' labour collective. The primary collective was the workers of a brigade, while the main collective consisted of the whole workforce of the enterprise. The implementation of this conception is discussed in Chapter 5. Here the question of the two levels is discussed briefly in relation to the operational application of the initial concept of the labour collective. In Bulgaria, the typical industrial enterprise employs between 500 to 1,000 people and the inclusion of all workers, specialists and employees in the administration in a single collective would entail serious practical difficulties. This became clear in the late 1970s, with the mass implementation of brigade organisation. A brigade can only be an autonomous economic unit based on cost accounting and applying direct forms of democracy if its members do not exceed 100. The problem is not simply one of numbers, but the impracticability of exercising day-to-day mutual control over the labour process in large communities. The application of the new mechanism of distribution in the brigade based on a brigade wage fund and individual wage determination through the coefficient for labour participation (see Chapter 7), also becomes impracticable. Thus practical necessity led to the solution of separating the labour collective into two structural levels. In this way the process of restructuring the Bulgarian industrial enterprise acquired its distinctive character of starting from the base upward. The other operational problem relates to the territorial boundaries of the main labour collective. In Bulgarian industry there were both single site enterprises and enterprises comprising units in different parts of a local authority district and also in different districts. This feature runs counter to the requirement that the collective should be integrated through forms of direct democracy. Hence the necessity of providing in the Labour Code that the main labour collectives should as a rule only be established in enterprises located on a single site.

In sociological theory the distinction between different levels of the collective was made during the 1970s. The collective was seen as being parallel to the structure of the enterprise which had three levels: primary (the brigade), intermediate (the department) and main (the enterprise as a whole). However, this perception was mainly confined to research studies in the fields of industrial sociology and the sociology of organisations, and the terms 'primary', 'intermediate' and 'main' collective were not adopted in organisational practice, in management theory or in legislation. The theoretical distinction between levels became operational in the new Labour Code which specified the criteria for 'Primary labour collective' (Arts. 18–23) and the 'Main labour collective' (Arts. 24–32) (Labour Code 1986). The definition of the concept of labour collective was elaborated, deductively, in the following sequence.

First, the collective was defined as a 'community' of people, a concept taken from sociological theory. To 'ground' this concept it was postulated that the workers in an enterprise become an organically integrated community when their relations are based on economic interests. In other words, the heterogeneous mass of individual workers can become integrated as a labour community only in conditions conducive to the rise of differentiated collective interests. Second, it follows that the collective should work on the basis of cost accounting and self-financing, as it is only in these conditions that it becomes an economically differentiated unit. Third, to operate on the basis of cost accounting and self-financing, the collective ought to have the right to dispose of the means of production. This in turn presupposes its economic power and responsibility for investment, for directly choosing the mix of products related to market demand, and some freedom in the field of price formation. In essence, therefore, it should operate as the manager of property. Thus the concept of labour collective adopted in Bulgaria led to the position that restructuring should provide an economic base for self-management. The economic rationality of the model of self-management has always been a key issue of strategic choice in socialist countries. However, priority can also be given to the enterprise as a self-managing unit (the Hungarian model), and not to the labour collective.

As a basic structure the labour collective needs organisational forums to integrate the other two structures of the enterprise-operational management and the social–political organisations. Accordingly, a new hierarchy of self-management bodies was established.

Structure of self-management bodies

Primary collective	*Main collective*
General assembly	General assembly
Brigade council	Plant council
Brigade leader	Director

This structure takes the form of an 'inverse pyramid' and implies a type of hierarchical link between the levels which differs from the hierarchy of the socialist enterprise. The supreme body is the general assembly (in enterprises employing more than 300 people a delegate assembly is elected). The general assembly of the primary collective elects a brigade council and a brigade leader, while the general assembly of the main collective (the delegate assembly) elects a plant council and a director. The brigade council and the plant council are executive bodies. The brigade leader and the director organise the activities of these executive bodies and the implementation of their decisions. The director, however, has to be considered as a special case. In the political documents and legal acts, the director is assigned a dual role – as a representative of the interests of the labour collective (being elected by the collective, he or she becomes its member) and as a representative of the interests of the state. This special status is still an open issue in managerial practice and legal regulation. The confusion derives from the traditional conception of the director as a one-man manager, a principle that could hardly be mechanically incorporated in the concept and model of self-management by the collective.

In summary, therefore, the development of the concept of labour collective and its operational implementation, required a reassessment of its place and role in the structure of the enterprise. The logic of development of the concept entailed an elaboration of new conceptions of the status of the collective from three aspects:

1 Economic status (manager)

2 Labour status (a party in labour relations)

3 Managerial status (self-managing unit)

STRATEGY FORMULATION AND STRATEGY IMPLEMENTATION: NORMATIVE LABOUR AND ECONOMIC REGULATION

The formulation of strategy and the development of concepts and structural solutions are processes carried out at national level and then imposed on structural units in different sectors and regions which have largely standardised internal structures. The labour reform (1982–7), like earlier changes in management, was carried out from the top downward, from the centre to the enterprise, and each enterprise was expected to implement changes in its structures and management in conformity with national standards. This unity of action was achieved through normative regulation, the process of developing a system of legal acts and their implementation in practice. From the standpoint of organisational design, a distinction should be made between three types of normative regulation concerning labour reform:

1 Labour legislation: including the Labour Code and its associated regulations.

2 Economic legislation: the Regulation on Economic Activity.

3 Internal (local) legislation: rules and regulations drawn up in the enterprises to implement the national labour and economic legislation in accordance with the specific conditions in each enterprise.

Here the first two types of legislation are discussed as they provided the general legal framework for the structural changes.

Before considering the process of formulating the Labour Code, the content of the economic legislation and the conception of the transfer of property need to be briefly explained. In the period 1982–6, while the Labour Code was being developed, the economic legislation in force was the Regulation on the Economic Mechanism (*Drzhaven Vestnik* 1982), which came into effect on 1 January 1982 (modified and amended in 1984). The main features of this regulation were a reduction in the role of ministries in economic management and an increase in the autonomy of enterprises. The brigade as a unit of internal structure was recognised and defined for the first time in a document of this status. Counterplanning was now seen as a central mechanism for the dynamics of the enterprise both internally and externally in relation to the organisations above it. At the beginning of 1988 a new regulation on economic activity took effect (Pravilnik za ikonomicheski deynost).[1] This became the main legal act covering economic relations both between the state and enterprises, and between enterprises themselves. Moreover, it regulated the economic relationships between the structural units in the enterprise: between brigades and enterprise management and among brigades themselves. For the first time economic organisations were termed 'self-managing'. It represented a more radical step in economic reform, as it granted greater autonomy to the enterprise and opened up possibilities for the operation of market mechanisms and commodity–money relations. The role of the state was envisaged as influencing the operation of the enterprise indirectly rather than through economic levers such as taxes, credits, prices etc. (Detailed analysis of the economic mechanism is outside the scope of this book.)

In parallel with the economic mechanism, the new mechanism of agreements for the transfer of property to the labour collective was being developed to consolidate self-managerial relations in enterprises. The declaration of intent was made by President Zhivkov at the Trade Union Congress in April 1987 (Zhivkov 1987a) and the decree was published in December to coincide with the Regulation on the Economic Mechanism. The underlying concept was that real economic power and autonomy should be vested in the labour collective, with the right to make independent decisions about the utilisation of the means of production. The right to utilise state property would be given to the labour collective by contract between the state and the main collective (within the enterprise there would be contracts between the main collective and the primary collective). Implementation is discussed in Chapter 8.

The new code was drafted in the period 1983–6, and all its provisions became effective at the beginning of 1987. (The old code of 1951, repeatedly modified and amended, was repealed.) In fact, the period of preparation for the new code was considerably longer, and needs to be described in the context of strategic changes. The need for a new code was first mentioned in the documents of the July Plenum of the CC of BCP (1968) (Zhivkov 1976a), but for four years no practical steps were taken. In 1972, the issue emerged again (Zhivkov 1976b) in connection with the December social programme. In the period 1972–82, the former Ministry of Labour and Social Affairs and the Central Council of the Bulgarian Trade Unions, prepared a draft of a new code, but it was not presented to the legislative bodies of the country for discussion. The next stage began in 1982 with the elaboration of the New Party Conception of Labour and Labour Relations, which was associated with a change in the approach to the drafting of labour legislation. Previously it had been dealt with by specialist state institutions and the trade unions, but now it was identified as an issue of political strategy, requiring a political line. This argument was explicit in the New Conception where it was noted that the reform in labour legislation should be taken as a basis for the renewal of the whole legislative system of the country (Zhivkov 1984: 120), including civil legislation. The process of strategy formulation from a concept in a political document to a legal act is not unusual in socialist practice, but in Bulgaria this was the first application in the field of labour law (Mrachkov 1987: 3–8). The process involved a number of stages:

1 National discussion of the New Conception (November 1982–January 1983).
2 Work by expert groups based on the political conception and the proposals made in the course of discussions (1983–5). The total number of proposals was about 150,000, of which 4,000 were selected as significant.
3 Discussion of the draft for a new code in the trade unions and the Commission on Legislation of the National Assembly (January–March 1986).
4 Submission of the draft to the National Assembly for discussion (the new Labour Code was adopted by the National Assembly on 21 March 1986, with a resolution that it should come into effect at the beginning of 1987).

Some of the proposals in the political conception relating to the collective bodies of management were implemented in enterprises before they were required by law. Thus in 1984 elections were held for brigade leaders. Members of brigade councils, delegate assemblies and plant councils were also elected. The 1986 election campaign was carried out in accordance with the provisions of the code (see Chapter 9) before the code became law. Some aspects of the four successive stages described above deserve special attention. First, once the political line has been approved, the decisive part is played by experts. Traditionally, their work had always been confined to the legal and technical aspects of drafting. In this case however, the problem proved to be much more complicated. Some of the proposals included in the conception of the new code were formulated only in very general terms. For example, the proposal that the trade unions should act as an organiser of the activities of the collective and of the collective bodies of management. Others like those on collective agreements, elections and competitions required a substantial reappraisal of existing legislative practice. Thus proposals such as those for the procedure for the placement of young specialists and skilled workers, could only be implemented by changing the system of planning and management. The code had to be written as a whole and only a few provisions could be taken directly from the old code. Second, in the formation of expert groups, the unusual step was taken of including not only lawyers, but economists, sociologists, political scientists and specialists in the field of management and organisation. The argument for this was that the code should not be a 'narrow legal document' (Zhivkov 1984: 133–42) but reflect a broader political and societal approach. In practice, achieving a common approach and language with specialists drawn from different disciplines was an extremely complicated task. There were differences in approach to the same problems not only between lawyers and non-lawyers, but also between legal experts. Third, the work of the experts in parallel with 'accelerated' practice (the establishment of collective bodies of management in accordance with the recommendations of the Party Conception) led to some modifications in the initial plans for the structure of labour legislation. Thus it was assumed initially that two other laws would be needed to accompany the code – a law on labour collectives and a law on elections and competitions. However, the results of experience in enterprises in 1984 and 1985 showed that the regulations on the collective bodies of management, and on elections and competitions could not be considered in isolation from the traditional issues of labour law such as the organisation of work and standardisation, payment, qualifications etc. V. Mrachkov (1987: 115–16) commented that the right to participation in management proceeds from labour law and cannot be implemented effectively apart from it. This shows that the drafting of the new code by expert groups was not a smooth process. In fact at the preparatory stage there was a divergence between different theoretical traditions and different sources of ideas, some even outside the sphere of law. From a sociological standpoint, it can be concluded that the role of the groups represented in this process and their interests is decisive in the drafting of labour legislation.

The relationship between labour and economic legislation merits discussion in terms of status and content. While the code is a law of the highest order (in status it comes next to the constitution), the economic regulation does not fall strictly within the category of law. According to Bulgarian legal terminology, such regulations should include a system of rules and norms operating within a basic legal framework. However, as shown by observations in the five core enterprises, disputes concerning the 'seniority' of the two documents were not uncommon. In terms of content, the code regulated labour relations at enterprise level; the regulation governed economic relations mainly above this level, though it also contained norms valid for the internal economic operation of the enterprise.

Comparison of the two kinds of economic legislation reveals another peculiarity. As explained, the 1982 Regulation on the Economic Mechanism was in operation before the new code had been drafted. This explains the inclusion in economic legislation of topics which strictly pertain to labour law, for example, brigade organisation and its mechanisms. With the new code, economic legislation has largely followed the practice of leaving all issues of labour relations, including those concerning the establishment and functioning of the bodies of self-management of the enterprises, to the sphere of labour law. Research shows that synchronisation of two kinds of legislation is difficult to achieve in practice. Contradictions in the interpretation and application of the norms arose in connection with the elections of directors of enterprises and of plant councils: the code provides for the elections to be held by the general assembly with a qualified majority (two-thirds of the votes), and the director is then appointed by the higher organisation. The regulation gives a slightly different solution – following the elections the director is appointed by the Minister of Economy and Planning or by the President of the Association. According to the code, workers and specialists can also be elected to the plant council of the economic organisation as representatives of the main labour collective besides the director of the enterprise; according to the Regulation on Economic Activity, the plant council of the organisation includes the enterprise director and the president of the trade union council of the organisation.

CONCLUSIONS

Strategy formulation from above and the dynamics of the self-managed enterprise

The process of strategy formulation throughout the period 1978–88 was one in which issues were identified and strategies developed at the national level and then imposed on the lower levels. There were no significant upward pressures for change from those lower levels, although on occasion prototypes of structures or mechanisms created at local level were taken up and used for the development of the national model. However, in the model of the enterprise which was being developed from 1978, the concept of pressure from below was seen as an element in enterprise dynamics. In Bulgaria the mechanism of counterplanning (see Chapter 6) was consciously promoted in order to mobilise internal pressure from below. The subsequent elaboration of the concept of the labour collective as *stopanin* and the accompanying redesign of structures and mechanisms were all intended to lead to the articulation of pressure from below as an integral element of enterprise dynamics. The changes in the economic mechanisms, especially that of 1988, were intended to shift the principal source of external pressure from that of the central plan towards that of the market. Consequently, the dynamics of the enterprise were designed to derive from two main sources of pressure – from the market and from the labour collective. Pressure from the labour collective, however, was seen as requiring the redesign of structures and mechanisms in such a way as to engage their interests both economic and social.

The synoptic and incremental models

At the beginning of this chapter, a distinction was made between the incremental and synoptic models of strategy formulation in socialist states, and it was suggested that the synoptic model requires a primary concept from which other concepts can be derived and which can be expressed in the redesign of structures and mechanisms in a logical sequence. In these conditions it is expected that practice will adapt to the legal changes and thus in turn facilitate subsequent restructuring. In Bulgaria it can be argued that the synoptic model, taking as its primary concept the labour collective as *stopanin*, was followed, though not completely, during the period 1981–8. Logically, the next stage in normative regulation would have been legislation integrating labour and economic relations. The preparation of a code of self-managing organisations was discussed at the National Party Conference of January 1988, but was not proceeded with. This chapter has shown that the primary concept from which other concepts could be elaborated deductively was that of the labour collective as *stopanin*. It is of interest to contrast the relationship of this concept in Bulgaria to that of self-management, which was not officially recognised until 1987, with the approach followed in Yugoslavia where the concept was first adopted in 1949–50. In Yugoslavia strategy formulation can be seen as proceeding incrementally until 1974 when the Law on Associated Labour integrated economic and labour relations and facilitated the synoptic model. Although the synoptic model has clearly been possible in socialist societies, the incremental model equally has a place, and has the advantage of reducing the risk of errors in design.

Alternative models of societal change in socialist societies

The theoretical assumption underlying the restructuring of labour relations in Bulgaria was that this provided the basis and starting-point for societal change and the restructuring of social relations. Consequently, redesigning the dynamic of labour relations became the core strategic issue and the primary criterion in the process of strategy formulation. The Marxist assumption is that socialist society is a labour society, that its wealth and development are based on the people's work and that the social status of each individual is determined by his personal labour contribution. Consequently, no social or individual prosperity is possible if there is no dynamic in the labour sector. In *A new conception of labour and labour relations*, this connection was defined in the following way:

> We are a society of labour and two main pillars are embedded in its foundations: working man and the work force. Labour is necessary to produce value, it is the source of social wealth and of man's personal well-being. But labour is also a crucial sector of the socialist way of life, it is a means of shaping man, his values and behaviour.
>
> (Zhivkov 1982: 9)

Although this formulation is generally accepted (it is also provided in the Bulgarian Constitution and the labour legislation and often used in political documents), different views of its significance have been expressed in the debate on the formulation of the strategy and its implementation in practice. Tomov, for example, sees labour self-management as a trend in the socialist democracy which leads only to some limited changes in only one social area and at the level only of the enterprise and the labour collective (Tomov 1987: 144–5). Other authors emphasise the importance of political reform, assuming that it will act as a catalyst for changes in two ways: first, that the party's withdrawal from direct economic management and the abolition of the administrative-command system reduces the pressure exerted by the centre on the enterprises and the labour collective, and leaves space for economic initiative and the creation of direct relations between producers and between producers and the market; and second, that the extension of democracy in the political arena creates a new social environment which is in itself a stimulus to promote work discipline and economic participation (Prodanov 1988: 36–8). The economic determinism thesis, traditionally dominant in management theory, also has its supporters. They assume that since economic welfare determines living standards and the achievement of common goals, economic reform should play the decisive role, and the technological development of production should come first. From this position changes in labour relations are seen only as a derivative of the restructuring of economic management, which is mainly seen as a greater degree of decentralisation These different approaches reflect alternative models of societal change which can be summarised as follows:

1 from labour to society.
2 from the economy to society.
3 from the political system to society.

Some implications of these alternative sequences are discussed in Chapter 12.

The present chapter has discussed the process of strategy formulation at the national level.[2] The following chapter explains the approach adopted for the conduct of the fieldwork which was intended to show the process of implementing national strategy in enterprises.

NOTES

1   In January 1989 a further regulation on economic activity (Decree 56 of the State Council, 9 January 1989) was adopted. This took as its primary concept the enterprise as a self-managing economic unit that is in effect a firm and not a labour-managed organisation.

2   The process of strategy formulation in Bulgaria: until 1989 T. Zhivkov held the posts of General Secretary of the Party and President of the State Council. The first public stage in national strategy formulation was the identification of an issue by Zhivkov, usually in a speech. Identification was based on proposals put to him by individual specialists or groups of specialists, and the speech, recorded in Zhivkov's complete works, legitimated further work on the issue by specialists. Decisions based on such work were made by the Party Central Committee and were published in reports presented by Zhivkov. Thus almost all policy statements related to strategy formulation were made under Zhivkov's name, irrespective of their origin.

4 Case studies and fieldwork in Bulgarian enterprises – research methodology

The previous chapter explained the process of strategy formulation in Bulgaria at the national level. The succeeding chapters discuss the dynamics of structures and mechanisms at the level of the enterprise using empirical evidence mainly drawn from fieldwork undertaken by the research collective. This chapter sets out the approach adopted for the fieldwork in Bulgarian enterprises. It discusses four main aspects of this: (1) the reasons for the choice of the extended case study as the principal research method; (2) the significance and use of this method for both the testing and development of theory; (3) an explanation of the concepts that were not defined in previous chapters and were considered to be necessary for the application of the case-study method; (4) the research strategy for the selection of enterprises and the gathering of evidence. The history and principal features of the enterprises are then briefly described.

CHOICE OF THE EXTENDED CASE-STUDY METHOD

In Bulgaria the predominant method of sociological research since the 1960s has been the survey based on questionnaires administered to samples of individual respondents selected according to statistical criteria; and analysis has typically been based on the tabulation of individual responses to particular questions. Generally, discussion of the significance of data from such surveys has been used in an aggregated form rather than disaggregated, to provide a basis for relating the responses of individual respondents to the structural characteristics and the mechanisms of the organisational unit – be it enterprise, brigade, family or household – to which they belong. Although Marinov (1987) and Botev (1987) have both discussed the place of studies of 'problem situations', there is no established tradition of organisation-based studies in Bulgaria. In the Soviet Union, according to Rutland (1986: 191, 206), published case studies of industrial organisations are relatively few, although there have been unpublished doctoral dissertations, concentrating on individual plants. In opting for the extended case study rather than surveys as the principal research method, the authors were influenced by two general considerations: first, and most importantly, by their conception of the nature of the research problem which they were investigating; and, second, by their positive evaluation of the results obtained by other researchers who had used this method. As explained in the previous chapter, the development of changes in enterprise structures and mechanisms were closely related to the elaboration of the concepts of the labour collective as *stopanin* of socialist property. From this, it followed that the main focus of the research must be the labour collective, which in the terminology of research methods, therefore became the main unit of analysis. It was clear that the development of the labour collective would take place over a period of time and that this process would depend on events originating in the political arena as much as within the enterprises themselves. It was assumed that while some changes in organisation would be clearly apparent because they were required by normative regulations, other changes emerging directly or indirectly from political decisions might be less easy to detect. The aim of the fieldwork was to identify changes in social action as an aspect of change in organisational dynamics (as explained in the Introduction). It was considered that the extended case-study method was one which was more likely to be effective in detecting changes in organisational processes than other methods such as surveys based on structured questionnaires. Surveys can provide a snapshot of opinions and perceptions at a particular point in time, but do not usually provide data on the context of issues and actions. The case study was seen as essential for the study of the processes of action and the emergence of issues. Comparison of case studies was seen as the most effective way of reaching some explanation of why actions occurred in one case and not in another. (The value of comparisons of this kind is shown by Crenson's study (1971) of the emergence of environmental pollution as a political issue in one American city but not in another.) At a different level, the case-study method in relation to the study of organisational design, can be seen as analogous to the historical approach advocated in the Introduction.

As presented by Mitchell (1983: 194):

> The particular significance of the extended case study is that since it traces the events in which the same set of main actors in the case study are involved over a relatively long period, the processual aspect is given particular emphasis. The extended case study enables the analyst to trace how events chain on to one another and how therefore events are necessarily linked to one another through time.

Mitchell also draws attention to Goode and Hatt's comments on case studies as a method which preserves:

> the unitary character of the social object being studied. . . . Expressed somewhat differently, it is an approach which views any social unit as a whole. Almost always this means of approach includes the development of that unit, which may be a person, a family or other social group, a set of relationships or processes . . . or even an entire culture.
>
> (Mitchell 1983: 191–2)

In contrast, the survey method usually replaces the person with the trait as the unit of analysis.

In opting for the case-study method, the authors were also influenced by research on which *Strategies, issues and events* was based, drawing as it did on case studies of thirteen British manufacturing firms. It was seen as important that although the published case studies of enterprises in socialist countries were comparatively few in number, the significance of the insights found in some of them indicated their potential value. Thus John Thirkell had been impressed by the results obtained by Adizes (1971) in his classic study of two Yugoslav textile plants over a six-month period in 1967. This provided insights into the organisational processes which could occur in self-managed enterprises and confirmed his own impressions from short visits to two Yugoslav enterprises in 1971. It seemed to him that the insights from Adizes and from Comisso's study of a Zagreb factory in 1974 (Comisso 1979), were essential to an understanding of the organisational dynamics of the self-managed enterprise, and that this revealed a major gap in much of the extensive Yugoslav sociological research conducted and published in the late 1960s and early 1970s. The predominant method used in these studies were questionnaires administered to workers as individuals and designed to elicit their perceptions of such issues as the relative power of the director and the workers council and other bodies. While such surveys provided aggregated distributions of the perceptions of individuals, they did not attempt to provide, any more than similar surveys of western workers, any real indication of the nature and content of the process of issue mobilisation, the operation of mechanisms and the opportunities and constraints deriving from particular patterns of organisational structure. In Hungary the pioneering study of organisational changes in the Raba plant in 1969 by Hethy and Mako (1989) initiated a series of plant-based studies, but most of these have been published only in Hungarian. A very important exception is Hethy's recent case study based on an enterprise in the construction industry (1989).

Mitchell's definition of case studies as being focused on 'events' shows that their central feature is a concern with social action (the concept of 'event' used in this book is explained below). Case studies of this kind seek to explain social actions principally by deploying and analysing the interpretations of the participants themselves or of those members of an organisation who may be presumed to have sufficient knowledge to offer some account of the events in question. (It follows that it is often desirable to compare the explanations and accounts offered by persons in different positions.) Van Velsen, in his (1967) paper discussing 'situational analysis', highlights an intrinsic concern with the process of 'optation' in this research approach.[1] Clearly this type of study must seek explanations of why a particular action was not taken either because that action was demonstrably taken on other occasions in apparently similar contexts, or because there are cogent theoretical grounds for expecting it to be taken on this particular occasion.

To obtain evidence for explanations of this type, using the case-study method, the principal source is key informants or what Hethy terms 'strategic informers'. Tremblay (1982: 99) defines key informants as those 'who might be expected to have specialised information on particular topics'. Hethy argues that for researching and analysing the behaviour of workers 'A strategic informer means that the researcher selects from the real, genuine participants in the events . . . a person who has a kind of researcher's way of thinking and approach' (Hethy 1989: 38). Not all key informants meet this criterion, but it is a central task of the fieldworker to seek out informants who can offer explanations of why a particular sequence of events unfolded, the conditions under which a possible course of action might be followed, and about the opportunities and constraints deriving from a particular set of structures and mechanisms. In this research the main characteristics of key informants were, first, that they usually held key positions such as deputy director, *nachalnik*, trade union chairman, brigade leader, and, second, that they were often active in incidents, episodes and events. (However there were some workers among the latter.) Their importance for the research was that they could give coherent accounts of systems and sequences of action. It is of course axiomatic that in this approach the perceptions of any individual informant must be grounded in the specific organisational context in which he or she participates.

Generalisation from case studies and the relationship of case studies to theory and theorising

The question of the validity of inferences drawn from a single or small number of case studies has long been a subject of discussion in the literature on research methods in sociology. (For a review of this discussion see

Mitchell 1983.) Mitchell argues that the debate between advocates of quantitative and non-quantitative methods of research has been clouded by 'confusion between the procedures appropriate to making inferences from statistical data and those appropriate to the study of an idiosyncratic combination of elements or events which constitute a "case"' (1983: 188). Mitchell makes clear that the analysis of data and material collected for case studies necessarily requires the application of some general theoretical principles. However, there are a number of different ways in which case studies can be used in relation to theorising. One of these is to compare or test the usefulness of established theory against the reality of practice in one or more case studies. For example, the general importance of Hethy and Mako's (1989) study of the Raba factory in 1969–70, was to show that the real structure of interests and groups in the factory diverged substantially from the theoretical model of the socialist enterprise which had been endorsed at the political level and formed the basis on which the structures and mechanisms of the enterprise were designed. Hethy's case study from the construction industry, on the other hand, is used to 'present the characteristics of the notion of interest relations in a factory' (1989: 38). As explained in the previous chapter, the theory of the labour collective as *stopanin* was developed deductively though related to empirical evidence obtained by surveys and observation in Bulgarian enterprises and from recognition at the political level of the necessity of change. Evidence from case studies, however, was not available. It was recognised in designing the research on which this book is based that the possibility of in-depth research using the case-study method, offered opportunities for detecting shifts in organisational processes which were more difficult to obtain by other methods and that the case studies could provide helpful 'illustrations' of the changes that were taking place in Bulgarian enterprises. However, as Mitchell makes clear, case studies can also be used to develop theory. This was not a primary aim of the research, but the development and elaboration of concepts seen as necessary for analysis of the empirical evidence has led to some theorising, for example, on the place and operation of mechanisms in relation to organisational processes and consequently to their place in the theory of organisational design. As other writers have noted, while the researchers will often have a set of some initial concepts to apply to the analysis of the information collected, consideration of the empirical evidence will often require the development of further concepts to inform the analysis of the evidence.

Concepts and the extended case-study method

In the Introduction the paradigm of organisational design and the concepts used for the historical analysis of the Soviet enterprise and labour relations were defined. However, it was recognised that further concepts would be needed for the analysis of information collected from the extended case studies. As explained above, in his discussion of different types of case study, Mitchell frequently refers to 'events' as constituting the main content of case studies. However, it was considered desirable to define and distinguish between different categories of occurrences that could illustrate the nature of organisational processes in enterprises. Three categories were therefore defined: events, incidents and episodes. Events are seen as arising from the environment external to the enterprise. They include the decisions of state and other higher bodies, for example to make the election of managers compulsory or, more specifically for some enterprises, changes in the exchange rate of the Bulgarian lev for foreign currency. Events may also, especially with more economic decentralisation, arise from market relations. The significance of events is that they may provide both challenges to existing structures and mechanisms and opportunities for the emergence of new issues, the creation of new mechanisms and the redesign of structures. In contrast to events, 'incidents' are seen as arising within the enterprise – their essence is that their occurrence may be seen as a challenge to established routines and patterns of action, so providing an opportunity to create new mechanisms and for the mobilisation of issues. 'Episodes' are closed sequences of action which may precede or follow an event – they may also, though less frequently, follow an incident. The following is an illustration of an incident which led to an episode. In 1983, John Thirkell visited a Bulgarian factory where the young director had recently died very suddenly. The trade union chairman related that the plant party, trade union and management organisations had responded to this incident by taking the position that the director's successor should be appointed from among the managers in the plant, and not as formerly, be an outside appointment imposed by higher authorities. Of course, the ensuing episode (the outcome of which is not known), although triggered by the internal incident, is only intelligible in the context of the wider discussion then emerging on the mechanisms for appointing managers.

In studying social action, the concept of the action field is used to analyse processes in relation to structure. In his study of the Konds of Northern India, Bailey (1960) saw the concept of 'field' as necessary for an analysis of process which he saw as precluded by the structural–functionalist approach. Kapferer (1972) developed the concept of an action field in his study of a Zambian clothing factory, and defined it as 'the resources, and the interaction between them which are activated in the course of social interaction'. The definition of resources, developed from *Strategies, issues and events*, is that they consist of: workers and position holders (management, trade union and party representatives); forums (e.g. brigade assembly, general assembly, plant council); and rules and norms. A central empirical question is, of course, how and to what extent these resources may be mobilised in response to events and incidents and in ensuing episodes. The redesign of structures and mechanisms in Bulgaria was intended to shift the balance of resources in the enterprise action field by creating new resources to establish the labour collective, and to create more space for the mobilisation of these resources in relation to issues. Events, episodes and incidents are all characterised by increased mobilisation of resources in the action field. In Chapter 1 the concept of interests was introduced. Empirically interests are revealed only in action through the mobilisation of resources; and events, episodes and incidents often reveal conflicts of interests and how resources are perceived by the social actors.

RESEARCH STRATEGY

The initial planning of the research took place in September 1985. The authors and a team of research assistants met daily over a period of ten days discussing concepts and the case study as a research method. This 'extended research seminar' was seen by the authors as essential for the successful initiation of the project as they conceived it. Since the researchers would not be administering previously prepared questionnaires, it was fundamental that they should understand the research aims and approach, and be able to recognise the significance of incidents, episodes and events in the plants, to conduct semi-structured interviews, to select key informants and evaluate their evidence, and to write reports which were both factual and analytical. It was made clear that their active contribution to the development of the concepts both as individual researchers and as a research collective was essential for the project to succeed. The demands placed on the researchers can be illustrated by the following example: the authors asked the researchers to look for examples of organic mechanisms, but they could not specify what these mechanisms would look like. It was, therefore, the responsibility of the researchers to find actual illustrations in the processes of social action within their enterprises with only an abstract definition to guide them. (In this instance the researchers were practising 'situational analysis'.)[1]

It was estimated that the availability of resources for fieldwork would make it possible to produce in-depth case studies for four or five plants, based on research in the period 1985–8. Given the relative standardisation of structures in Bulgarian industry (in contrast to the heterogeneity of management and trade union structures in British industry), it was felt that this would be a sufficient basis for drawing conclusions of the kind that the extended case method makes possible. Moreover, it was decided that the case studies of the 'core' plants might be supplemented by short visits to other plants. The standardisation of structures meant that the routine processes were common to most plants but the occurrence of episodes and events was more random. The purpose of such visits therefore would be to provide further illustrations of events and episodes. As the research proceeded the importance of such supplementary visits became clearer; responses to national events, such as the election campaign in 1986, or local events, such as the closure of a product line in a particular plant, and the occurrence of episodes inevitably produced sequences of action which were specific to those plants. Consequently, although the research in the five plants provided the basic evidence, examples of events and episodes are taken from a wider range of plants which were investigated by Krastyn Petkov or members of the research collective; evidence from these plants is used in Chapters 5 to 10.

Initially, 8 plants were selected from a list of 40 to which the Georgi Dimitrov Institute had research access. The criteria for selection included the need to have plants from the main sectors of Bulgarian industry: examples of plants producing consumer goods (market pressure) and for export; examples of plants with a significant proportion of qualified white-collar design staff; and plants with a high proportion of women workers. Preliminary studies were made of the 8 plants, and on the basis of these, 5 were selected as 'core' plants. Each of the plants was made the responsibility of one of the five research assistants (all members of the academic staff of the Georgi Dimitrov Institute). The research assistants made regular visits to their enterprises to collect information. The focus of each visit was topic centred. The initial visits in 1985 were focused on the history of the enterprise, the development of brigade organisation and the mechanisms associated with counterplanning. Later visits focused on events such as elections and the transfer of property and the mechanisms of distribution. The main sources of information were interviews with key informants at both top and base. However, the researchers also collected data from records and observed elections and other meetings. Both authors also conducted some interviews in the plants.

The enterprises

Assembly

This plant is a part of a combine for the manufacture of communications equipment in the engineering and electronics branch. It was founded in

1967 to manufacture parts for equipment produced in other plants. In 1979 the plant expanded and began to make complete systems of communications equipment. Most of the components are made within the plant and are then assembled into systems. The output is more than sufficient to meet domestic needs, and over 50 per cent of production is exported. There were about 2,000 workers at the plant (of whom 75 per cent were women), and work was organised in seven departments.

Chemicals

This enterprise became a combine in 1979. Before then there had been an enterprise with two main product lines and two departments. A new type of product line with its associated technology was opened in 1983. The combine employed 1,300 and there were, in effect, four separate plants on the site, each producing a different type of product.

Heavy engineering

The original engineering works was founded in 1935 through the merger of two co-operatives. Following nationalisation in 1948, there was major investment in equipment and the workforce increased. The enterprise now comprises a main plant, three subsidiary plants and a research and design institute. The main plant (where the research was conducted) employed 2,500, of whom one-third were women, and was organised in four departments: foundry, machinery 1 and 2, and assembly. A large part of the machinery produced is exported.

Metals

The enterprise opened in 1969 in one of the oldest industrial centres in Bulgaria. In 1979 it achieved combine status when a department from a metallurgical works integrated with it. There are now three main production departments and auxiliary departments producing equipment and spare parts. The workforce totalled 3,000 in 1985. The combine was selected because of its pioneering and autonomous role in the introduction of changes in the organisation of work.

Textiles

Before nationalisation in 1947, this had been a private factory with a workforce of about 50. By 1955, with new investment it employed over 500, and had become the first enterprise specialising in the large-scale production of children's clothing. Further investment in production technology led to increases in output and in the workforce – which in 1985 totalled 1,000. This plant was selected as a case from the light-industry sector with a predominantly female workforce in direct production jobs. It was also seen as significant that it was located in a rural community and not in an industrial centre.

NOTE

1   Situational analysis as a research method was developed by social anthropologists studying societies in Africa, as a result of the perceived inadequacies of the structuralist approach, which concentrated on the analysis of social structures. As Mitchell explains in his foreword to *The politics of kinship among the Tonga of central Africa*, Van Velsen found that:

> In order to be able to study the process through which people select some of a wide range of possible relationships in order to achieve their ends, we must observe people in a wide variety of social situations. We can then analyse the behaviour of the individual in terms of the factors which constrain him to choose a particular mode of action in one situation, and a different one in another. This process is what Dr Van Velsen calls 'Situational Analysis'.
>
> (Van Velsen 1964: xi)

On the relationship of the extended case study to social structure, Mitchell points out that:

> the extended case method can only be used in conjunction with a statement of the structure of the society for it deals with the way in which individuals are able to exercise choices within the limits of a specified social structure. . . . The typicality of the material is irrelevant since the regularities are set out in the description of the overall social structure. In a sense, the more atypical the actions and events described in the case history, the more instructive they are since the anthropologist uses case material to show how variations can be contained within the structure.
>
> (Van Velsen 1964: xiii)

Although Van Velsen and his fellow anthropologists were primarily concerned with the process of optation by individuals in social situations, it can be argued that the approach is equally valid and useful in analysing processes in industrial organisations. In the case of Bulgarian enterprises, the structures were centrally determined. The study of events, episodes and incidents shows how, within those structures, groups (or individuals) were able to choose different courses of social action.

While there is no sharp distinction between the case study and situational analysis as research methods, they do reflect certain differences in the approaches to fieldwork. Thus in the case study the researcher usually has some concepts or hypotheses which are to be tested or developed in the cases selected. In situational analysis the researcher enters the situation more in order to discover its internal operation than to test or develop previously formulated concepts and hypotheses. The empirical research in this book reflects elements of both approaches. Thus while the approach to the study of brigade organisation and such imposed mechanisms as counterplanning, which were already known in general terms, reflected the case-study method, the search for examples of organic mechanisms which could not be specified in advance was more characteristic of situational analysis.

5 Redesigning structures to establish the labour collective

Chapter 3 explained the process of strategy formulation at the political level and the significance of the concept of the labour collective as *stopanin* in this process. This chapter is centred on the process of transition from concepts to the redesign of structures within enterprises. However, the decision to establish brigade organisation as the generic structure for the organisation of work was made by the party conference in 1978, before the concept of *stopanin* was adopted. The decision of the conference drew on the experience of prototypes established during the 1970s and the design process of establishing one of these prototype brigades is illustrated first. Redesign of structures as a national strategy, however, requires the articulation and recognition of design criteria and their incorporation in normative regulations. The process by which criteria were developed and implemented, initially at the level of the brigade, is therefore discussed. The general implementation of brigade organisation is illustrated with particular reference to the five plants. The cases of Heavy Engineering and Metals are described in more detail as examples, though atypical, of enterprise level strategy formulation followed by restructuring. This is followed by an explanation of the measures to restructure the intermediate level of the enterprise which is illustrated by the cases of Heavy Engineering and Materials. Finally, since restructuring requires agencies of organisational change, the general role of management – and the party and trade union organisations as agencies – is discussed.

ESTABLISHING A PROTOTYPE BRIGADE OF THE NEW TYPE

In Chapter 3 it was explained that the Party Conference of 1978 endorsed the strategy of making brigades of the new type the generic structure for the organisation of work. The strategy was based on the experience with some prototypes in Bulgaria. The case of one such prototype is used to illustrate the design process at the base in the 1970s. The case is based on an interview with Miloushev who was brigade leader in the docks at Varna.

The idea of establishing our brigade originated in the seventies long before any attempt to introduce brigade organisation of work of the new type on a national scale. Our biggest problem at that time was that of integrating the activities of the different skill groups in the brigade and making each group into an important link in the overall work of the brigade as a whole. We had some serious problems in this respect, even conflicts, as each group regarded its own work as the most important and indispensable. Our second problem was training all workers in the brigade up to the level of the best ones and making them multimachine operators with further training. We also met difficulties in our relations with the other brigades which adhered to the old organisation of work and refused to adopt the methods of managing the new type brigade. An attitude of disregard and even scorn was clearly felt by us. They tried continuously to create barriers and obstacles in the work of the complex brigades. We had sharply increased labour productivity [and earnings] in loading and unloading and they had to catch up with us. The norms for the different types of loading jobs went up and they could not fulfill them. . . . Besides the old type of brigade hired their technical equipment on a daily basis. Whenever they had to reorganise themselves during the shift they were unable to replace the equipment and continue with the job while our brigade could send machines and workers from one job to another any time of the day. I cannot but mention also the negative attitude of the middle level of management at the docks and our conflict with them. As they received their salaries regularly, they did not depend on the results of the work of the brigades. They even put obstacles in our way, though not openly, as they had to work with us much harder than with the brigades of the old type. There were also conflicts with top management when they failed to provide the machines and equipment necessary for loading and unloading operations.

(interview 1987)

An essential mechanism in the operation of this brigade was that of the monthly distribution of earnings: the brigade leader put his proposals for the earnings of each worker on a notice board and later all the members met as an assembly and voted on them. The experience and approach of Miloushev in the Varna docks has many similarities with those of brigade leader Nikolayev, described in Chapter 2, in the Baltic shipyard in Leningrad in 1931. Both were worker-activists who redesigned structures on their own initiative without the support of top management. One of the constraints on prototypes such as Miloushev's was that the collective form

of work organisation ran counter to the philosophy of the scientific organisation of work, which centred on norming the tasks of individuals. Without
the support of normative regulation, prototypes of new forms were difficult
to maintain.

DESIGN CRITERIA

The redesign of organisational structures from above requires the
elaboration of design criteria according to which restructuring can be
carried out. For the brigade organisation the criteria were necessary for
determining their boundaries, their size and their composition. The
appropriate size of organisations has long attracted the attention of both
theorists (Bell 1956) and practitioners. Evidence of the latter is the current
tendency to establish small and medium-size enterprises with more flexible
structures and programmes. The question of the size and composition of
collectives is also discussed in the academic literature in the context of the
collective (group) forms of organization of work. From the start of restructuring in Bulgaria, two different perspectives on design criteria
emerged. These can be characterised as the organisational and the sociological. The former considered it necessary to make the boundary of the
brigade coincide with the complete technological cycle, while the latter
emphasised the size of the brigade not in its purely quantitative, but in its
social aspect, pointing to the advantages of small working groups as more
socially integrated and more amenable to self-regulating mechanisms. In
this way the issue of design criteria and their priority in the structuring of
brigades became a central one. It has also emerged in other socialist
countries. Thus in the model regulations on brigade organisation in the
Soviet Union the criteria are technological (complete technological cycle)
and economic (accounting and self-financing). The Bulgarian Labour Code
(and the internal enterprise regulations on brigade organisation) specified a
set of criteria. These were the economic, which had priority, the technological, the managerial and the social. (In the 1982 Regulation on the
Economic Mechanism the design criteria were technological and
economic. The brigade was recognised as a social unit but this was not a
design criterion nor was there any explicit managerial or self-managerial
criterion.)

The economic criterion meant that the brigade had to adhere to the
principle of accounting for its work (internal brigade cost accounting was
recommended) and to be self-sufficient. This meant calculating the costs of
labour, raw materials, fuel, energy, depreciation etc., and comparing them
with the overall results (the contribution) of the brigade measured on the

basis of the final or intermediate product – a machine, a single unit or part, or of services. It is obvious that the contribution of the brigade has to be sufficiently high to enable it to support itself by forming its own wage fund and other social welfare funds. Experience has shown, however, that accounting for both costs and the contribution of the brigade to the final product is extremely difficult to achieve, and in some cases, with the existing technology and accounting systems, impossible. This has made the requirements deriving from the economic criterion very hard to implement. It is significant that after nearly ten years of experience of the new type of brigade, only about 60 per cent operate on the basis of cost accounting and the proportion of those which are self-supporting is much smaller.

The technological criterion means that the brigade should be based on the complete technological cycle of a measurable intermediate or final product. The dual aim is to involve directly all workers and specialists in the production cycle and to plan the costs and the contribution of the brigade. In this way the technological criterion and the economic one are combined. In enterprises the general response to this criterion was initially mechanistic. The department, the traditional internal structure, was in most cases originally designed to comprise a complete technological cycle and manufacture a final or intermediate product. The tendency therefore was to make the department into a brigade. 'Department-brigades' consisted of 300–400 (or even more) workers and specialists, and were difficult to manage on the basis of full internal cost accounting. These very large brigades were even less capable of satisfying the social criterion and the requirements of direct democracy. The arguments put forward by advocates of departmental boundaries for brigades seemed convincing: the department is the complete technological and economic unit and it is a reality which cannot be changed. This was 'valid', especially for the mechanical engineering and chemical industries. However, particularly in light industry, brigades began to be established on the basis of one of several shifts. This type was the most successful and it was centrally promoted. In the context of the election campaign for the bodies of self-management in 1986, when the first serious attempt at restructuring was undertaken, the priority was to eliminate departmental brigades and research showed that this happened in most enterprises. In enterprises operating on shifts, 51 per cent of the brigades were based on the principle 'one shift – one brigade', while the remainder comprised all the shifts (2, 3 or 4).

The management (self-management) criterion expressed the objective of transforming the brigade into a self-managing unit. (Theoretically, the potential of the brigade as a self-managing unit was first postulated by Petkov and Kolev (1982: 140–56).) This criterion required the creation of bodies of direct, not representative democracy. It is clear that if the brigade has 300 or more members, it can only have an assembly of representatives and not a general assembly. So from the standpoint of self-management smaller brigades are required. This coincides with the management criterion because operational management is easier when the brigade works in one place, operates on one shift and does not have a large number of workers. The validity of this criterion has been proved many times in practice when the brigade council or the general assembly has had to make an immediate decision.

The social criterion was initially contested as operationally inefficient. However, sociologists and social psychologists have always emphasised the significance of the phenomenon of 'internal group solidarity', and it was eventually included as one of the criteria in the Labour Code. Empirical studies suggest different answers as to the bases of group cohesion, but the most frequent ones are: close contact and mutual control; the possibility for creating organic mechanisms of self-regulation; and more flexibility between jobs and greater mutual assistance. A number of investigations have shown that the optimum size for small working groups is between 10 and 30; groups of 50–60 are also acceptable, but above this limit the indices of group unity decrease. At the other extreme, while groups of 5–10 people are often the best for internal group integration, they do not satisfy the first three criteria. However, although the social criterion is a legal criterion for structural design, research into Bulgarian enterprises showed that it was mentioned in general terms rather than used operationally for determining the boundaries, size and composition of brigades. In terms of the criteria as a whole and in the light of 'the ideal model' of the brigade of a new type, it should be noted that the economic criterion is the primary one which underlies the others and expresses the concept of transforming the brigade into an economic unit. The self-management criterion is decisive in that without self-management the brigade is not able to exercise its economic rights and influence the higher levels of the enterprise (the dynamic of the 'pressure from below'). The technological and the social criteria are subordinated to the first two. However, to create the 'ideal model' in reality, it is necessary for all four of them to be applied as a set. Restructuring to create new-type brigades required, and was supported by, strong legal standards, especially the Labour Code of 1986 and the Regulation on Economic Activity of 1987, which were mandatory. This contrasts with other socialist countries where the standards have been limited to model rules and guidelines. It also contrasts with the approach to establishing traditional brigades in the 1960s and 1970s, when political and administrative, but not legal, pressure was applied.

THE IMPLEMENTATION OF BRIGADE ORGANISATION

The first year for which national statistics on brigade organisation were compiled was 1980. Table 5. 1 shows the overall diffusion of brigade organisation (data for 1988 are for the first six months).

Table 5.1   The diffusion of brigade organisation

	1980	1984	1988	Complex	Specialised
Number of brigades	39,883	31,872	27,622	16,506	11,116
Number of workers in brigades	850,981	934,430	948,034	725,439	223,395
Average number of workers per brigade	21.3	29.3	34.3	44.0	20.1

Source: Statisticheski godishnak

The 1988 statistics distinguished for the first time between complex brigades (generally larger) and specialist brigades (generally smaller). However, the distinction, in practice, had existed since the inception of the new type of brigade in 1978. Generally, complex brigades are those engaged in direct production while specialist brigades are composed of ancillary or maintenance workers. Complex brigades by definition comprise workers of different skill grades. However, implementation of the economic criterion could favour, in specific conditions, the inclusion of production and maintenance workers in a single brigade. Equally, in some cases, junior clerical and administrative workers could be in a complex production brigade to provide service functions for the operations of the brigade.

The process of implementation is illustrated in practice by the evidence from the five plants. At Textiles, Chemicals and Assembly, management complied with the central directives on the implementation of brigade organisation. Heavy Engineering and Metals, on the other hand, show local management developing brigade organisation autonomously as an element of their strategy for the organisational development of their enterprises. At Textiles the introduction of western technology in 1977 was accompanied by the formation of brigades which was completed in 1980. The sixteen brigades were based on the production principle, following the layout of the machines, and on the implementation of the principle of cost accounting. The male maintenance workers were not integrated into the production brigades made up of women workers. At Chemicals the introduction of brigades was constrained by the organisation of production into four separate production plants (on the same site) with different technologies. Initially, each plant was constituted as a single brigade operating on three shifts, each with a section leader, so that these brigades were large, generally with over 100 members. The major constraint on making each shift a brigade was the difficulty of accounting for partially completed products so that the work done by one shift or brigade could be evaluated separately from that done by the succeeding shift or brigade. In one continuous-process plant with a single final product, it was particularly difficult to allocate costs to the different stages of the process, but this was eventually overcome. Auxiliary workers, power engineers and drivers were in specialised brigades. At Assembly the researcher found that although brigades had been introduced in all departments, they did not operate on cost accounting, and they were generally large and in his opinion functioned formally. A major constraint was the specific form of work organisation in engineering.

Strategy formulation and redesign at enterprise level

The process by which the national strategy could be used by enterprise management as an opportunity to formulate an enterprise strategy is illustrated by the cases of Heavy Engineering and Metals. The managements of both enterprises came to recognise that the concept of the labour collective as a *stopanin* adopted at the political level at the Party Congress in 1981 was an opportunity to formulate strategies for enterprise development based on internal restructuring and the design of mechanisms. The catalyst at Heavy Engineering was a journalist who visited the enterprise in 1981, and floated the idea that the enterprise should set up a movement to establish the labour collective as *stopanin*. The party bureau of the plant considered the idea and discussed it with the district party committee to ensure their support for the initiative. When an understanding had been reached between the enterprise party and trade union leadership and the district party committee the issue was taken to the base: three brigades which declared for the initiative wrote an open letter to *Trud* (the trade union daily paper) in support of the proposal. The enterprise party secretary was then called to report to President Zhivkov and the initiative received national backing. This meant a campaign mobilised by management, party and trade union to implement goals identified at the political level. Thus the possibility of linking the concept to structural redesign by developing the traditional brigades into brigades of the new type was recognised.

There were three main stages in the implementation of brigade organisation. In the first stage from 1978 to 1980 brigades were introduced throughout the enterprise which operated the co-efficient of labour participation in the distribution of earnings (see Chapter 7) according to internal rules drawn up for each brigade. The second stage began in 1981 with the campaign and lasted until 1986, progressing through a series of steps. Brigades were categorised as complex or specialised. The introduction of 'normed plan tasks' was associated with the establishment of the brigade as an accounting unit with its own wage fund. Quality, as well as quantity, of production was progressively introduced as a criterion for wages, together with housekeeping and innovation. A special technique for measuring energy and materials costs for each brigade was introduced in 1982. In the same year the enterprise instituted brigade councils for the first time in Bulgaria so that it established the prototype. The brigade assembly elected both the council and the brigade leader, though by an open vote and not a secret ballot, as was later required by the Labour Code. As early as 1983 one brigade rejected the director's nominee for the position of brigade leader. In 1986 in the third stage the boundaries of the production brigades were changed to conform to the complete production cycle so that the number of these brigades was reduced from 50 to 30 with an increase in the size of brigade membership. Half of the brigades, however, had 25 or fewer members.

At Metals the management took up the idea of a movement and used it as the basis for elaborating a comprehensive strategy for the redesign of work organisation and the internal structures and mechanisms of the enterprise. Here the initiative was taken by the director and the deputy economic director (with, of course, the endorsement of the party organisation) but the president of the trade union took a very active part in strategy formulation and the trade union committee was used as a major agency in the implementation of the strategy. At one level the strategy can be seen as a response to the economic problems deriving from low utilisation of machinery, high labour turnover and absenteeism. These conditions, however, while necessary to an understanding of developments are not sufficient to explain the emergence of strategic thinking in these key individuals in the management team, who saw the identification of the workforce with the means of production – their machines – as the strategic issue which required the transformation of relationships between top and base. Chapter 3 explained how the adoption of the concept of the labour collective as *stopanin* made possible the development of the process of strategy formulation at national level according to the synoptic rather than the incremental model. Metals provides an example of how the same concept was used by local management to formulate enterprise strategy synoptically beginning in 1984. The evidence for the synoptic approach is that key members of the management team were able to identify a series of issues and to articulate a sequence of changes in structures and mechanisms. This facilitated separation of the process of redesign into different stages, each of which was preceded by intensive analysis and preparation. Management recognised that the dynamic of 'pressure from below' was a necessary element for the success of their strategy, but they also envisaged the brigades organising operations, competing between themselves and generating lateral as well as vertical pressures. By 1985, 98 per cent of the workers had been organised into 46 complex brigades and 30 specialist brigades. Management recognised that to make the structure work as they intended, a comprehensive set of mechanisms was necessary. They therefore designed a series of mechanisms including counterplanning, agreements, arbitration and internal distribution to provide the dynamics of the new structures and the relationships between them. Most of these mechanisms, which are discussed in Chapters 6 to 8, were to be found in other enterprises. The distinguishing feature at Metals was that a network of mechanisms was developed as a complete set with the creation of secondary mechanisms to support the operation of primary mechanisms – see, for example, the public defence of the counterplan described in Chapter 6.

Management strategy was related to two general design criteria, in addition to that of accounting: first, that brigade organisation should be as complete as practicable, including the widest possible range of occupations found within the enterprise; second, that brigades should be relatively small – for example, a brigade for each shift rather than covering two or more shifts – thus implementing the social criterion. At the base, the implementation of the first criterion led to the inclusion of clerical and lower-level administrative personnel within production brigades instead of servicing the operational management of the department as in the previous structure. Restructuring was not confined to the base: attempts were made to apply a form of brigade organisation to managers at the levels of the department and enterprise. The dynamics of these brigades were derived from the mechanisms of payment with bonuses distributed according to the co-efficient of participation. Although organisational development was consciously based on the mobilisation of economic interests through stronger and more direct material incentives, it was still located within the traditional framework of a movement and economic performance was linked to the traditional mechanisms of socialist emulation. Thus in model workplaces flags inscribed '*stopanin* of socialist property' were displayed; machines carried photographs of the workers and plates stating their commitment to the idea of *stopanin*; and each department had a marble plaque recording the acceptance of the machines by the collective. The novel element was that the balance between moral and material incentives was shifted decisively to the material. At a more general level the use of the traditional campaign approach initially contrasted with the strategy of innovation, so that major changes in structures and mechanisms were consciously located within a traditional framework. The explanation of this paradox offered by the researcher covering this enterprise was that since the strategy being implemented was well in advance of what was provided by normative regulation, location of the changes within a movement provided a basis for legitimation in relation to the labour collective which otherwise would have been lacking.

REDESIGNING THE INTERMEDIATE LEVEL OF THE ENTERPRISE

So far this chapter has discussed restructuring at the base. However, in 1986, accompanying the strategy of eliminating department brigades, an attempt was made to eliminate the department as an administrative level within the enterprise thus making the enterprise a structure with two main tiers of authority corresponding (as explained in Chapter 3) with the concepts of primary and main collective. In relation to the elaboration of the theory of the labour collective as *stopanin* this was derived deductively as a strategic issue from the theory of interests. Although the traditional enterprise had three main levels of structure – top, middle and base – and, consequently, three main levels of interests, the redesign of structures to strengthen the base raised the issue of how far it was appropriate for the middle level to continue as a significant level of interests. This also clearly had implications for the conceptions of operational authority and hierarchy at the middle level. This questioning of the future place of the department in the structure of the enterprise ran parallel to some emerging ideas of western management theorists on the effectiveness of different types of internal structure in industrial organisations. Thus Gustavsen in his work on the future of the enterprise (1986: 367–82) has discussed the possibilities for eliminating static hierarchical structures and replacing them with more flexible integrating mechanisms, moving from a rigid hierarchy towards 'softer' forms of vertical relations. Similar themes are discussed by Naisbitt and Aburdene, who also claim that in the United States, West Germany and Japan computers are replacing middle managers so that 'We are witnessing the beginnings of a tremendous whittling away of middle management, a flattening out of those hierarchies that were the norm in industrial America' (Naisbitt and Aburdene 1972: 15). In socialist societies, however, the only general strategy for reducing the power of the middle level occurred in

China during the Cultural Revolution where 'organisationally, the management system was two level . . . the middle level of control and coordination was reduced' (Andors 1977: 226).

The restructuring of the middle (intermediate) level of management in Bulgaria following the introduction of the Labour Code is illustrated in Figure 5.1.

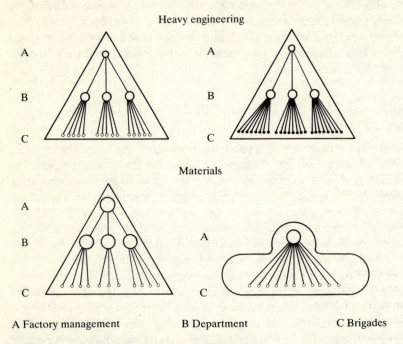

A: Factory management. B: Department. C: Brigades.
Figure 5.1   Redesign of intermediate level

At Heavy Engineering changes in internal structure occurred as one of the responses to the event of the campaign for managerial elections in September–October 1986 (see Chapter 9). Figure 5.1 shows that in the first half of 1986 there were 3 departments, each with 5 brigades. Restructuring was carried out, resulting in the segmentation of some brigades so that there were now 8 in each department. This altered the structure of the department but it remained in existence. The new feature was the change in the status of the elected departmental heads from that of administrative managers to that of co-ordinators of the activities of the brigades working with an *operativka* composed of representatives from the brigades. Similar changes in the status of departmental managers were made in 30 per cent of enterprises.

At Materials, a factory in the textile sector, Figure 5.1 shows a more radical restructuring with the abolition of the departmental level, so that the structure of the enterprise became a two-level one of primary collective (brigade) and main collective (enterprise) thus conforming to what Gustavsen (1986) has called 'the clothes hanger' model of enterprise organisation. This happened in 14 per cent of enterprises – mainly smaller ones. At Materials, a plant studied by a member of the research collective, the abolition of the middle level of management was a central feature of the director's strategy for enterprise development. The critical event here was a serious fire which destroyed part of the factory and led to a high turnover of workers. Management faced the challenge of reconstructing the building, restoring previous production levels and attracting back workers who had left. The director, who had previously worked at the factory before transferring to the district party organisation, restructured the way in which work was organised and remunerated. The main factory was rebuilt as a single large hall with the stores located in the middle. The production process was the responsibility of two large brigades, one of 300 and the other of about 200 located on either side of the store from which raw materials were taken and to which finished or semi-finished products were returned and accounted for. (This is an example of the implementation of Brigadier Nikolayev's concept, described in Chapter 2, of a *khozraschet* brigade buying materials from the stores and selling its products back to it.) The main change in managerial structure was that the middle level of management was abolished and most managers at this level were trans-ferred down into the two brigades, or in few cases became members of the management brigade of about 60 members at the top of the enterprise. These structural changes were intended to resolve the issues of linking the interests of managerial staff with the overall results of production, and of increasing productivity and quality through material interests and extended collectivity in the production process. The restructuring resolved these issues: previous production levels were achieved with fewer workers and quality control and earnings increased. The director had also developed a product strategy for manufacturing finished products for sale to the market as well as materials sold to other enterprises. The inclusion of managerial and engineering staff in the brigades had, the researcher found, unforeseen consequences for the dynamics of brigade organisation: in these big brigades with large brigade councils the influence of the engineers was perceived by the workers as strong and this led to the trade union organisers in the brigades assuming a much stronger role in representing worker interests than in smaller, less qualificationally differentiated brigades where direct democracy was more common.

THE AGENCIES OF RESTRUCTURING

Any process of restructuring based on external design requires internal agencies to implement it. In the socialist enterprise there are, in principle, four possible agencies – line management and the three social–political organisations, that is, party, trade union and Komsomol. Although in the special circumstances of industrialisation in the Soviet Union in 1928–30 the Komsomol were a leading agent in mobilisation, their role has normally been secondary and subordinate to the other social–political organisations. The implementation of the standards for the restructuring which brigade organisation required, rested on enterprise management and the party and trade union organisations. The aim here is to present a general picture of the actions and attitudes of these agencies in the process of restructuring and the diffusion of brigade organisation. Since implementation of the brigade organisation was party and state policy, it became one of the criteria for the performance appraisal of the local management and the party and trade union leadership. To some extent this led to mechanical implementation of the criteria for the new type of brigades. This meant not taking account of the specific features of the enterprise and the economic criterion's requirement that the operation of each brigade should be organised on the basis of cost accounting and self-support.

The general attitude of management can be characterised as positive but not very active in practice. Studies conducted in enterprises in 1982–4 showed that while most managers preferred brigade organisation, there were some who preferred the individual form of work organisation. Interviews with directors, their deputies and departmental managers in a number of factories showed that there were three categories of manager: those, a minority, who accepted the brigade organisation as an element of their own strategy for the development of the enterprise; those who accepted the brigade organisation as a measure imposed from above – it was in this category that the mechanistic, quantitative approach was most common; and those with a negative attitude towards brigade organisation. In the latter category there were two main groups: middle-level operational managers, especially departmental heads, and the heads of service departments such as planning, accounting and wages. For the former, brigade organisation meant the loss of some administrative power: for instance, the right to appoint and dismiss workers, to sanction them (although formally this was done by the director, the opinion of the departmental heads was decisive), and reduction of his power in relation to the allocation of tasks and distribution of wages among groups and among individual workers. For the latter, brigades involved additional work: for example, in bringing the indices of the plan down to the level of the brigade (before 1982 they were set only for the enterprise as a whole), calculation of the wage fund of each individual brigade, and in working out complex brigade quotas and rates.

The party and the trade unions

The political decision to introduce brigade organisation by the National Party Conference meant that party organisations were committed to supporting this initiative. However, in the succeeding period the party organisations in some regions and enterprises shifted from direct leadership in the work of implementing brigade organisation towards one of political oversight and assistance. The trade unions were very active in the process of implementing the strategy for the new type of brigades. Their activity is understandable as the brigade organisation involved the whole range of labour relations within their sphere of responsibility – wages, norms, training, employment, labour legislation etc. Firm support was given to this strategy and the implementation of brigade organisation was proclaimed to be a priority task for the trade unions. This was the platform endorsed by the 9th Congress of the Bulgarian Trade Unions held in 1982. The concentration of the efforts of trade union activists and leaders in the collective, mainly in the primary collective, became a kind of an organisational norm and the basis on which the results of their work was assessed. In the period 1982–7 brigade organisation was discussed as a problem of central importance at almost all trade union forums. In 1984 structural changes in trade union organisation were introduced in enterprises with the establishment of two levels of organisation: the primary one in the brigade and the main one in the enterprise. In this way, at least formally, the trade union structure in the enterprise was redesigned to conform with the concept and design of brigade organisation.

The trade unions took an active part in the preparation of legal and other regulations at all levels: national (the Labour Code and associated legislation); sector (regulations); and enterprise (internal regulations). The enterprise trade union became involved in the practical organisation of brigades: they convinced workers and managers of the advantages of the brigades; they assisted in the elaboration and introduction of the new model of wage distribution (through the co-efficient of participation – see Chapter 7); they intervened to resolve conflict situations; and they organised training of brigade leaders, exchange of experience, etc. The trade unions initiated two successful campaigns for the election of collective bodies of management including the brigade level, in 1982 and 1984, and organised a third one in 1986. This activity should not be overestimated, nor should it give the impression of a smooth process of involvement of the trade unions as an agent of change without conflicts and internal differences. The dynamic of their activity derived from the pressures arising from the requirements placed on them as the organisational 'guarantor of the economic mechanisms' and an 'organiser of the collective'.

The introduction of brigade organisation was imposed from above and this leads to the question of how workers responded. One national survey of workers attitudes showed that 43 per cent were in favour of the new form of organisation. However, there were significant differences in the responses of different skill groups. Highly skilled workers and especially frontrankers were more reluctant to join a brigade, while unskilled and those with average skills were more willing. These attitudes derive from differences of interest: the former recognised that the operation of the new mechanism for the distribution of earnings would tend to reduce their earnings, whereas the latter hoped that it would enhance theirs.

CONCLUSIONS

This chapter has described the introduction of a new internal structure for the organisation of work, and the elaboration of the criteria for designing the structure. As a centrally conceived and imposed strategy, this raises the question of how far it was congruent with emerging trends and conditions in the enterprises on which it was imposed. Thus it can be argued that trends in technological change favoured collective rather than individual forms of work organisation, and to this extent there was an internal dynamic that was already present in some enterprises. While this was true, in strategy formulation at national level from 1982, any internal dynamic of technological change was subordinated to the economic and managerial (self-management) criteria imposed from above. The other operational condition which is sometimes seen as facilitating collective forms of work organisation derives from the effects of the shortage economy which often leads to an irregular production process and in these conditions it may be easier to achieve the flexibility that such conditions require with a collective rather than an individual form of work organisation. Although this may be true as far as the level of operational management is concerned, there is no evidence that it was identified as a significant factor in the process of national strategy formulation.

At a more general level, the process of introducing brigade organisation according to design criteria elaborated at the national level and imposed on enterprises raised issues about the interrelationship between production engineering (the way technology is laid out), accounting for costs and income, and the social organisation of work. The last two criteria were, inevitably, imposed on existing layouts. The case of Materials shows how the destruction of the plant was used as an opportunity to redesign the layout and the organisation of work. At Metals and Heavy Engineering, on the other hand, enterprise management were able to restructure work without major changes in technology. Generally, the evidence suggests that when the accounting problems were overcome, by devising effective techniques for recording and allocating costs, the creation of smaller brigades was made possible. However, changes in technology, as at Textiles, could facilitate the introduction of brigades. Consequently, when the technology in an enterprise is changed there may be, at least in some technologies, an opportunity to arrange the layout of the machines in such a way as to meet the social criterion.

Finally, it is necessary to consider the relationship between changes in structure and changes in the norms and behaviour of the individuals brought together in the structure. As might be expected, existing norms and patterns of behaviour were often transferred to the new structure, so that the situation can be characterised as one of old content within a new structure. The key issue for norms and patterns of behaviour is the relationship between structures and mechanisms. Although changes in structure are necessary for organisational change, they are not sufficient unless they are accompanied by changes in the mechanisms which make the structures work and which, over time, influence and shape patterns of behaviour. On the other hand, new mechanisms often require a change in structure to operate effectively. (However, as the case of Metals shows, the legitimation of new structures and mechanisms was judged by enterprise management to require the traditional mechanisms of socialist emulation.) Effective redesign of organisations requires the integration of changes in structure with changes in mechanisms. The succeeding chapters discuss the changes in mechanisms which were imposed from above and their relationship to organisational change within enterprises.

6 Counterplanning and worker proposals – designed pressure from below

IMPOSED MECHANISMS

Chapters 6, 7, 8 and 9 on counterplanning, distribution, agreements and elections are conceived as a set. They analyse the process by which a series of imposed mechanisms were developed and introduced in order to shift the internal dynamics of enterprises and to develop the labour collective. In a process of redesign, the sequence in which mechanisms are introduced and the process by which they are, or are not, effectively linked together are of critical importance. In the presentation a general aim is to relate the development of each mechanism to the main economic models – the centralised model of the 1960s, and the intermediate models of the 1970s. The logic of development is seen as proceeding towards the self-management model (economic autonomy) introduced in 1988. The discussion of each mechanism is intended to show its significance in terms of organisational design, organisational dynamics (in relation to pressures and interests) and of labour relations. To provide an overview for the four chapters, Table 6.1 sets out the sequence and timing of the main changes in mechanisms.

COUNTERPLANNING AND WORKER PROPOSALS – DESIGNED PRESSURE FROM BELOW

This chapter seeks to explain the changes in organisational processes arising from changes in the structures of economic organisation and the mechanisms associated with the processes of planning. Discussions in both the western and socialist academic and specialist literatures on centrally planned economies tend to assess the planning mechanisms in terms of economic criteria, that is, their effectiveness in promoting economic goals of growth, productivity, and the efficient allocation of resources. The approach to the planning process adopted here is sociological and sees it as an organisational process. This means that it deals with the process by which the political balance of the organisation is shifted through redesign of the structures and mechanisms associated with the planning process which affect the dynamics of the relationships between different levels and units of structures within the enterprise and outside it. Therefore, particular attention is given to the effects of the changes on the different levels of enterprise management – top, intermediate and first line – on the participation of shop-floor workers, and on the role of the party and trade union organisations.

Table 6.1 Sequence and timing of changes in mechanisms

Counterplanning	*Distribution*	*Agreements*	*Elections*
1971 Promoted within centralised model		Collective agreement as component of centralised model	
	1978 Co-efficient of participation as basis of distribution of earnings in brigade		
1982 Counterplan as brigade mechanism linked to proposals	Residual income recognised as concept	Agreement as mechanism linking top and base	
1985 Counterplan as only plan of enterprise	Attempts to implement concept of residual income		
		1986 New type of collective agreement	Elections of directors and brigade leaders (full form)
1988 Abolition of counterplan	1988–9 Reduction in number of wages and salary grades begins	Agreements on transfer of property	Second round of elections

The academic and specialist literature on the planning process in centrally planned economies has tended to assume that the planning process is one which is relatively smooth and undisturbed and that the rationality of plans centrally determined in the interests of society is accepted by the active participants in the process. Participants in the process and specialists concerned with it have, however, accepted that in reality 'plan bargaining' is an integral element of planning as an organisational process. In Hungary there is an academic literature (Kornai 1980; Laky 1979: 227–46, 261) which has developed and discussed economic models of the bargaining process and its economic implications. In Bulgaria, among participants in the planning process – economists, planners and workers – the term 'hot spot' (point of tension) has established usage, though it has rarely been discussed in the literature. 'Hot spot' is related to the recognition that in the actual process of allocating tasks, competing criteria reflecting the differing interests and perceptions of interests result in a process of negotiation and accommodation. 'Hot spots' are the focus of the action field when there is an open meeting of different interests, and resources are mobilised to resolve the issues which emerge and are identified. 'Hot spots' emerge in the process of relationships between levels of organisational hierarchy – for example, between the enterprise and the ministry or between the department and the top management of the enterprise. They emerge from the issue of fixing the targets and allocating the resources for the mechanisms of the state plan and of the counterplan. The way in which these 'hot spots' are resolved is related to changes in structures and mechanisms and this in turn is related to the structures of power and authority and the extent to which different levels of interests are recognised formally and in reality. 'Hot spots' may be resolved by hierarchical command and authority or by dialogue resulting in agreement. One aim of this chapter is to show the dynamics of 'hot spots' for the three models and how transition from one model to another may alter both the levels at which 'hot spots' emerge and the way in which they are resolved.

In analysing the process of redesign and the development of alternatives to the centralised model, counterplanning is seen as a mechanism which changes its nature as other mechanisms are redesigned. As shown in Chapter 2 counterplanning originated in the Soviet Union in the 1930s, as an organic mechanism in response to the decision that the planning mechanism should be taken below the level of the department to the brigades. It was then sponsored as a campaign to act as a complementary mechanism to the main planning mechanisms. Worker proposals also developed in the Soviet Union in the 1930s as an organic mechanism which then received endorsement as a movement at the political level and which took various forms at different times – thus Stakhanov can be seen as the author of a worker proposal. In this chapter, worker proposals are seen as a secondary mechanism which in the course of redesign became linked to counterplanning. This mechanism had various forms but it is interesting to note that at the Baltic shipyard in Leningrad in 1931, brigade proposals for rationalising of work were set in the context of the counterplan which in turn was set in the context of socialist emulation (see Chapter 2). The process of separating and linking mechanisms – and the consequences – is one of the themes of this chapter. Equally, the directions in which mechanisms operate is another central concern: thus the main direction of the command central-planning mechanisms was from the top downward; the theory of counterplanning is that it entails some reversal of this direction through mobilisation of pressure from below.

THE CENTRALISED COMMAND MODEL OF THE 1960s

In the 1960s there were two or three main levels and units of structure: the enterprise and the ministry, though in some cases the trust (*obednenie*) was an intermediate unit between the enterprise and the ministry, which in turn was subordinate to the State Planning Commission. In the assignment of plan targets and the allocation of resources for investment, the main 'hot spot' was between the enterprise and the ministry. The enterprise through its director would submit proposals for targets and investment to the ministry (or trust) which in turn would often seek to impose a tauter plan with tighter targets. To a certain extent it was in the interests of the enterprise to secure investment for new projects since these were more difficult for the higher level to control than the established products for which historical cost information was available. Thus the direction of the mechanism of determining plan targets was downward from above. However, the direction of the mechanism for allocating funds for investment was at least in part, upwards, from the enterprise to the higher bodies. The allocation of supplies was the responsibility of the higher level. The process of establishing targets thus required dialogue, but the authority of the higher level over the enterprise was clear: the plan targets were authorised by the higher level and the director did not sign them, although he was accountable for their achievement. In practice, plan targets were frequently revised to take account of both national interests (as determined by the State Planning Commission) and the failure of supplies. Although the director was accountable to the state bodies, the enterprise party organisation was also accountable for plan fulfilment to the district party organisation and consequently specialists attached to the enterprise party bureau were closely involved in the planning process. The party organisation, which in socialist theory represented the interests of society, was charged with ensuring that the director and his planning staff were not pressing for unduly loose targets. At times the director and the party organisation might act in coalition to promote the interests of the enterprise – for example, in using both party and state channels to press for more investment. However, the district party organisation was responsible for ensuring that the enterprise party organisation did not operate in such a way as to promote enterprise interests at the expense of societal interests as set out in party documents. From 1956 the enterprise trade union was legally entitled to participate in the planning process. However, its role except on social and welfare issues was essentially subordinate to that of the party and of management. Unlike the party, it did not have planning specialists and its channel of access to the district trade union committee was of less significance in securing resources.

In the internal allocation of plan targets and resources the key unit for planning and accounting was the department headed by its *nachalnik*. The *nachalnik* participated in the process of dialogue on targets with the director and the enterprise planning staff (in large departments the *nachalnik* would have the assistance of his own planners) but the document which eventually specified the targets was signed by the director alone on the basis of his authority. Within the department there was, of course, a party organisation, but in the opinion of one experienced specialist the status of the *nachalnik* in relation to that of the party secretary was relatively high because of the *nachalnik*'s technical qualifications, whereas the balance between the director and the enterprise party secretary was more equal. In the distribution of tasks to the different sections of the workforce supervised by *majstors*, the authority of the *nachalnik* was high not least because work-group cohesion was limited by the predominance of individual payment systems and because he had influence over the distribution of bonuses and tasks and the supplies which could affect earnings. In this system of reward, leading workers who had achieved high performance through their skill in organising their work were accorded the status of 'frontranker'. Frontrankers were, or often became, party members and were encouraged to act as tutors to their fellow workers and to set an example to be followed. As 'core' workers they would tend to form a coalition with the *nachalnik* on problems relating to plan targets, although they might also be informal spokesmen for the interests of groups of workers. In the 1960s in the context of socialist emulation, frontrankers and other workers might offer proposals beyond the state plan, that is, as a pledge to overfulfil the allocated tasks, but at this period counterplans were the result of initiatives in particular factories and not part of a national movement. The infrequent existence of the mechanism of counterplanning at this time had consequences for the way in which worker proposals operated as a mechanism. The direction of both of these mechanisms was intended to be upward, but there was significant external support from outside the enterprise only for the rationaliser's movement. This was originally initiated in 1947 and supported by a national network linking technical and engineering specialists in enterprises with those in research and other institutes. By the 1960s this movement was integrated with the national five-year plan. Sociologically, this can be described as an elite movement in that its participants were necessarily drawn (within the enterprise) from the stratum of engineers and technical specialists. The second movement for worker proposals was intended to mobilise proposals from the shop floor (from within the department) and it was one aspect of the movement for socialist emulation. The presentation of worker proposals at this level was closely linked to the institution of frontrankers and other core workers who were rewarded for rationalising working methods within the department. Within the enterprise such proposals were mobilised through production meetings. The initiative for both movements came from the centre so that they can be seen as mechanisms operating from the top to the base.

THE 1970s – INTERMEDIATE MODEL, STAGE 1

The redesign of the 1960s model to meet the conditions of the 1970s involved one major change in structure and one major mechanism, although there were also modifications to other mechanisms and changes in the relationship between some mechanisms. The DSO was larger than the trusts of the 1960s – a total of seventeen was created for the whole economy. On average they employed 34,000 people. They became a major planning unit, so that there were now two 'hot spots' external to the enterprise, in the process of fixing state plan targets and allocating resources: between the enterprise and DSO and between the DSO and the ministry.

The theory of counterplanning, as developed during the 1970s was intended to redesign the planning process so that there was pressure from below from within the enterprise as well as pressure from above. The planning mechanisms were now to operate in two directions: the assignment of state-planned tasks from top to bottom, and the mechanisms of counterplanning from bottom to top. This redesign of mechanisms was related to the recognition that the centralised command model of the 1960s was no longer successful in combining and integrating different levels of interests. As explained in the preceding section, under the centralised command model, it was in the interests of the enterprise to secure planned tasks that were not too difficult and to keep 'reserves', for example, in the form of labour to safeguard itself against increases imposed by higher authorities in the planned tasks already fixed or to offset the adverse consequences of unplanned shortages of raw materials or semi-finished products needed for the manufacturing process. The theory of counter-planning was based on the assumption that enterprises needed incentives to reveal and make more efficient use of reserves. The combination of state-planned tasks with counterplanning assumed that the enterprise would be given an incentive, and more freedom to enjoy the results of achieved counterplan proposals above and outside the state-planned tasks. It could also imply that state-planned tasks would not be set so tightly as to inhibit the mobilisation of counterplan proposals. Implicit in the theory of counter-planning was the recognition that there were two levels of interest in the enterprise: the top level of the whole enterprise and the department. Consequently, it was necessary for the mechanism of counterplanning to operate in such a way as to provide incentives at the level of the department as well as the level of the enterprise. It was, therefore, decided that at the level of the department the counterplan should be directly linked to worker proposals designed to improve the organisation of work. The announce-ment of this policy by President Zhivkov in December 1971 showed how the mobilisation of those mechanisms was intended to develop. The occasion was a mass meeting of frontrankers from different regions of the country and branches of the economy held at Pernik (such gatherings were held periodically). The significance of this was that frontrankers were clearly identified as the leading agency for the operation of the linked mechanisms of counterplanning and worker proposals.

The dynamics implicit in the process of counterplanning had consequences for the different structures within the enterprise. Thus for the party organisation the implementation and development of the mechanisms as an aspect of party policy meant that it was responsible for ensuring that top management promoted and facilitated its operation within the enterprise and that it was supported by party members in specialist departments and those working on the shop-floor. However, since it was regarded as essential for the success of counterplanning that there should be mass shop-floor involvement in the development of worker proposals, the trade union organisation had to be involved. In the opinion of a senior trade union specialist the implication of the counterplanning mechanism with the need for mass explanation brought the enterprise trade union organisation into the planning process as an active agency. (Previously its involvement had been linked to the planning process mainly through the social plans and the plant collective agreement.)

The mechanism of counterplanning linked to worker proposals led to significant changes in the dynamics of the department which revealed the duality of the mechanism. For the *nachalnik* it meant, on the one hand, that the increased mobilisation of workers reduced the uncertainty in which he operated; on the other hand, recognition that proposals could come from the workers could alter his status as a source of technical authority and could require his collaboration with workers on a more equal basis. However, at this period the mode of work organisation was still individual rather than the collective form of the brigade. Consequently, frontrankers remained the leading agents among the workers in counterplanning and worker proposals, and the operation of these mechanisms led to an increase in the number of frontrankers. One specialist with experience of department management suggested that whereas in the 1960s there might have been 2 workers out of 10 who were frontrankers, in the 1970s there would be 3 or 4 who to some extent would be competing with one another and putting pressure on the *nachalnik*.

THE INTERMEDIATE MODEL, STAGE II: BRIGADE ORGANISATION OF WORK AND THE TRANSFORMATION OF THE COUNTERPLAN INTO THE COMPULSORY STATE PLAN, 1982–1987

The New Economic Mechanism of 1982 marked the next stage in the redesign of the planning mechanisms. However, since the Party Conference of 1978 had decided that brigade organisation of work of the new type should be the generic unit for the organisation of work within the department, the changes in 1982 were about redesigning mechanisms to conform to a structure that was already being introduced. The New Economic Mechanism provided that the brigade was to be a unit of planning and accounting, and also that the brigade should have its own counterplan. This shift in levels meant a shift in the level of the 'hot spot', so that it would now be between the brigade and the department (or the brigade and top management). In terms of mobilising pressure from the base through the counterplanning mechanism, what was later to be recognised as the self-managing brigade, and a 'unit of interests' seemed to have a greater dynamic potential than the department.

The external structure of the DSO remained intact, but the redesign of mechanisms altered the relative significance of the DSO and the enterprise in the planning process. Whereas in the 1970s model the DSO was the most important unit for planning, in the 1980s model the enterprise was in the process of becoming the core unit. The redesign of mechanisms that produced this change was directly connected with the shift in the balance between the importance given to the compulsory state tasks and to the tasks set out in the counterplan generated within the enterprise. At first, state tasks and counterplan co-existed; then in the redesign of the model the counterplan became the only plan of the enterprise.

In the process of extending and developing the operation of counter-planning as a mechanism after 1982, the trade unions at national, district and plant level became a leading agency in the process. Specifically, from 1983 to 1986 the trade unions organised a series of regional conferences at which representatives of enterprise management, party and trade union organisations discussed with specialists and other representatives from the national level the issues arising from the introduction of counterplanning and ways of resolving them. Recognition of the need for such forums was triggered partly by pressure arising from the labour collective at the base (the new 'hot spot' centred on the brigade counterplan), the resolution of which required action initiated by the trade union as the organiser of the labour collective. Such regional-level activity was, of course, a reflection of the problems the trade union organisation was facing in the enterprises.

It was generally accepted that both the enterprise and the brigade would include counterplan targets higher than those allocated to them. The economic profitability of counterplanning lay in the tapping of additional resources, which the state (central) bodies could not foresee, hence the term 'extension' plan widely used at that time. As an incentive for this, the enterprise which exceeded the state targets had the right to keep a greater proportion of the additional profit. In principle, this was also valid for the counterplan of the brigade. The economic mechanism allowed for updating of the enterprise plan and the brigade plan in the course of the year, on condition that if the targets were increased, they would be compensated with additional material resources and that the marketing of the additional output would be guaranteed. In an attempt to restrict centralisation in planning, the number of compulsory targets of the enterprises was reduced, which in turn offered more space to the management in negotiating the plan targets with the brigades. Another new feature was the right of the brigade to determine the number of workers needed to fulfil the plan and, in the case of manpower savings, to re-allocate the wages of the transferred workers to the brigade wage fund. For this purpose, the individual workers at the brigade as a whole were encouraged to come forward with proposals for technological improvements, economies and other measures that would lead to the preparation of a more economically effective plan. Worker proposals and the right of the brigade to vote on its counterplan were mechanisms for securing the active participation of more workers at the base.

The mechanism of counterplanning should in theory provide higher economic results. In the 1983–4 period analysis by Bulgarian specialists showed that it led to improvements of the economic situation in a number of enterprises. At the same time, however, some deviations from the new method of planning began to emerge. Thus, the practice of 'reserve appropriation' emerged. This occurred in two ways: first, administratively – the superior organisation appropriated by directive a considerable part of the additional profit of the enterprise; and second, through the planning system – the state planning bodies used the targets laid down in the enterprises' counterplan as the basis for the following year. In some cases, in the process of updating the plan during the year, the higher organisations did not adhere to the requirement of ensuring additional financial and material resources. Constraints from above on enterprise managements curtailed internal relations with brigades. An example of this in response to pressure from below deriving from the process of counterplanning in a consumer durables plant is explained in Chapter 8.

The empirical evidence from the five plants is drawn mainly from accounts of what happened in the years 1984–6. The general procedure was that when state tasks had been received from the higher authorities (usually the DSO), and the enterprise had negotiated the indicators for the counterplan, a number of commissions composed mainly of managerial specialists were set up to discuss and allocate the targets to the internal production units of the enterprise and to integrate worker proposals into the counterplan. In considering this evidence, the main aims are: first, to show the constraints arising from the external environment which limited the operation of the counterplanning mechanism as it was designed; second, to indicate the existence and the level of structure at which 'hot spots' emerge – that is between the enterprise and the higher bodies or internally within the enterprise; and third, to consider the actual relationship between counterplanning as a primary, imposed mechanism and worker proposals as a secondary, and potentially organic mechanism. The sequence of presentation is that the plants where the evidence shows that counterplanning was less developed are discussed first.

Assembly

In 1986 the bargaining between the enterprise and the DSO over the state-planned tasks, was protracted. When these were finally accepted, commissions in the different departments collated and incorporated them in the counterplan of the enterprise. The enterprise counterplan was not completed until April, three months after the beginning of the accounting year. This plan was approved by the plant council, but was not discussed or approved by the general assembly. Subsequently, plan tasks were worked out for each brigade. Two factors underlay the limitations and formality of the counterplanning process: the commissioning of a large new department with more modern technology, which, in part, explains the long negotiations with the DSO, and the approach of management which did not seek to foster the development of the labour collective.

Heavy Engineering

In 1985 the main factory did not adopt a counterplan for two principal reasons: first, continuing disagreements about some costings in the state tasks; and second, problems in ensuring supplies of components from another factory. However, the procedure for worker proposals was put into operation. This involved the encouragement of workers to submit suggestions for both social development – improvement of conditions, recreational facilities and safety – and technical proposals designed to improve work organisation and reduce energy and material costs. The annual average of such proposals was about 900, of which about half were for social development. In 1986 special forms were prepared for worker proposals which set out the state tasks for each sub-unit and space for worker proposals of both kinds. These forms were widely distributed within the department with the intention that they should be accessible to every worker. Proposals were discussed by brigades and then submitted for the consideration of an *ad hoc* departmental commission. In the opinion of the researcher, the imposed mechanism of counterplanning was for both top and base an obligation rather than an opportunity. For the management, strong pressure from the central state authorities to fulfil state orders was a major constraint on the development of the internal counterplanning process. For the workers, the opportunity of making proposals was often offset by uncertainty about securing their acceptance. It appeared to the researcher that the trade union committee were more concerned with the number of proposals rather than their content, that is, with quantity rather than quality. This approach may be seen as a response to the external criteria for assessing their work.

Chemicals

In 1985 it had been the intention to start the counterplanning process in June, but this was delayed because the state tasks were not received until November. The major constraint on the operation of the plant was the supply of raw materials and this restricted the scope of counterplanning. The recognition of this constraint was general within the enterprise, and the formation of counterplan targets was seen as primarily a task for top management. Although worker proposals were collected, the process of counterplanning was not one of dynamic interaction between the levels of internal structure.

Textiles

The report of the researcher describes the details of the counterplanning procedure. As soon as the state-planned tasks are received at the enterprise, the director issues an order for the elaboration of the counterplan. On the basis of this order a commission for the counterplan is set up including the deputy directors, specialists for the plant, representatives of the trade union organisation, shop foremen and heads of departments. The commission for the counterplanning has the task of rendering practical assistance to the brigades and shops in the drafting of the counterplans and of explaining and acquainting the individual labour collectives with the specific characteristics, content and possible ways of fulfilment and overfulfilment of the state plan assignment. Some members of the commission are appointed to see to the preparation of counterplans in the individual brigades. The counterplans of the brigades are worked out on the basis of personal creative plans. These were a traditional mechanism derived from the movement approach of socialist emulation so that there was a mixture of mechanisms here.

The counterplan of the brigade contains the following indices:

1 Number of workers, economy of materials, wages, labour productivity;
2 Measures for training and qualification;
3 Demands to the economic management of the enterprise.

After the counterplans are finalised at the brigade level, they are considered by the plant council and the trade union committee and then sent back to the brigade councils with the comments of these two institutions. They are finally approved by the general assembly of the brigade. The counterplan of the enterprise as a whole is drawn up on the basis of the brigade counterplans worked out in this manner. It also includes workers' proposals accepted in the course of the year. In 1985 their number was 743, covering a wide range of problems. Although the procedures for counterplanning and worker proposals were well developed, the researcher noted that the enterprise was frequently subjected to pressure from the DSO to undertake additional production to that in the state-planned tasks because of high demand for the products. Consequently, the interests of top management in achieving a high counterplan were limited. The researcher also thought that the content of many of the worker proposals was very slight.

Metals

As explained in Chapter 5, top management had taken initiatives in establishing brigade organisation which was well developed and they saw the imposition of counterplanning as an opportunity to strengthen the dynamics of relationships between the top and the base, although the scope of counterplanning was limited by the rules retricting the funds available as a result of the counterplanning process. As in other plants, there were commissions for all five departments which were responsible for developing counterplans with the assistance of enterprise specialists. In 1984 the participants – specialists, representatives of brigade councils – attended a two-day seminar on counterplanning, a mechanism for linking levels of structure as well as being educational. The draft counterplans developed by brigades with the assistance of specialists were debated by representatives of the brigade and the departmental commission for counterplanning in the presence of top management representatives. This public defence can be seen as an organic mechanism created by the top to link the three levels of structure to meet the emerging needs of the base. If the commission was not satisfied that the brigade's counterplan adequately represented the potential of the brigade, it was referred back to the brigade for further discussion. The most effective counterplan was awarded a prize. The enterprise counterplan was aggregated from the departmental counterplans. Worker proposals were examined by a separate commission on the basis of forms for proposals which were distributed to each worker. Since the procedure was instituted in 1981 the number of both proposals and approved proposals had increased significantly. An important shift in the content of proposals was noted: at the beginning most of the proposals were related to social and welfare problems; over time, they became more related to the technical problems of production. Proposals were, however, constrained by external conditions. Thus in one department the workers would have liked new machines, but it was not possible for the enterprise to obtain them. Consequently, worker proposals in this department were designed to alleviate the problems with the old machines.

The evidence from the five plants shows clearly that in the first three the environment constrained the development of counterplanning as a mechanism operating to engage the interests of the internal structures of the labour collective. In the first two plants the evidence shows that the real 'hot spots' were between the enterprise and the higher bodies. At Chemicals there was no clear evidence of such 'hot spots' and in the opinion of the researcher the interests of top and base were integrated by a tacit agreement. The base saw the role of top management as that of ensuring regular supplies and in return their role was to work.

Counterplanning did not operate to disturb the basis of this reciprocity. At Metals, where the redesign of structures and mechanisms was more developed than in the other plants, the main internal hot spot was between the enterprise and the department. Here, however, the recognition that counterplanning required the emergence of 'hot spots' between the brigade and the department had led to the creation of the public defence of brigade counterplans with representation from the top level of structure as well as the two levels directly involved. This forum operated as a mechanism facilitating the identification of issues and their resolution with an element of dialogue.

CONCLUSIONS – DESIGN, DYNAMICS AND LABOUR RELATIONS

The central purpose of this chapter has been to analyse the successive changes in models and mechanisms. It is clear that in the process of transition from one model to another only some structures and mechanisms can be redesigned, so that the process of change is necessarily incremental. New mechanisms operate in old structures and new structures have to operate with old mechanisms, at least until the next stage of redesign is introduced. The main structures of enterprises and the mechanisms of counterplanning and worker proposals originated under the centralised command model and the fieldwork was conducted at the time of the intermediate model, stage 2, when many of the external mechanisms of central planning were still in operation. In particular, counterplanning was introduced without any change in the mechanisms of forming the wage fund (see Chapter 7) so that increases in earnings could come only from the discovery of 'reserves'. For this reason, it had to operate within the traditional framework and mechanisms of a movement. This partly explains why hot spots emerged mainly between the enterprise and the external bodies. It can be argued that when external constraints were dominant there was insufficient space for the emergence of internal hot spots, and that, conversely, when external constraints were less dominating there was more space for internal hot spots to appear, as at Metals. Space measured in financial terms, that is, the extra funds available from the revealing of reserves, was quite small. At Metals it was about 3 per cent. However, the existence of brigades as a collective structure and unit for both counterplanning and worker proposals, that is a new structure for mechanisms from earlier models, could, in some cases, provide pressure from below. In terms of design, counterplanning contributed to the linking of levels within the enterprise, especially between the brigade and top management and in this way it influenced labour relations. It also operated as a mechanism which concentrated on the results of work and not simply on work done.

The procedures for counterplanning operated principally through the same two structures as the planning procedures, that is, through the operational structure supplemented by mobilisation of the 'movement' type through the social-political structures, especially the trade union. In practice, counterplanning was generally only related in a formal way to the institutions of the third structure, that is, the general assembly and the plant council. The linking of worker proposals to counterplanning was designed to provide a more specific focus and point of action for them than had been available with previous mechanisms, such as production conferences, by relating to a potentially stronger mechanism. Worker proposals had always been designed to operate upwards; counterplanning as an adjunct to the mechanisms of allocating the state-planned tasks which generally operated downwards, was designed to provide some counter pressure upwards on top management. They had, therefore, for top management, a strong potential element of duality: on the one hand, successful proposals and counterplans were to the advantage of the enterprise, the top management and the workers involved; on the other hand, there was the possibility of generating unexpected pressure from the base on top management, and of creating frustration at the base when proposals were rejected as unfeasible.

7   Distribution – wage funds, wage interests and pressures from below

Distribution is a complex process in which a series of mechanisms are interlinked. The operation of these mechanisms is a sensitive regulator of worker behaviour and labour relations. Every redesign of these mechanisms shapes the interests of individuals, groups and collectives and influences their responses to economic, organisational and technological change. The principal aspect of distribution to be discussed is wage payment, concentrating on payment within the enterprise but setting it in the context of macro-distributional relations. At enterprise level the dynamics of wage payment derive not only from the method of payment and the distribution between grades and categories of worker but also from the mechanisms for establishing the enterprise funds from which wages are paid. At societal level wage payment has a special significance in socialist societies. As Kornai remarks:

> Nowadays every government in the world has a wages policy, whether enforced or not. In a socialist economy the analysis of wages has to start from central wage policy because the latter is actually enforced. Hardly any indicator in the economy-wide plan is fulfilled more precisely or with smaller relative deviations than the targets for wages.
>
> (Kornai 1980: 377)

Consequently, the significance of wage mechanisms in the enterprise cannot be understood without an explanation of the macro-system. From this are derived the conflicts of interests over the size and differentials of wages, the generation of pressures from individuals and groups when the operation of the mechanisms of distribution produces results which run counter to their perceptions and criteria of what is a fair reward for their skills and contribution.

Academic study of the mechanisms of distribution in socialist economies has been dominated by the work of labour economists who have concentrated on payment systems and their relation to the overall economic performance of the enterprise, and little attention has been given to the social and informal aspects of worker behaviour. (A notable exception is the study by Hethy and Mako (1989).) The aims of this chapter are: first, to show the sequence of shifts in the models of payment systems in the Bulgarian enterprise; second, to assess the significance of changes in the mechanisms of distribution for the restructuring of labour relations in the period 1982–7; and, third, to relate the mechanisms of distribution to other mechanisms of planning and agreements and also to norming (although these are not the main subject of analysis). It should be noted that the analysis in this chapter does not deal with social funds and supplementary incomes which are important aspects of socialist wage distribution. In the period 1982–8 the growth of social funds continuously outstripped the growth of wages. The proportion of wages to general income which was 60-65 per cent in the 1970s fell to 47 per cent in 1985. This could only diminish the interest in wages as a source of income and an incentive to work. Analysis of this, however, goes beyond wage behaviour and concerns the operation of economic behaviour as a whole.

THE CENTRALISED MODEL

As explained in Chapter 2 the transfer and establishment of the Soviet model of labour relations in Bulgaria was completed in the early 1950s. For distribution, the model included integrated and centralised institutions for the control of the mechanisms of enterprise income formation and of individual remuneration. There were four main levers for these mechanisms. The first was the manual of grades and wage rates. This set out as state standards the specifications for all jobs in each industrial sector, the skills required by the worker to undertake a given job, and the requirements for upgrading within a skill group (the so-called tariff section). The second was the manual of salary scales, a similar document covering non-manual workers – specialists and white-collar workers. On the basis of this the administrative–management personnel of the enterprise were classified into different categories and it was used to determine the complements and the salary scale for every position. The third were the standards for remuneration included in the Labour Code. The code contained such principles as 'all work shall be remunerated according to the quantity and quality of work done', and 'bonuses will be paid for the fulfilment and overfulfilment of production plans'. It also included standards for overtime and shiftwork and for the minimum wage. The fourth were internal enterprise regulations on payment – every industrial organisation had internal rules on the formation of its wage fund and for the individual payment of manual and non-manual workers. Together, these four sources of standards provided the normative base for the system of remuneration in the enterprise. To operationalise them, standards for assessing the work done were needed for every occupation and workplace. This required the establishment of a national network of institutions responsible for developing and controlling standards according to the principles of what was termed the 'scientific organisation of work'. There were norming departments for every industrial sector and enterprise, and enterprises and their production departments had work-study engineers to measure and time all jobs. Specialists working for these institutions were responsible for the periodic revision of norms at national, sectoral and local level. It was standard practice to review and revise enterprise norms at the end of the year so that the new plan year started with corrected norms. A specialist with experience of this in the 1950s and 1960s described it as 'a painful process'. In this way, norming was the base for assessing the work of every worker and brigade and hence for establishing their wages.

The payment system for individual workers was a central area of concern. The most widespread were time-rates and piecework. The proportions varied between periods. Thus in the mid 1950s, 22 per cent were on time-rates and 78 per cent on piecework; in the 1960s time-rates increased to 32 per cent while piecework decreased to 68 per cent. The operation of the system is illustrated by the following example: a turner in grade 5 would have a grade rate (fallback rate) of 6.31 leva per day. For 100 per cent fulfilment of the standard over a working month of 22 days he would receive 138.82 leva, for 90 per cent 124.94, for 80 per cent 111.06, and so on. If the turner overfulfilled the norms his earnings would increase. However, the increase in wages for a specified percentage of overfulfilment, was not proportional. This was termed the 'wage ceiling', an issue to be considered below. There were also increments for length of service and supplements for work in difficult conditions. In addition, at the end of the quarter or the year, bonuses were paid depending on the overall results of the enterprise. This presentation of the method of calculating the individual wage has been deliberately simplified. The essence of wage determination depends on the general method of generating enterprise funds and specifically on the determinants of the amount of the wage fund. For the traditional centralised model of economic management the income of the enterprise was calculated and distributed as shown in Figure 7.1.

The distribution of enterprise income into its funds depended on what was provided in the plan. The remainder was appropriated by the state for social needs – investment and equipment. As Figure 7.1 shows the greater proportion of profits was taken by the state. Part of the appropriated income was redistributed to the enterprise in the form of investments or subsidies. The latter were given to economically weak, that is, unprofitable

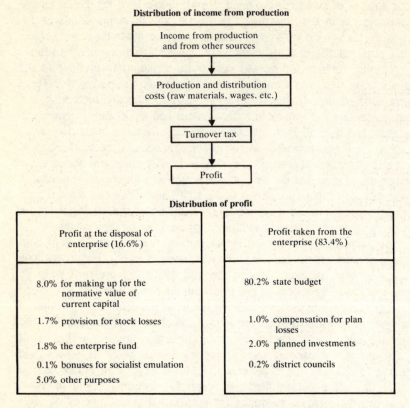

Distribution of income from production

Income from production
and from other sources

Production and distribution
costs (raw materials, wages, etc.)

Turnover tax

Profit

Distribution of profit

Profit at the disposal of enterprise (16.6%)	Profit taken from the enterprise (83.4%)
8.0% for making up for the normative value of current capital	80.2% state budget
1.7% provision for stock losses	1.0% compensation for plan losses
1.8% the enterprise fund	2.0% planned investments
0.1% bonuses for socialist emulation	0.2% district councils
5.0% other purposes	

Figure 7.1 Distribution of income and profit (industrial enterprises)

enterprises. The justification for this was that the production of every enterprise was important for the national economy. Thus through artificial redistribution by the state using administrative methods, production became the basic criterion for economic activity, and profit did not function as a regulator of production or an indicator of the financial state of the enterprise. In these conditions the main economic interest of a given enterprise was the size of its wage fund. The amount provided in the fund by the plan was in practice always fully utilised though, as explained later, there were often subsequent pressures from the enterprise for upward revision. In the centralised model this fund was determined in two ways: first, as a tightly fixed amount, and, second, as a norm-related amount, for example, as a percentage of gross enterprise income. In the first method the interest of the enterprise was to increase the size of the fund using the argument of its manpower requirements – the size of the wage fund was directly proportional to the number on the payroll and to their skills and qualifications. It followed from this that there was internal pressure to increase the proportion of skilled workers and counter-pressure by the state to control not only the total complement but also the distribution of skill groups within that total. At the same time the centre aimed to control the ratio between production workers and engineering–technical staff and the administrative–managerial stratum. In the second method the interest of the enterprise was to increase gross income, for which the basic source was an increase in the price of its products. To counter such pressure, the state-control mechanism was to fix the prices of products or to set upper limits which a given enterprise could not exceed. There was one further index in the plan to ensure strict control of the wage fund by the central institutions. This was to ensure that 'the correlation between the rate of growth of wages and the rate of growth in labour productivity' was maintained, as it was considered imperative that wages did not increase faster than labour productivity.

The amount of individual remuneration depended in the first place on the industrial sector. It was determined, first, by an assessment of the differences in the conditions and difficulties of work in particular sectors, and, second, by the importance attached to a particular sector for the development of the national economy. Thus in mining, construction and metallurgy and certain other sectors, the level of wages was significantly above the national average. This reflected the principle of the Soviet model of industrialisation that heavy industry should be given priority.

Once established, the network of normative regulations on wage payment did not change often. By the end of the 1970s, changes in wage policy occurred generally every five years in conjunction with the five-year plan. Typically, changes were related to the minimum wage and the wage and salary scales. They were initiated by the central economic planning institutions and associated with the projected development of the economy. Changes were associated with campaigns carried out from top to base – from the ministries to the enterprises and then to different occupations and workplaces. The last reform of this kind began in 1979 with an integrated wage and salary scale for all sectors. The strategic aim was to remove disproportions in wages which were considered to arise from inadequate criteria for job evaluation in different sectors and projects. In retrospect this step can be seen as the culmination of the development of the traditional model of payment. It was presented by the centre as an 'ideal' normative instrument for management – a universal and common measure for evaluating the complexity and weight of every kind of job in the national economy. This reform set limits on variations in wages and had a negative effect on the interests of workers and collectives in securing steady improvements in overall results.

The centralised model of distribution with its complicated system of principles, regulations and norms gave rise to doubts about its effectiveness and led to many contradictions. On the one hand, the model made it possible for the central institutions to seek to control the amount and growth of wages in every workplace. However, given the multiplicity of occupations and work situations, the control was formal and often illusory. As Hethy and Mako point out: 'Even in the small or medium sized economic organisations, work tasks are characterised by such quantitative and qualitative differences that even plant managers who possess specific knowledge and experience find it difficult to evaluate them' (Hethy and Mako 1989: 31). The centre was thus under constant pressure from enterprises and departments to amend the regulations in their favour. This pressure was supported by 'objective' arguments. However, the exclusive authority of the central institutions to make decisions on the normative system of payment and the actual process of distribution did not engage the interests of the base (the enterprise and the collective) in controlling the relationship between overall performance and the wages of individual workers and categories of employees.

In addition to periodic reforms of the whole system, the central institutions responded to symptoms of the disengagement of the interests of producers in overall results by introducing experiments designed to improve the micromodel. Thus a multifactor wage system was tried in a number of enterprises in the 1970s. This was a modification of the classical model in which, in addition to the fulfilment of norms, qualifications and length of service, factors such as economy in the use of raw materials, energy, quality of work, care of machinery, work and technological discipline, and responsibility and initiative in the labour process, were taken into account. Essentially, however, the centralised model remained unchanged, in that the conditions for determining the wages of workers were planned and imposed by the centre and controlled by it. The emphasis in wage policy was on the funds of the enterprise and the individual system of payment associated with the predominance of the individual form of work organisation.

THE INTERMEDIATE MODEL

Discussions in the economic literature on the need for alternative approaches to payment emerged in the early 1960s in the context of the economic reforms undertaken at that time which partly affected the system of payment. Critics of the traditional model argued that it was vulnerable on the grounds that wage policy did not account for the objective nature of wage payment as the monetary expression of the value of labour power and that the wage fund of the enterprise and the individual wage did not depend directly on the overall results. Elimination of the first disadvantage implied a re-evaluation of one of the basic postulates of economic theory under socialism – that labour power is not a commodity and consequently wages are dependent solely on the quantity and quality of the work done. More specifically, the critics of this postulate argued that the basis of wage determination should take account of the costs necessary for the normal reproduction of labour power (these include all social costs such as education, training and social provision needed to develop and produce workers for employment). They argued that this should be adopted as a principle, and that the specific method of determining the individual employee's wage was a matter of applying effective techniques of distribution. As an alternative to the second disadvantage, it was argued that the wage fund of the enterprise should be transformed into a residual sum. This meant that the enterprise would be free to allocate the resources for wages, once the material costs of production, payment of bank interest, state taxes and provision for investment funds had been met.

The two alternatives had different outcomes in the economic reforms in Bulgaria during the 1960s and the 1980s. The first alternative was not adopted in the wage policy of the reforms and this showed their partial nature. To use the socially necessary costs for the reproduction of labour power as a base for determining wages would have meant a fundamental shift in the approach to the formation and distribution of the incomes of enterprises and of the employed population. Wages would have taken on a normative character and their size and dynamic would be the subject of agreements between the state and the trade unions as representatives of the workers. The second alternative became one of the bases of economic reform in 1982–8. The principle of residual income was firmly established as a policy in the reform and in the normative regulations of the New Economic Mechanism. This can be seen in the following scheme of the formation and distribution of enterprise income, set out in the Regulation on Economic Activity which came into operation at the beginning of 1988 (see Figure 7.2).

The real implementation of the principle of residual income required substantial changes in both the system of economic relations and in the status of the enterprise. As the economist Mateev has pointed out (1987: 300–30), once the enterprise freely disposes of the funds which remain after what is due to the state has been paid, in essence property is transformed either into co-operative or group ownership. It also means that enterprises

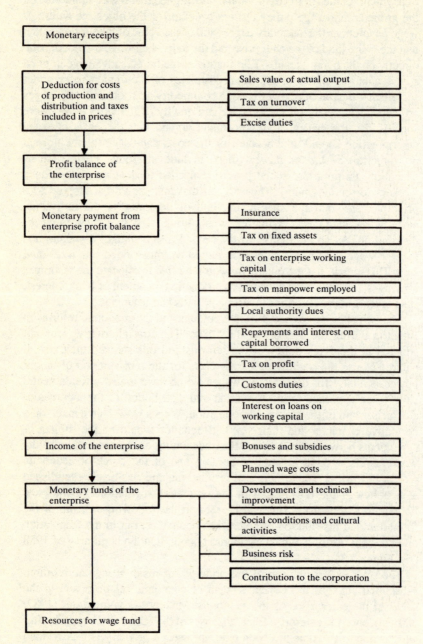

Figure 7.2 Calculation and distribution of profit and income

which get into financial difficulties and cannot secure subsidies or credit, will go bankrupt. Neither of these possibilities materialised entirely in the period 1982–7. The traditional conception of unified state property was reassessed only in 1988 with the attempt to transfer the means of production to the labour collective to manage and control. In the same year, for the first time, the state left enterprises in deficit to find their own way out of the situation. As a result, in the first half of 1988 about 10 per cent of industrial enterprises had insufficient funds to pay wages and had to obtain credit from the banks. The principle of residual income during the first six years of the economic reform which began in 1982 was not implemented consistently. It was proclaimed as a principle of the 'new' wage policy and included in normative regulations but was not put into operation. The reasons for this hesitation are complex. In part, they were ideological in that bankruptcy would lead to the issue of unemployment which was contrary to the political values of the working class, but at the same time the system for the management of the economy on the basis of enterprise financial autonomy had not been created.

A new stage in the design of the intermediate model was the attempt to establish the brigade as a level of material interest, that is as an economic unit, forming its own wage fund and distributing it autonomously among its members according to their individual contribution. The significance of this becomes clear when the internal mechanism of distribution for the intermediate model is compared with that of the traditional centralised model. In the latter, distribution was carried out at two levels: enterprise and department. The department did not generate its own fund but the means for remuneration were calculated on the basis of fulfilment of its plan and were distributed between the internal units – sections and shifts – and between the workers as mentioned above. In the intermediate model the resources for remuneration were allocated directly to the brigade and every month a wage fund was calculated for the brigade. This was generated on the basis of what were termed the 'normed plan tasks' which the brigade was assigned each month as part of the enterprise production plan. In enterprises with well developed brigade organisation, the normed plan tasks were accompanied by an agreement between it and the management. The essence of the agreement was to guarantee the wage fund if the brigade was not in a position to fulfil the planned tasks for reasons outside its control: for example, lack of supplies and materials. At the same time, the agreement provided the basis for management to penalise the brigade if it failed to fulfil the tasks for reasons within its control (see Chapter 8).

THE CO-EFFICIENT OF LABOUR PARTICIPATION AS THE MECHANISM FOR THE DISTRIBUTION OF EARNINGS WITHIN THE BRIGADE

The mechanism of the co-efficient was introduced as an imposed mechanism to accompany the establishment of the new-type brigade in the strategy formulated by the 1978 party conference. In terms of organisational design the co-efficient is a significant illustration of the need to integrate structures and the mechanisms to make them work. Thus in the 1960s experimental attempts to introduce a co-efficient had not been successful. Essentially, this was because at that time an appropriate structure of work organisation in which the mechanism could work had not yet been designed. However, the brigade organisation of work with its general assembly and brigade council proved to be an appropriate structure. Moreover, although as explained below, some specialists were critical of the mechanism, the evidence showed that it was the process of determining the co-efficient in the monthly distribution of earnings that provided the dynamics of the general assembly of the brigade. In other words, without the engagement of interests through the co-efficient, the meetings of the assembly – which had been created as a democratic forum and for the promotion of self-management – would have been relatively formal, except when there were specific incidents or episodes to engage the interests of its members.

An illustration of the operation of the mechanism of distribution based on evidence from one of the five enterprises is given below. The brigade had a detailed statement of the monthly planned tasks for the fulfilment of which by the end of the month its wage fund would total 2534.54 leva. Distribution between the workers was based on the co-efficient. Table 7.1 shows time worked (col. 6) and qualifications (col. 7). Before applying the coefficient of labour participation the quality of work is evaluated (col. 8) and compliance with labour and technological discipline (col. 9). In the table two workers, nos 3 and 5, were penalised for unsatisfactory quality of production and one, no. 6, for breaches of labour and technological discipline. It is possible to have other criteria for the coefficient of participation which varies between enterprises and even between brigades in a single enterprise.

The operation of the coefficient is more than the application of a technical formula; it is essentially a mechanism for regulating labour and economic relations in the brigade. This is clear if the interests which underlie the quantitative mechanism are analysed. As a rule, at the end of every month a proposal for the co-efficient of each worker is put forward by the brigade leader and then discussed by the brigade council. The

Table 7.1 Calculation of individual earnings in brigade 'A' according to the co-efficient of labour participation

Worker	Occupation	Grade	Working time (hours)	Basic	Working time	Skill level	Quality	Labour and technological discipline	Total co-efficient (5+6+7+8+9)	Total in leva for co-eff. as a whole	Individual wage (10 x 11)
1	2	3	4	5	6	7	8	9	10	11	12
1	Turner	7	129	1	–	+0.30			1.30	262.65	341.44
2	Fitter	3	176	1	+0.37	+0.10			1.47	262.65	386.09
3	Welder	4	176	1	+0.37	+0.15	– 0.05		1.47	262.65	386.09
4	Fitter	6	166	1	+0.29	+0.25			1.54	262.65	404.48
5	Fitter	6	128	1	–	– 0.25	– 0.05		1.20	262.65	315.18
6	Turner	5	144	1	+0.13	+0.20		– 0.10	1.23	262.65	323.06
7	Turner	4	166	1	+0.29	+0.15			1.44	262.65	378.20

Notes: Number of workers: 7. Fund for the month: 2534.54 leva.

brigade leader makes his proposal on the basis of records in which he has made assessments of each worker. Based on the total of the wage fund earned during the month, the brigade council, after discussion, presents the earnings proposed for each worker to the general assembly of the brigade. The proposals are put to the vote and a record is prepared which constitutes the basis on which payment is made (the record of the assembly serves as an accounting document). It is clear that this procedure both integrates and opposes the interests of the individual and those of the collective. The brigade as a whole makes a decision on the earnings of every worker (it is the new 'subject' in the relations of distribution); the worker in turn has the right to express his opinion and is obliged to vote on the assessments (for or against) together with all the other workers. The role of the management is confined to intervening only in cases where internal regulations have been broken. The trade union, and in some enterprises a specially created arbitration commission, has the right to intervene in such cases.

The distribution of earnings through the mechanism of the co-efficient has been a contested issue. Its introduction was strongly criticised by some specialists in wage-payment systems and by the workers themselves. These criticisms were directed against both the technique of calculation and the principles on which the formation of the co-efficient were based. The arguments were that the co-efficient encourages both a subjective approach to assessment and *uravnilovka* (wage levelling). It is true that some of the criteria shown in the table such as labour and technological discipline have a subjective element and this made it necessary for most brigades to maintain an accurate daily record of unauthorised absence and other breaches of labour discipline and, wherever possible, of the quantity and quality of production. It became common practice to enter daily, weekly and monthly results on a special board prominently displayed in the workplace. In the initial period it was not uncommon for the brigade leader to determine the co-efficient on his own or with the agreement of the brigade council alone, that is, without the agreement of the brigade assembly. There were also cases of attempts at direct intervention from above by departmental managers. (In one enterprise such an incident developed into an episode in which top management became involved. Pressure from the brigade eventually led to the replacement of the departmental manager.) At a more general level, as well as providing the dynamics of the monthly meeting of the brigade assembly, the co-efficient took away some of the upward pressure on management on routine wage issues – in fact the mechanism altered the direction of pressure.

THE EMERGING SELF-MANAGEMENT MODEL

The new wage system is the one designed to come into operation gradually from the beginning of 1988, depending on the preparedness of the enterprise and particularly on the availability of sufficient resources for the wage fund. However, at the end of 1988 only some enterprises were in a position to operate the new system, so the presentation here is based on the provisions of the regulations rather than on empirical data. Compared with the previous one, the new model can be seen as a combination of old and new components. It follows the tradition of the periodic reforms of the wage system, in that strategy was formulated by the central institutions which developed the normative regulations and guidelines on the basis of which every enterprise drew up its internal regulations. Specifically the state laid down the wage rates (in leva) for the different categories as shown in Table 7.2.

Table 7.2 Wage rates (in leva) for different categories of workers

Category	Grade		
	I	II	III
Workers	140	200	300
Specialists and employees with higher education	230	350	450
Managers	350	450	550

The first grade in each category comprises those with below-average qualifications, the second grade is for those with average and higher qualifications, while the third is for those with the highest qualifications. It was envisaged that everyone would be on the first grade of the scale in the first year. At the end of the year an appraisal would be carried out and further appraisals would be carried out at least every three years. Payment would be based on the results of the appraisal and transfers to a different grade could be made. The appraisal criteria are the nature of the work and the skills of the worker. The idea is to combine the two aspects of assessment to see whether the individual's qualifications correspond to the requirements of the post. Implementation of the new system, in 1988, was conceived as applicable only to enterprises to which property had been transferred (see Chapter 8). In 1989 it was decided that only enterprises which had adopted the 'firm' model of organisation should operate the new wage system.

The model is unified and universal in that it is a single system of job evaluation and wage payment for the whole economy. It differs from the previous model in its relative simplicity. The previous model consisted of seven categories and four subsystems – differentiated according to industrial sectors with salary scales and a handbook of more than a thousand job titles. Now there are only three scales: for workers, specialists and managers, each with three grades. The model allows more enterprise autonomy and discretion in determining wage rate, although this autonomy is governed by central parameters. In theory, wage ceilings are abolished and wages can increase without limits subject to the overall results of the enterprise and the contribution of the individual. Thus the maximum wage of the worker is 540 leva, of the specialist 814 leva, and of the manager 990 leva. In practice, however, the maximum increase is 80 per cent. When earnings exceed this limit they have to be deposited in a special fund which cannot be distributed. The enterprise has the right to differentiate the basic wages for different categories of workers. Previously the lowest rate was 120 leva, and the highest 172 leva, that is, a ratio of 1:1.43, the new ratio is 1:3.85 for workers; and for specialists 1:1.6 (previously 1:1.4). Finally, the state withdraws from administrative control of the enterprise wage fund and the growth of individual wages, but retains its regulatory functions. The new feature is that they are exercised in an indirect way: there are different rules for the distribution of the enterprise wage fund for different sectors and there is a tax on the wage fund which varies according to its growth.

This review shows that the impending reform of wages is a symbiosis of old and new components, in which the former have good prospects of predominating. There is a clear tendency for the centre to maintain its grasp of the levers of intervention and regulation of the direction in which the mechanism of distribution operates. In comparison with the other radical redesigns of labour relations in the period 1982–8, changes in wages have been undertaken at a slower pace and more cautiously. This leads to the reasons for this caution which may retard the whole economic reform. The logic of economic thought offers the apparently convincing answer that in the shortage economy the uncontrolled growth of wages will fuel the inflationary process, and open more sharply the 'scissors' between the fund of commodities and the financial resources of the population. This aspect of the link between wages and social policy has been stressed by Kornai (1980: 405). There is the additional argument that the transition from centralised regulation to self-regulation of wages should be gradual and flexible to prevent disorder arising from the disruption of organisational links. While there is some truth in these arguments, they do not explain the total situation because such analyses of the problems arising in the course of reform relate only to the macrosystem. They ignore the processes which take place at the base in enterprises and underestimate the informal aspects of the mechanisms of distribution in the socialist economy. These aspects of the operation of the mechanisms of distribution are dealt with in the following section.

BEYOND NORMATIVE MODELS: PRESSURE FROM BELOW AND *URAVNILOVKA*

In the preceding discussion of the three models of wage distribution the emphasis was deliberately placed on the process of direct normative regulation from the centre, one of the essential features of socialist labour relations. This approach is relevant for the periods of routine operation of the wage system and when redesign is being attempted, but it leaves open the questions of what provides the bases of the internal dynamics of the model and the social links between organisational levels in the system of labour relations. To consider these questions it is necessary to go beyond the external and visible side of distributional relations to the internal and generally uninstitutionalised mechanisms. Four years' study of wage behaviour conducted in industrial enterprises suggests that the dynamic of the models derives essentially from pressure from below and from *uravnilovka*. Pressure from the base means the influence of the lower levels of the hierarchy on the upper levels to modify the operation of the normative regulations on wages or to change these rules. These pressures operate at all levels and in all organisations: the enterprise puts pressure on the corporation, the latter on the ministry and finally on the top bodies of the state. The paradox is that the pressure is directed against the powerful instruments of state wage regulation: plans, (which have the status of law) funds, and the classification and evaluation of living labour.

The role of the plans in the centralised model is well known. Through the plans begun and completed every year and for each five-year cycle, the centre sets out detailed parameters for the production programme of every state enterprise; and the plan indicators at the end of the cycle assess the fulfilment of the production programme. These indices are the primary criteria for the performance appraisals of enterprise management which are made by the higher state bodies and by the regional party committees. The labour collective has a direct interest in the formation and fulfilment of the plan because it determines the level of remuneration. If the plan is fulfilled the collective receives the planned wage fund to the full amount. For overfulfilment it receives a bonus, while for a shortfall the management's earnings are usually reduced proportionately to the shortfall and in some cases receive no payment in the following month. Krastyn Petkov recalls a case from the 1980s. In an interview with the director at Chemicals on counterplanning he noticed that on the wall of the director's office were three coins with a total value of 50 *stotinki* (equivalent to about 12 English pence). Asked what this was the director answered: 'My pay for last month.' Beyond such results from shortfalls in plan fulfilment, there are other problems from such failures which lead to tensions in the enterprise. During the period covered by the research, in two of the five enterprises there were changes in management associated with non-fulfilment of plans. At Heavy Engineering there were two changes of director as a result of pressure from above and tensions within the collective.

The centre controls the financial resources of the enterprise through control over the funds. Table 7.3 shows the reduction in the number of funds with the successive models.

Table 7.3   Changes in funds

Centralised model	Intermediate model	Self-management model
Wage	Wage	Wage
Social welfare and cultural activities	Social welfare and cultural activities	Social welfare and cultural activities
Technical improvement	Technical improvement	Development and technical renewal
Economic efficiency	Economic risk	
Foreign exchange	Foreign exchange	
Inventions and rationalisation	Inventions and rationalisation	
District development		

The essential nature of the funds did not change; what changed was the way in which they were formed. In the centralised model funds were formed directly through the plan; in the intermediate model a part was formed indirectly through normatives differentiated according to branches. This applied to the funds related to the distribution of income: the wage fund, and the fund for social welfare and cultural activities. With the establishment of the self-managed model the character of the two funds is retained, but the basis of forming the wage fund is changed by relating it to total output.

In the event of a deficit in the wage fund, the enterprise has to choose between borrowing from the bank or asking for an adjustment in the plan indicators. In the centralised model the second course was the one most commonly initiated by the management and this was often associated with pressure from below. At Heavy Engineering, which had several directors in the period 1983–8, the best and most successful were judged to be the ones who knew how to present to the central planning institutes a realistic plan and to negotiate corrections at the end of the plan period.

If it is accepted that the plan for the economy as a whole is essentially realistic after such 'corrections', the balance is restored in a purely administrative way: administrative decisions from above take away funds from the economically strong enterprises to subsidise the weaker ones. Moreover, this process of redistribution occurs not only at the level of the centre but at the level of the sector ministry and the corporation. Although they depend on plan fulfilment the corporations and ministries struggle to avoid having redundant enterprises and this adds to the pressures for the redistribution of funds. These practices were normal throughout the operation of the intermediate model in 1982–8 in the five enterprises under investigation.

From a general standpoint *uravnilovka* or wage levelling is the conscious maintenance of determined differences in wages within a prescribed range. On the question of the ratio between the minimum and the maximum, Lenin argued that under socialism it was necessary to have 'fair' wage differentials and that the maximum should not be more than three times the minimum. Later he allowed higher wages for the 'bourgeois' specialists. Thus 'fair differentials' entered socialist labour theory and practice. The criterion of 'fairness' became postulated not from work itself but from the sphere of moral values. 'Fairness' was a feature of socialist morality and 'fairness' came to be defined in relation to equality – and inequality was seen as unfair. The contemporary interpretation of this value is that inequality is fair only within defined limits and these depend on the quantity and quality of work done. The moral criteria directly influence distributional relations. On the one hand, wage differentials are maintained within defined limits through normative regulation. Thus the greatest difference between the minimum and maximum wage rates in the enterprises investigated were in the ratio 1:4.5. On the other hand, through the distribution of funds every organisational unit at every level struggles to a greater or lesser extent to level its income and reward, regarding this as fair and necessary. As Kornai remarks:

> in a socialist economy the management in firms . . . act in wage negotiations with superior authorities as trade union officials and not as employers. There may arise conflicts between superiors and subordinates over a number of questions. But they are in agreement that every manager tries to wring higher wages for his shop, section etc., from his superior.

> (Kornai 1980: 402)

The wage behaviour of workers also reflects a deeply egalitarian psychology. This became especially clear with the brigade organisation of work during the period of the research. The operation of the mechanism of the co-efficient of labour participation revealed that the range between minimum and maximum values was generally insignificant. It was apparent that most brigade leaders preferred to have a steady average and not a high co-efficient of labour participation. Fairness and stability achieved in this way ensured the confidence and support of their brigades.

If there was some tendency for *uravnilovka* to develop within brigades the question of *uravnilovka* between brigades has also to be considered. The general conclusion was that the pressures for this were not strong and this requires some explanation. In British labour relations it is a well known phenomenon that wage groups use closely related groups as points of reference in exercising and legitimating wage pressure. Increases in the salaries of managers, that is, a vertical reference group, are rarely seen as an appropriate source of legitimation. On the contrary, in the Bulgarian enterprise there has been a strong tendency for units at the base to compare their earnings with the top as well as with other units at the base. This is to be explained as a product of ideology and values – the working class has always been presented as the main productive force and this legitimates their concern with the salaries of higher officials.

CONCLUSIONS

Compared with changes in other mechanisms, those in the mechanisms of distribution were less significant, so that the dynamics of wage distribution were not greatly modified. In all three models powerful principles, regarded as fundamental, continued to operate. Thus the principle of 'distribution according to work' was not reassessed as a principle and the primary concern was with its consistent implementation. Similarly, the correlation between the growth of wages and the productivity of labour operated as a standard for assessing the results of individual and collective work and as a limit for increases in remuneration. Throughout the period under investigation the mechanisms of distribution remained a principal instrument of the centre for influencing the behaviour of industrial organisations. They were used as a means of exerting pressure for greater labour efficiency, for maintaining defined proportions in the growth of wages in different sectors and professions, and between the growth of incomes and the growth in the supply of goods. The centralised system of distribution allowed little scope for organisational strategy. As a result of the absence of alternative strategies, pressures from below were expressed in the form of pressure for specific changes in the system to satisfy the interests of particular sectors and enterprises and through the general pressure for *uravnilovka* in distribution.

Changes in structure however, meant that there were some changes in the bases of pressures within the enterprise between the different models. The centralised model was characterised by a large number of grades and categories within grades and the individual organisation of work mainly paid by piece-rates. Typically, pressures were from individuals seeking higher grades and from groups seeking higher earnings. When a group within a department improved its earnings, there would be some *uravnilovka* pressure from other groups in the department which might be transmitted upwards to the top of the enterprise. With the creation of brigades in the intermediate model, a new level and unit of interests was established. The brigade as a structure exercised some upward pressure on the higher levels, partly deriving from *uravnilovka* pressures between brigades. On the other hand, it operated as a managerial mechanism for internal distribution by which some of the earlier upward pressures were contained within the brigade. Brigade organisation transformed individual into collective pressure and the size of the individual's wage level lost its significance. This led to a new contradiction between the highly skilled and the other workers in the brigade. The latter were satisfied with the mechanism of distribution while the former were not. The direction in which the mechanism of the co-efficient operated would reflect the balance of power within the brigade between higher-skilled and lower-skilled and between older and younger workers. Thus the whole foundation of labour relations among workers at the base of the enterprise was changed quite radically.

The emerging self-management model shifted the basis of distribution from a wage-fund based model to that of an enterprise-income based model. This would facilitate the release of surplus labour power and lead to the failure of unprofitable enterprises. In practice, this possibility remained unrealised up to 1988 although it was implicit in the normative regulations. The shift in the direction of reducing administrative pressures and replacing them by market pressures is clear. In terms of distribution it could lead to new choices within the enterprise between expenditure on wages and investment for the future, that is, a trade-off between the long-term interests and immediate interests of the collective. However, this would also depend on the level of structure at which investment decisions are made – whether at plant or above.

Finally, at a more theoretical level, it is appropriate to comment on the relationship between interests and distribution. A theory of distribution is a theory of interests and how interests are legitimated at the level of society. The mechanisms of distribution express the theory of interests at the societal level. Interests are expressed through pressure and pressures are the main source of organisational dynamics. Changes in the mechanisms of distribution to be legitimated require societal and political legitimation and by definition recognition of a different structure of interests. This in turn feeds back to the redesign of mechanisms and a shift in the dynamics of organisations.

8 Agreements and the engagement of interests

This chapter examines the successive stages in which agreements have operated as mechanisms in Bulgarian enterprises. The general aim is to show how agreements are related to structures and how they influence the relationships between units and levels of structure. The creation of agreements as an aspect of organisational design was both a part of the national strategy and an expression of primary theoretical concepts for the management of the economy and the organisation of the labour process and labour relations. Designed changes in the nature and scope of agreements as a mechanism are always a significant indicator of shifts in theory even though in practice their significance may be constrained by inadequate synchronisation with the redesign of other structures and mechanisms. In Bulgaria, agreements have at certain times been seen as a lever to advance the process of organisational change. At the conceptual level the essential features of agreements are: first, the existence of two or more parties and the recognition of the legitimacy of their interests; second, the process of reaching agreement is one of dialogue and negotiation rather than of administrative command, even though the balance of power between the parties may differ substantially and this may be reflected in the content of the agreement and, in particular, implementation; third, the possibility of sanctions for non-compliance; and fourth, a procedure for arbitration when there is disagreement between the parties about the terms of the agreement or its interpretation in practice.

COLLECTIVE AGREEMENTS UNDER THE CENTRALISED MODEL

As explained in Chapter 2, collective agreements at the level of the enterprise had been a mechanism of labour relations since 1950. These agreements were signed each year between the director of the enterprise and the trade union chairman after the state plan targets for the enterprise had been fixed at the end of the year. In form they were a reflection of the enterprise plan; in content the collective agreement was 'social' and covered such matters as training for qualifications, health and safety, housing, kindergartens, holiday homes and the number of holiday places for workers, and transport to and from work. In the same way as the enterprise plan specified production and other programmes for the different periods of the year, the collective agreement was a series of quantified programmes for each heading – so many workers to be trained, flats built and health and safety projects to be completed, and so on. Wages were paid from the wage fund which was linked to plan performance and had no place in the collective agreement, which was financed from the social fund of the enterprise. The size of both the wage and social funds was differentiated according to sector: higher in leading sectors, such as mining and heavy industry, and lower in light and consumer industries.

The theoretical explanation of the collective agreement was that it was to satisfy the social interests of the enterprise workforce in parallel with the satisfaction of the interests of society through the fulfilment of the enterprise production plan, and this can be seen as the basis of the exchange. The proposals for the contents of the different programmes in the agreement were drawn up by the trade union committee in consultation with the general meeting of the trade union members. The distribution of items in some programmes such as holidays and housing was through the trade union and the results of socialist emulation were taken into account. Sanctions for non-fulfilment of the terms of the agreement were weak. A specialist commented that although there were many cases of directors being disciplined for not fulfilling the production plan, there were none for breaches of the collective agreement, although the trade union had the right to propose the removal of a director, and the threat of this could be related to the fulfilment of the terms of the collective agreement. For the labour collective, fulfilment of the agreement was one of their criteria for the director – this was revealed later in the elections in 1986. Generally, the enterprise party organisation did not take an active interest in the collective agreement.

AGREEMENTS UNDER THE INTERMEDIATE MODEL

As explained in Chapter 3, the 1982 Regulation gave the first legal recognition to the brigade as a unit of structure and provided that brigades should be parties to agreements with top management and, in sequential production processes, with other brigades. The traditional collective agreement disappeared at this time as the result of changes in the approach to social funds and in the role of the trade union. In some brigades funds for social purposes were set up – the so-called 'fund brigadier' – though its size was generally small. Underlying the conception of brigades as parties to agreements was the idea that the brigade should operate as an economic unit as well as an organisational one but in practice this was often difficult to establish. The essence of the exchange between the brigade and the top management was that the brigade would carry out planned tasks negotiated with management (this was then related to the size of the brigade wage fund – created for the first time), and in return management was responsible for ensuring the regular supplies necessary for the planned tasks. In practice, management's inability to ensure supplies proved to be the biggest constraint on the development of this mechanism. (The brigade had freedom to carry out the tasks with fewer workers if it wished and so to divide the wage fund among a smaller number.) The actual agreements, although written down, were very open; there were no sanctions on management and generally no provisions for arbitration. The history of agreements at Chemicals provides a representative example of the atrophy of this imposed mechanism. In accordance with the normative regulations, management introduced agreements between them and the brigades. The enterprise periodically faced the problem of maintaining the regular flow of supplies necessary to ensure continuous production. In this technology it was not easy to find alternative work when production in a plant was held up for lack of supplies and at first management had to pay the workers for doing nothing. This put pressure on management to resolve the supply problem, but in reality it could not be fully resolved. The provisions of the agreements were, therefore, allowed to lapse and the brigades did not consider it in their interests to seek to enforce the agreements, which could of course be used at other times by management as a mechanism for exerting pressure on them. There was, therefore, a tacit agreement between management and the brigades to allow this externally imposed mechanism to lapse.

Apart from supplies, there were other constraints on the mechanism, illustrated by the following episode investigated by Krastyn Petkov. In a factory making domestic durable goods, the process of counterplanning led to a brigade proposing that the guarantee period to customers for the electrical appliances it produced should be doubled, while it would meet claims for poor quality products from its own funds. In exchange the collective of the brigade wanted management to transfer part of the savings resulting from the reduced number of claims to the brigade wage fund and to incorporate this exchange in a signed agreement. Management rejected this proposal. In the course of discussions with the management, it became clear that the main reason for this was the lack of funds and the limited economic independence of the enterprise. As one of the directors put it: 'If all our brigades switched over to such a way of working we should not be in a position to pay them.' At one level this episode illustrates the significance of constraints deriving from the environment. In terms of organisational design it is an illustration of the organic linkage of two imposed mechanisms: the process was that of counterplanning but the brigade sought to consolidate this by an agreement.

At Metals, where the process of strategy formulation has been described in Chapter 5, a system of agreements had been developed by 1985. There were agreements between complex brigades, between complex and specialist brigades, and between brigades and departmental management. Because of the salience given to the department in managerial strategy at Metals there were no agreements between brigades and enterprise management so that the agreement between the brigade and the department was the most significant. Logically there should have been agreements between the department and the enterprise (as there were between departments which were linked by the supply of products), but although models of such agreements had been prepared, they were not implemented. However, the head of a new department drafted an agreement between the department and top management. Top management refused to sign because they said they could not meet the proposed obligations. The head of department then said he would act as if the agreement had been signed. This can be seen as an example of an organic mechanism at the intermediate level. The general content of the agreements at Metals was similar: management agreed to provide the brigade with the machines and materials needed for the planned tasks; the brigade was responsible for meeting them and was liable for deduction from its wage fund if failure to meet the targets was judged to have been its responsibility. In cases of disagreement there was provision for arbitration at three levels of structure – department, enterprise (top management) and plant council. The agreement between departments provided for exchange on the basis of internal prices fixed at enterprise level and for fines from the departmental wage fund in the event of culpable failure. There were also provisions for fines on the engineering design department if it was judged responsible for design failures which affected brigade or departmental performance.

The Labour Code of 1986 (Labour Code 1986: arts 50–60) provided for a new type of collective agreement, its main new elements were:

1 It was to be made vertically between the primary collective (brigade) and the main collective (plant council).
2 The representation of the collective in making the agreement was through two channels: directly, through its elected bodies, the brigade council and the brigade leader (this was the main channel); and indirectly, through the trade unions.

3 The emphasis was now placed on rights and duties of an economic nature and the responsibilities deriving from them, with strict definitions on compensation for breach of the agreement by one of the parties.

The intention was to give agreements real economic importance and thus overcome the formalism of the old type, which created serious difficulties when it came to implementation in practice. The initial intention was that the agreement between the brigades and the plant council should be worked out in parallel with the preparation of the plans of the enterprise for 1987 and for the 9th Five-Year Plan period. The partial implementation of the new variant of the economic mechanism from the beginning of 1987 placed the management of enterprises in an insecure and ambiguous situation. Ignorant of what the system of prices, taxes and credits would be, management did not conclude agreements with the brigades. This process is illustrated by the case of Heavy Engineering. Of the brigade leaders there, 30 per cent judged that the collective labour agreements were potentially the most significant mechanism for the self-managing brigade. Towards the end of 1986 there were discussions in the brigades about the planned tasks for 1987. Some brigades argued that to fulfil them they would need new machines or the repair of existing ones, extra workers and the resolution of some social problems. Every brigade held an assembly which discussed the plan for 1987 and agreed a list of concrete demands. Representatives of the brigades put these to management in discussions about the terms of collective agreements in December. Management, with the assistance of the trade union committee, drew up a draft model agreement, but this was rejected by the brigades. In further discussions the brigades identified the basic issue as that of supplies and they wanted a clause in the agreement that management would ensure regular supplies and so secure their earnings. Management rejected this and blamed the brigades but conceded a lowering of the plan tasks. Essentially the management was afraid that they could not rely on supplies from other enterprises, and under these circumstances it was impossible to make real agreements with the brigades.

AGREEMENTS FOR THE TRANSFER OF PROPERTY – THE SELF-MANAGEMENT MODEL

In April 1987 President Zhivkov's speeches to the Trade Union Congress (1987a) and to the National Assembly (1987b) set out the strategy for transfer of property to the labour collectives. This was presented as the final step in the process of developing the collective as *stopanin* and the occasion was used to characterise the collective as *pulnovlastin stopanin* (translated as 'sovereign master'). Zhivkov outlined a new approach to strategy implementation:

> Let us imagine society's structure as a pyramid. It has an apex and a base. Managerial echelons are aligned from the pyramid's apex to its base. The millions of people are at the pyramid's base. Two approaches are possible – either to start restructuring from the top downward or vice versa, from the base upwards.
>
> (Zhivkov 1987b: 16)

He declared that the second approach was necessary: 'Work should start from the grass-roots where the working people are, those who realise the ideas' (Zhivkov 1987b: 17). The strategy was to be implemented through the transfer of property to the labour collectives governed by the mechanism of agreements/contracts specifying the rights and duties of 'the two subjects of management – of the state which by proxy of the people is the owner of socialist property and of the labour collective which will run this property' (Zhivkov 1987b: 27). A series of model agreements was published (*Trudovijat* 1987: 31–43). The main ones were for transfer from the Council of Ministers to the main collective, and from the main collective to the primary collective. These were signed by representatives of the collectives. There was also a model of an agreement to be signed by each individual worker as a member of a primary collective. The essence of the agreements was the transfer of funds and property. For the brigades this meant the transfer to them of the machines they worked with.

In relation to the established theory of socialist property, the concept of transfer adopted in Bulgaria in 1988 represented, at that time, the most radical revision in property relations in European socialist countries since changes adopted in Yugoslavia in 1953 made the enterprise 'social property' (see Chapter 12). Implementation of the strategy was to be initially confined to 55 selected enterprises. The preparations in these enterprises began at the end of 1987 and the transfers to the main collective were implemented in the first half of 1988. In August 1988 the process of transfer was terminated. The explanation given on Bulgarian television related this decision to the problems of the economy. The improvement in economic performance that transfer was intended to promote would take too long to materialise and an alternative strategy to produce quicker results was necessary. This alternative was Decree 56, which came into force on 1 January 1989.

Transfer of property was, therefore, an uncompleted process. However, the process was researched by staff of the Georgi Dimitrov Institute and a whole issue of 'Trade Unions and Self-Management' (*Profsiosite* 1988) was devoted to the subject of the transfer of socialist property to the labour collective. The process required, in the first place, extensive investigation and preparation by accountants, economists and lawyers to draw up an inventory of the assets to be transferred and then to make an assessment of their value. Among the technical but very significant issues which had to be resolved were the absence of any legal precedents for a transfer of this nature, the problems of accounting especially those relating to the valuation of buildings, machinery and equipment and the land occupied by the enterprise. The statement of assets and their assessment was the basis then of the agreement which was placed before the general assembly of representatives for approval before being signed by the representative of the state and the director as representative of the main collective. Observations of these meetings indicated that their character was predominantly formal with little scope for participation by the delegates – the problems having been dealt with by specialists in the preparatory period.

Transfer within the enterprise from the main to the primary collective, usually the brigade, equally posed many technical and especially accounting problems. Transfer required accounting for costs and contributions, and the establishment of internal (transfer) prices. Full implementation of *stopanska smetka* at the level of the brigade, had as explained in Chapter 5, been difficult to achieve with some technologies. The act of transfer in these conditions generated some pressures to make the department, for which it was easier to prepare fuller accounting information, the unit to which the transfer was made rather than the brigade. Potentially there was more scope for the active involvement of the labour collective at this level than at the level of the main collective. The kind of issue that could emerge from this process can be illustrated from Textiles, where the technology was not a significant constraint on accounting. The basic difference that emerged was between brigades with new machines and those with older ones. Agreements with the former were reached quite easily. With the latter, however, there was an episode of negotiations in which the brigades sought, successfully, to secure undertakings from management about the eventual replacement of their machines as part of the transfer agreement.

CONCLUSIONS

Theoretically, agreements are a necessary and appropriate mechanism for self-management because they become an expression of the interests of the labour collective. A leading Bulgarian legal specialist commented that self-management cannot be developed on the basis of normative regulation alone and that self-management requires agreements as an essential mechanism (Mrachkov 1988). This view expresses a conception of the internal dynamics of the self-managed enterprise and the nature of the interests and pressures which provide those dynamics. Agreements recognise the existence of different parties with interests which may differ. However, the agreements between brigades and management were rarely implemented, while the much more radical agreements on the transfer of property were suspended before they became operational.

Agreements between brigades and management were designed to change labour relations by providing a mechanism linking the two levels of the base, the brigade, and the top without the middle level being a party. However, considered as an event attached to the 1982 regulation the significance of agreements was small as an element of redesign compared to the restructuring of work organisation to establish complex brigades which the regulation required. Nevertheless, it set a precedent as a mechanism linking the base to the top without the direct involvement of the intermediate level of the department. Whereas counterplanning as a mechanism was designed to operate upwards from the base, the theory of agreements in terms of organisational dynamics was that they should produce pressure in both directions, from the base to the top and from the top to the base, with the terms of the agreement as the outcome of the two sources of pressure. The fact they did not operate generally in this way indicates a design problem that was not resolved in Bulgaria. In part, as this chapter has shown, the problem derived from external constraints but equally there were problems of internal accounting. Theoretically, this failure is an example of a mechanism that failed to engage the interests of either party or to put it differently the interests of both parties were perceived as promoted by not enforcing them.

In theory, agreements on transfer, by changing the relationship of the labour collective to the means of production, represented a fundamental change in the basis of labour relations and modified the 'hired labour' status of the worker. The evidence on the preparation for transfer implies that in the initial stage episodes were primarily confined to specialists from the top of the enterprise and from organisational levels above the enterprise and that the labour collective was relatively passive. However, it is arguable that if the process of transfer had been taken to the brigades on a wider scale a dynamic would have developed as brigades came to recognise and assert their interests. Imposed mechanisms of this kind necessarily take time to become established and rooted in organisations. It is, however, interesting to note that at Metals the top were opposed to the top–down strategy of implementation in relation to their enterprise. Their position was that transfer should be implemented as something to be earned by the brigades and not as something handed down. This would have meant that transfer would have been a change of status that brigades could achieve if their performance justified it.

9 Elections – interests, representation and conflicts

The selection, appointment and career development of managers and supervisors in western industrial enterprises is a process carried out through a variety of mechanisms. However, although ability to secure the support of subordinates may be a criterion for some managerial positions, the election of managers by the workforce is extremely rare and would generally be regarded as incompatible with the rights of ownership and managerial control. On the other hand, in socialist countries the party organisation has played a leading role in the appointment and promotion of managerial cadres through the mechanism of the *nomenklatura* system. Recently however, there has been a significant increase in the use of the electoral mechanism for managerial appointments in some socialist countries. In Bulgaria the Labour Code of 1986 included provisions for elections and competition for both worker representatives on plant councils and for the holders of managerial positions – directors, departmental managers and brigade leaders (Labour Code 1986). In September–October 1986 these provisions were put into operation in all industrial enterprises in Bulgaria and elections by secret ballot were held for 5,000 plant directors and 50,000 brigade leaders as well as representatives on plant councils and other bodies.

The preceding chapters on mechanisms have dealt with those which have an economic base. Elections as a mechanism have only an indirect economic base and are more directly related to the politics of the enterprise as an organisation. On the other hand, elections can be analysed more clearly as an event than other imposed mechanisms such as agreements and as such it is of particular interest to see under what conditions they led to 'episodes', as defined in Chapter 4. In analysing election as a mechanism, the aims are to assess how it operates in three main aspects: first, in securing the representation of the interests of the different groups created by the structures of labour organisation within the enterprise; second, in modifying the structure of hierarchical relationships between top and base;

and, third, as a mechanism for organisational change and development in the context of self-management.

ELECTIONS – THE PROTOTYPES

The election of managers in industrial enterprises first emerged as an idea in 1968 in the wider context of proposals for economic reform. However, it was not until 1978 that the prototype for the mechanism of competition and elections in industry was developed in the district of Ruse as described by Tsonev (1982). This development has to be set in the context of the mechanism of *nomenklatura* and reserve cadres as they apply in industrial organisations. The essence of *nomenklatura* is a list of posts the appointments to which require the approval of the appropriate level of the party organisation. Thus, in a factory, the posts of director and deputy director are usually on the *nomenklatura* list of the district party organisation; lower posts in the factory, such as departmental manager and brigade leader, are on the *nomenklatura* list of the plant party organisation. Reserve cadres consist of those who hold *nomenklatura* posts and those who are listed as potential candidates for such posts. According to Tsonev, there are four main groups which provide reserve cadres: first, holders of positions such as deputies or assistants and members of elected bodies such as the plant council, trade union and party committees; second, those extending their education or improving qualifications; third, members of the Komsomol (age limit 30); and those from the base of the working class, especially young leading workers (Tsonev 1982: 32). In Bulgarian enterprises the percentage of total employees who are members of the Communist Party is usually in the range 12–15 per cent (the majority of workers under the age of 30 are members of the Komsomol). The issue of reserve cadres had been raised at the 11th Party Congress (1976) and the Ruse District Party Committee were given approval by the Secretariat of the Central Committee of the party to proceed with innovations in December 1977. The District Party Committee decided to develop a more systematic approach for the selection, preparation and development of cadres and reserve cadres, especially from the ranks of manual workers. The principal mechanism was the establishment of commissions by the primary party organisation (in a plant the organisational unit in which the primary party organisation operates is the department, though in some cases it may be the smaller unit of the brigade). The commissions were composed of the party secretary, the president of the departmental trade union committee and the departmental manager. Their task was to identify younger workers with potential for development and to make a register of them and then to produce plans for their development. As a result, in many of the plants in the Ruse district the number of reserve cadres drawn from manual workers was significantly increased. When posts became vacant it was open to members of the reserve cadres to apply to enter the competition. Evaluation of candidates was made on a series of forms and written and oral examinations assessed by the Party Committee and representatives of management. A shortlist of candidates with a summary assessment was put to the assembly of workers who voted by secret ballot. In the period 1978–83 in the Ruse district, 211 competitions for managerial positions were held with 656 candidates competing (Tsonev 1982: 126). The significance of the Ruse experiment is: first, that it originated as a move to widen the base of cadre recruitment, second, that elections were chosen as the mechanism; third, that by the early 1980s there was a real process of competition; and, finally, that it showed that such changes could operate successfully. Although the development of competition and elections was most marked in the Ruse district, the process was also being established elsewhere. Thus, in 1983, John Thirkell visited a chemical plant where a procedure similar to that in Ruse was being developed by the plant sociologist; procedures were also being developed in the Pleven and Plovdiv districts.

Political endorsement of managerial elections as a principle to be applied generally was given at the 12th Congress of the Communist Party in 1981. Application of the electoral mechanism then began at brigade level and its gradual implementation was associated with the introduction of other mechanisms. In 1982 the election of brigade leaders was introduced as an option. There was no procedure and in practice this meant that the assembly of brigade members was given the opportunity to approve a candidate proposed from above by management. In 1984 there was a national campaign organised by the trade unions for the mandatory election of brigade leaders which was associated with the mechanism of counterplanning, which involved the brigade leader in negotiating with higher management (a brigade council was also elected at this time). The main development regarding elections in the Labour Code of 1986 was that elections of directors and members of the plant council as well as brigade leaders, were now mandatory; elections were, moreover, by secret ballot, and to be valid required a two-thirds majority. Of particular importance was the introduction of competition as well as elections. Implicitly, competition was seen as a mechanism for the assessment of candidates by management and the party organisation according to the criterion of professional competence; election was the mechanism to ensure that a candidate was acceptable in terms of the social criteria of the workforce. The Council of Ministers and the Central Council of the Bulgarian Trade Unions decided that the sections of the Labour Code on elections should be put into effect in September/October 1986 throughout industry, and that the trade unions should be responsible for organising them. In practice, the principle of competition was only possible in districts such as Ruse, where the practice was already well established, though it was also applied elsewhere in some cases.

BRIGADE ELECTIONS

National data collected for the Central Council of the Bulgarian Trade Unions showed that there were 50, 000 elections for brigade leaders and in 26 per cent of these elections there was more than one candidate. Management and the party or trade union nominated 87 per cent of the candidates; the remaining 13 per cent being nominated by the collective (the brigade). Of the existing brigade leaders 1,134 (2.2 per cent) were not re-elected. Data of this kind, however, cannot provide significant insights into the dynamics of the electoral process in plants, which requires illustrations taken from the five plants, and from other plants visited by the researchers. In selecting these, the aim has been to choose those which show evidence of a dynamic process rather than those in which the proceedings were more formal. In particular, they are intended to show the potential significance of elections for the representation of interests, the emergence of conflicts and the relationship between the top of the enterprise and the base.

Chemicals provides an example of an election assembly; it was observed by both authors and was calm and without apparent conflict. About sixty workers (men and women) were present and the assembly was chaired by a representative of the trade union. The brigade leader read a report of his work and that of the brigade which was adopted on a show of hands. The chairman of the party group then presented the report of the commission appointed from members of the brigade to assess the work of the brigade leader. (His offer to withdraw during the discussion of this report was rejected by the assembly.) In the ensuing secret ballot he received a unanimous vote. The proceedings were relatively formal but it was pointed out by the plant trade union chairman that the endorsement of this brigade leader was to be expected. In the past the brigade's performance had been low and this had been reflected in its earnings, but during the last two years under the leadership of this brigade leader, there had been significant improvements in both. At this meeting the only issue identified by the workers in the assembly was the list of nominations for the brigade council – a proposal for replacement of one nominee was accepted and then the candidates were elected by a show of hands. This was an example of a concern frequently expressed in these elections that the composition of the brigade council should be representative of the interests of the various occupational groups within the brigade.

Elections and internal conflicts

A case from Textiles shows how a potential challenge to the brigade leader could emerge. In a brigade with poor results there were internal tensions between long established and newer members, and informal proposals were made by older workers to the party and trade union committees that the brigade leader should be changed. However, they did not put forward an alternative candidate and the vote for the brigade leader was unanimous. It appears that the majority who had expressed dissatisfaction initially had become convinced that the brigade leader would make changes to resolve the tensions. Latent conflicts between different groups within brigades also became manifest in one of the departments at Metals. There the introduction of brigade organisation led to the establishment of two brigades in the department and the integration of production and maintenance workers. The earnings of the latter had been affected as the new organisation of work meant that they worked during the week instead of at weekends. There was also tension over the distribution of earnings between highly qualified workers and those, mainly younger, workers with lower formal qualifications. The party-management candidate in one brigade was elected, but in the other was rejected, the opposition centring on the division between older and younger workers.

Another example from Textiles, observed by John Thirkell, shows how internal issues, not necessarily related to specific sub-group interests, could be mobilised in the assembly. The election of the brigade leader by the assembly of thirty women followed the same procedural pattern as that at Chemicals. However, there were significant differences in the response of the workers in the way in which the election was used as a mechanism for the mobilisation of internal issues. After the brigade leader had given her report, five women rose to their feet in succession and although not criticising the brigade leader directly, identified a series of issues which either had not been satisfactorily resolved in the past or which should be accepted as requiring resolution in the future. These included the allocation of holidays, the conditions in the canteens and toilets, problems of work organisation which had led to loss of earnings and the need to encourage members of lower educational qualifications to improve them and thus qualify for improved pensions. When the results of the secret ballot were announced, five votes against the brigade leader were recorded.

Another case from Textiles shows how an election could produce a direct challenge to top management and the party organisation. The existing brigade leader declined to accept nomination for election – an indication of conflicts present within the brigade. Management and the party organisation considered that an engineer with good technical qualifications but no experience in the brigade and so unknown to its members would be able to solve the production problems in the brigade, and they nominated her at the assembly. Workers asked if they had the right to nominate another candidate and when this was confirmed they put forward a candidate from the brigade. In the ballot the management/party nominee received only a single vote, all the rest going to the brigade nominee. This meant that the party and Komsomol members had voted against the party candidate. It appears that initially they had been prepared to follow the party line, but when it came to the vote they followed the weight of opinion in the collective, which was influenced by the criterion that the brigade leader should be an 'insider' and not an 'outsider'.

Two cases of elections of departmental managers show how elections at this level could be used. At Assembly the members of one brigade felt that the departmental manager had exercised unfair influence on the mechanism for the internal distribution of earnings among the brigade's members. This had been a recurring issue and, in the view of the brigade members, one which the departmental manager had not sought to resolve; in the election he was voted out. At Metals in one department the manager was re-elected by a large majority. However, the director of the enterprise was present at the assembly and workers used it as an opportunity to emphasise the importance of reducing the problem of labour shortage by resolving a wage structure issue. The election was used as an opportunity for the base to put pressure on the top.

More complex processes are revealed in two excerpts from the report of one of the researchers who studied the written statements on elections in a processing-industry enterprise and conducted follow-up interviews. The first situation was defined by the investigator as 'pessimistic', the second as 'optimistic'.

Pessimistic case

The brigade is in a department with the oldest technology and with most production rejects, the lowest economic indices in the plan, some of the lowest wages and the highest labour turnover. At present it is undergoing a technological reconstruction to improve this situation. The report of the brigade leader is probably the best of all those available both in structure and content. The problems discussed in it are accurately defined and analysed. The most important are:

1 Three-shift working creates difficulties in convening the general assembly of the brigade (157 persons). The duties of the assembly have been taken over by the assemblies of the shifts, their decisions being considered later by the brigade council. Consequently, the members of the brigade as a whole did not have a clear idea overall of the tasks assigned and their fulfilment.

2 The participation of the brigade in counterplanning is formal. The approach is administrative, without the participation of the brigade council.

3 The brigade council does not observe its duty to report on its work twice a year at the brigade's general assembly since it cannot bring together two-thirds of the brigade.

4 The brigade council falls below standard in its activities on the counterplan and the determination of the CLP (Co-efficient of Labour Participation). The approach to the solution of problems is often administrative.

5 Socialist emulation is not sufficiently promoted.

6 An objective difficulty is the lack of sufficiently qualified personnel to fill the jobs (but this is a problem for the whole district).

This report prompted no reaction from the collective (104 persons were present) and no one was willing to take the floor and comment on it. The meeting then proceeded with the election of brigade leader and brigade council. It is not clear from the written report whether an evaluation of the work of the brigade leader was read out or not but at this point there was some movement and a second nomination for brigade leader was proposed by the collective. The new candidate nominated, an engineer from the same department, did not agree to stand and the initial proposal was passed by 84 votes to 12. The representative on the plant council was elected by 54 votes to 34.

In subsequent interviews it was established that after the meeting the brigade leader called a meeting of the brigade council and forced its members to vote openly for the second time. He then declared that having elected him they would have to obey him from now on. This was followed by a sequence of actions by the elected brigade leader:

1 While there was permission only for a 6-hour working day, he compelled the brigade to work 8 hours each on the last Saturday of the month.

2 After the proposals for the co-efficient had been agreed by the brigade council, the final results were later adjusted (probably by the brigade leader).

3 He issued orders for sanctions on his own authority, without notifying the brigade council and the general director.

The response of the brigade members to the actions of the brigade leader, noted by the researcher at the time of his visit, were that they were considering whether to extend the action field by seeking help from Bulgarian Television or from the Central Council of the Bulgarian Trade Unions.

Optimistic case

The brigade has 62 members and is traditionally a successful one, but during the period under review difficulties have arisen and the results have deteriorated. The report of the brigade leader gives a detailed and critical evaluation of the situation. The reasons for the failure are also sought in the poor labour and technological discipline, and in the slack control on the part of the group and department heads. Following the report, a proposal was made to re-elect the brigade leader, and it then proceeded with the discussion of these two areas for failure.

If one is looking for maturity, it is probably in this brigade that it can be best felt. The minutes contain a very important note made by the meeting: 'All statements having a production orientation will not be written down. They are the subject for discussion at the departmental meeting.' This was probably one of the factors that created an atmosphere of liveliness (a total of six statements) and gave an altogether different orientation to the debates – an outspoken, comradely, critical and constructive spirit. They contain the following assessments and recommendations:

1 The brigade leader should be more exacting towards the persons he has given tasks to and should not do instead of them jobs that he is not obliged to do.
2 The group leaders do nothing to improve the psychological climate of the workshop. They should be among the workers more often instead of building prestige by exploiting their mistakes.
3 Some incompetent people have participated in the brigade council. The council should be made up of people well informed on the work of the previous month.
4 Business is not going well because there is a clear pressure towards activities bringing a higher co-efficient, i.e. higher wages.
5 More workers should take part in the brigade council.

In spite of these critical notes, the brigade leader was unanimously re-elected by the collective. Two additions were made to the nominations for the brigade council, one of the new candidates finally remaining in the elected council.

It can be seen that both cases are episodes with their own internal dynamics and tensions. In the pessimistic case there is mobilisation of the workers in the course of the elections (a new nomination was put forward but the nominated engineer did not give his written consent as required by the Labour Code), but the 'official candidate' elected responds with a series of administrative measures outside his authority; in the second case, the criticism in the course of the discussion of the brigade's work was followed by support for the candidate and a conflict-free election. The general assessment by the researcher of the significance of elections as an event at this plant was that it changed the general climate from that characterised by the researcher as one of 'family relations' into one in which conflicts of interests became open.

The discussion so far has concentrated on responses to elections as an event leading in some cases to episodes. A different question is whether elections led to significant, lasting changes in internal processes. This question was investigated by the researcher for Heavy Engineering, who visited the plant four months after the elections. The researcher found that 50 per cent of the brigade leaders felt that there had been definite changes in the behaviour of workers: they were more involved, more ready to make proposals and demands and to participate in the management of the brigade. A consequence of this was that the role of the brigade council had increased in that it discussed a wider range of issues. Although this might have been seen as diminishing the power of the brigade leader, in fact all brigade leaders considered that their authority in relation to the collective had been enhanced by election. Some reported that workers had said they were afraid to desert their brigade leader by transferring to work elsewhere.

ELECTIONS AND RESTRUCTURING

The cases described so far have focused on brigade elections in the context of the existing structure established by top management. However, the provisions of the Labour Code encouraged the restructuring of brigades, and such restructuring (which involved changing the boundaries and membership of brigades) was an option for top management for other reasons, such as changes in production technology. This raises three questions: first, whether restructuring had any effect on elections; second, since elections could pose a challenge to management's preference for a particular brigade leader, whether management might choose to alter brigade structure in the hope of ensuring the election of what they perceive as acceptable brigade leaders, and equally whether elections could provide an opportunity for the collective itself to initiate any changes in organisational structure. There is some evidence from the five plants that recent changes in brigade structure could influence the results of elections. Thus, at Assembly the trade union chairman judged that in the five cases where existing brigade leaders were not re-elected, changes in brigade structure had been a significant factor. Similarly, at Heavy Engineering where only two of fifty-two brigade leaders were not elected, a change in structure was judged as important in the rejection of one brigade leader. There was no evidence from the five plants of top management 'changing' structures to influence election results, but at another textile plant the director refused to designate maintenance workers as a primary collective in order to prevent them electing a brigade leader.

From the standpoint of the labour collective, there were some indications of how elections might be used as a mechanism for mobilising issues related to organisation structure. In the election observed at Textiles one women identified an issue related to higher management's external control over the brigade's results: she argued that the brigade's quality of work compared favourably with that of other brigades and consequently they should be entitled to be responsible for their own quality supervision without external control (if this had happened the brigade's earnings would have been increased). The outcome of this proposal for the elimination of external supervision is unknown. At Chemicals a brigade used the election as an opportunity for changing the managerial structure. The Labour Code (Article 20) and the Regulation on Economic Activity guaranteed to the brigades the right to determine and regulate (increase or decrease) their number, without asking the agreement of the management. The brigade involved consisted of four shifts and, following the industry tradition, each was led by a shift manager (an administrative position). The brigade (it was obvious that the initiator was the brigade leader) arrived at the position that it could work without a shift manager by nominating for each shift a person to take charge from among the experienced workers. Thus the issue emerged of the dismissal of four line managers, which would give the brigades the opportunity to redistribute their wage fund among the rest of the workers. The strategy of the brigade was to use the elections and the right to internal structural changes given to it for the purpose of legalising its decision to dismiss the shift managers. Despite some reservations on the part of the management, the decision was taken by the general assembly and the dismissed managers were offered other jobs within the enterprise. This episode can be seen as an example of an imposed mechanism (elections) being complemented by an organic mechanism (the steps taken by the brigade). (Organic mechanisms are discussed in more detail in Chapter 10.)

An example of a different type of structural change associated with elections occurred among the dockers of one of the Danube river ports, investigated by Krastyn Petkov. For organisational purposes, the five ports had been established as a single managerial unit headed by a director. In accordance with the provisions of the Labour Code, this managerial unit became the main collective, and each of the five ports became a primary collective. The workers at one port, however, decided that it was not in their interest to remain a constituent unit of this main collective and the election provided them with a mechanism to assert their desire to be an autonomous unit.

ELECTIONS OF DIRECTORS

Nationally there were 5,500 elections for director, and 117 (2.1 per cent) were not elected. In the five plants the directors were elected with only occasional 'no' votes. The election of the general director at Metals was observed by a researcher and is representative of the elections in these plants. The electors were the members of the general assembly of representatives, of whom 143 were present. In addition, there were representatives of the regional and district party organisations, the district trade union and the corporation of which the enterprise was a part. The meeting lasted for two hours. The assessment of the director's performance was made by the regional/district party organisation and the director gave a report not only on the past performance of the enterprise but also on its future prospects. There were about a dozen contributions from the floor, mainly from departmental managers and supervisors, some congratulatory but others critical of the omissions of comments on their departments which they wished to see represented in the director's report. In the accompanying elections for the council of the corporation, concern was expressed about the need for stronger representation to solve the 'strategic problems' of the enterprise. Proposals were also made about the future strategy of the enterprise and the need for the research and development department to develop new technology. In the opinion of the researcher the meeting was used as an opportunity to press for the resolution of some issues by the corporation.

CONCLUSIONS – THE SIGNIFICANCE OF MANAGERIAL ELECTIONS

The significance of the 1986 elections was assessed in an official report to the Central Committee of the Party, the Council of Ministers and the Central Committee of the Bulgarian Trade Unions. This summarised the main official criticisms of the elections: they had been characterised by a formalism inconsistent with self-management, by interference and manipulation and by inertia and conservatism (*Pretsenka otnosno* 1986: 8–9). However, the cases cited in this chapter show that the election assemblies could provide opportunities for the representation of interests through changing managers (or voting against them) and for the mobilisation of issues. It is clear that it was possible for challenges to brigade leaders to emerge when brigade members felt that they had not effectively represented their interests. Equally, there was clear concern that the membership of the brigade council should adequately reflect the different occupational groups. When there were strong internal conflicts between competing groups within a brigade, this could become clearly manifest in the elections, though in such cases, whatever the result, the resolution of conflicts of interests of this type would probably require changes in structure to bring about their resolution. The cases also show how the assemblies could be used as a mechanism for the open mobilisation of issues seen as unresolved by the workers, that is, for the manifestation of latent conflicts. Sometimes the object seems to have been to draw them to the attention of higher management or representatives of other bodies present at the assembly. The assemblies were, therefore, used as a mechanism for bringing issues from the base to the notice of those at the top. In most cases mobilisation of such issues was not a direct threat to the election or re-election of the brigade leader or manager, but rather a public warning of the need for future action to resolve it. From this perspective the significance of elections, especially at brigade level, is not to be assessed simply in terms of the number of brigade leaders voted out or even in the number of votes against successful candidates.

Some of the cases cited and the results from a study by the Georgi Dimitrov Institute of 880 non-elected candidates (Aroyo 1987), show how elections lead to changes in the criteria for managerial appointment. Thus, in the election of a brigade leader the assembly may assess a candidate on criteria related both to his effectiveness in representing the interests of the brigade externally in relation to higher management, and internally by his perceived social skills and ability to reconcile the interests of different groups within the brigade. Higher management and the plant party and trade union organisations may be more inclined to apply criteria to a candidate in terms of technical qualifications. By thus altering the criteria for brigade leader appointments, elections may modify relationships between the top and the base.

At a more general level, elections introduce an explicit duality into managerial roles – that of a representative as well as manager. For the brigade leader election as a mechanism significantly shifts the essential nature of his position from that of a managerial appointment with strong upward accountability, to that of a leader and representative of the brigade with primary accountability to those who elected him. There is a similar shift in the role of the enterprise director, hitherto the representative of the state and accountable to state bodies, towards that of a representative of the collective. The potential conflict arising from the duality of this role has to be set in the context of the changes in economic organisation which are designed to increase enterprise autonomy and reduce the role of the state. The implied shift from management by command to management by consent does not necessarily entail a weakening of managerial authority. Engels (1962: 320) contrasted the 'authority' of the police officer with that of the clan chief and 'the uncoerced and undisputed respect that is paid to him. The one stands in the midst of society; the other is forced to attempt to represent something outside and above it'.

For the party organisation, elections meant a significant change in its role in the enterprise. It had to consult with the workforce and take account of their opinion, although the empirical evidence presented has clearly shown that in exercising its right to make an assessment, and in presenting candidates for election, the party organisation played an influential role. However, as Aroyo (1987: 64) reports in his article, 56 per cent of the 880 cases of managers who were not elected were members of the party or the Komsomol, while 76 per cent were on the party *nomenklatura* lists and hence had party approval. Elections, therefore, tend to modify the nature of the *nomenklatura* mechanism and with it the character of party organisation within the plant. The non-election of candidates approved by a party organisation presented it with the choice between accepting the will of the workforce or attempting to interfere with it. Although there were cases where the party set out to overturn the results, in the majority of cases it accepted them.

The responsibility of the trade unions for organising elections as an event had significant consequences for their role as an agency of organisational development. Since 1978 the trade unions had taken a leading part in the process of introducing and structuring the brigade organisation of work and the associated mechanisms of counterplanning and distribution of earnings. Their role in organising the elections further confirmed and strengthened this aspect of their work, but it could also be associated with a change in their style of work. Thus, a district trade union president interviewed at the time of the election campaign commented that he was receiving many calls from plant trade union officials asking for detailed instructions on how to carry out the electoral work. His response was that now it was their responsibility to work out the best local method of implementing the general guidelines and not to rely on higher authority for this.

10 The labour collective, the labour community and self-management – the emergence of organic mechanisms

COLLECTIVE AND COMMUNITY

Earlier chapters have focused on the redesign of structures and the introduction of imposed mechanisms designed to develop the labour collective. The essential characteristic of the labour collective is that it is created externally from above and established through the process of normative regulation. The labour community, which this chapter considers, may develop internally from below and emerge from the labour collective. Analysis of this process requires clarification of the concept of labour community and consideration of how its emergence may be illustrated empirically. The concept of community has a long tradition and an important place in western sociological writing. Nisbet (1966: 47) claims that: 'The most fundamental and far-reaching of sociology's unit-ideas is community. The rediscovery of community is unquestionably the most distinctive development in nineteenth-century social thought.' The main focus of recent western academic discourse on community, however, has been in relation to social groupings in territorial or ethnic units, that is, on community outside rather than within the workplace. Flanders (1975: 89), however, referred to: ' "The Plant Community" which evolves from below out of face to face relations based on shared interests, sentiments and beliefs, and relations among various groups of employees', but he did not seek to relate the concept of community to criteria which could show empirically its presence or development. Lee and Newby (1983: 57–8) suggest that there are two main sociological definitions of community (they reject the purely territorial definition as geographical rather than sociological): the first is community as a 'local social system – that is as a set of social relationships which take place wholly or mostly within a locality'; the second is community 'as a type of relationship – more particularly "community" is defined as a sense of identity between individuals'. A recent Bulgarian discussion of types of social community is to be found in Tilkidzhiev's work on 'social groups'. His approach is a contribution to a debate among Bulgarian sociologists which emerged in the late 1970s about the nature of social groups and social communities and the differences between them. The essential difference was considered to be that whereas social communities were integrated by common activities, social groups were not. One type of community discussed by Tilkidzhiev is the 'community of interests' integrated by a common value system, but he did not link his consideration of groups and community to the workplace (Tilkidzhiev 1989). Earlier Petkov and Kolev (1982) had discussed social relations in the labour collective and pointed to the potential for the development of community in the brigade organisation of work, and Petkov had discussed the labour community in the *Sociology of work* (1985: 318–26).

Discussion of the issue of the labour collective and its relation to the labour community emerged most clearly in Yugoslavia in the early 1980s in the context of academic debates on the evaluation of the Yugoslav experience of self-management (this was, of course, at a late stage in the development of self-management). In 1982 Horvat (1982a: 2–3) published an assessment of self-management which was in some respects critical. Reviewing 30 years of Yugoslav self-management in 1983, Rus argued that Horvat's assessment was over-critical and that this was because he had evaluated it according to criteria derived from the concept of community rather than criteria derived from the concept of collective: 'his ideal type of self-management is based on the community; therefore the fact that the social dynamic in Yugoslav enterprises is more like that of collectives than of communities, unavoidably provokes his negative evaluation' (Rus 1984: 375–6). As Rus saw it the Yugoslav enterprise was 'between a collective and community' and he then listed some criteria for distinguishing between collective and community in terms of social action:

Collectives are based on calculated reciprocity, and communities are based on unlimited reciprocity. Collectives are aggregations of groups and coalitions which are in mutual conflict and co-operation; communities are based on common values, and are socially non-differentiated co-operative entities. In collectives freedom and equality are negatively correlated since the freedom of one member represents the limitation of freedom of the others. In communities they are positively correlated; in collectives more equality means at the same time more uniform social arrangements which allows less individual or group freedom, while in a community more equality means also more co-operation and more individual freedom. In collectives co-operation and integration are externally motivated: individuals, groups and coalitions co-operate and limit their peculiarities because they try to increase security and decrease the risk or unpredictability of environment for the collective; in communities greater equality allows greater involvement of the individual and through this more creative inclusion in a broader social frame.

(Rus 1984: 376)

Three general comments may be made about Rus's approach. First, it is valuable that he sees both collective and community as about the nature of the internal relationships within a unit of organisational structure and the interests, norms and values which both reflect and influence these relationships. On the other hand, the criteria are very general, for example, the discussion about equality, freedom and the individual and it is not easy to see how they may be illustrated empirically. Second, the evaluation is a macro-level one based on 'collective' and 'community' as ideal types; and Rus does not seek to deal with the organisational processes by which a given organisation may move in one direction from collective towards community or in the reverse direction from community towards collective. Third, it is important to note that Rus confines his discussion to the enterprise as a whole and does not seek to relate 'community' and 'collective' to internal units of structure such as the work group and the Basic Organisation of Associated Labour. The legal distinction in Bulgaria between the two levels of structure, the primary and the main collective, means that the concept of community has to be related to each level and it seems reasonable to hypothesise that the features of community will be more frequently apparent at the level of the brigade, where-face-to-face interaction is normal, than in the much larger unit of the enterprise as a whole. As Fox (1971: 111) remarks in his discussion of collectivities: 'collectivity may mean very different things according to the goal being pursued and the level at which action is appropriate'.

In relation to the workplace the process may be seen in terms of the following sequence: a unit of organisational structure (externally designed) which is integrated by economic interests has the potential to develop the social relationships which integrate it as a community. Thus the basis of collective norms and values may be seen as economic, whereas the basis of community norms and values may be seen as social. This relates to the bases of reciprocity to which Rus refers. So when the problem facing an individual member is accepted as a matter of common concern by all, this may be seen as collective when the problem has a common economic base but as community when it is not. In reality collective–community is a continuum in which economic and social aspects are mixed – the collective is mainly economic but has some social aspects, while community is mainly social but has economic aspects. However, as Fox remarks, 'Once the collectivity is established it becomes a partly independent force in the situation' (1971: 109) and this independence can provide the opportunity for a shift from collective in the direction of community. The potential, for community, however, will depend in part upon the structures and imposed mechanisms incorporated in the design. It should also be noted that there may be exceptions to the sequence of development suggested above. Thus some brigades in Bulgaria, especially in construction and mining, are formed from family groups, so that the social unit and the relationships existing outside the workplace are taken into the workplace and enhanced in the labour process. In such cases, which are not considered here, the question arises of how the social norms are integrated with the rules of the organisation. Equally territorial ties, looser than those of the family, may be brought into the workplace and facilitate action based on community norms and values.

Empirically the presence of community in a unit of structure will, it is argued, be partially revealed by the creation of organic mechanisms at the base in response to issues. Organic mechanisms are indicators of collective social action, which is one of the preconditions of community. The concept of organic mechanism was developed deductively in the autumn of 1986 in the context of discussion and elaboration of the concept of mechanism and its relationship to organisational processes, design and strategy. It was recognised that the origins of mechanisms could clarify their significance and this led to the distinction between imposed and organic mechanisms. At that time the authors had no examples with which the concept could be illustrated empirically nor any certainty that such examples could be found in the five core plants. This posed a challenge for the researchers, who had to seek out concrete examples armed only with an abstract definition of a concept. The process of recognising organic mechanisms became easier as soon as the first examples had been identified. Subsequently, it was considered that the presence of organic mechanisms could be seen as an indicator of community, a concept that had been introduced at an early stage of the project but which had hitherto not been grounded empirically. However, although a number of illustrations were found in the core plants, these were supplemented by episodes from other plants which were investigated by the researchers and Krastyn Petkov and which were judged to be significant and relevant to the theme of this chapter. This evidence is set out below in three main categories: first, where the mechanisms were developed for issues internal to the brigade; second, where the mechanism was created by the brigade in response to externally generated issues; and third, those which involved the main collective.

THE EMERGENCE OF ORGANIC MECHANISMS

Issues internal to the brigade

In the first group the mechanisms are principally concerned with individual issues for which the brigade created a mechanism. At Textiles a primary party group organiser explained that the women workers in the brigades were usually sympathetic to the problems of women with small children and they would take over the work of a woman who was absent looking after a sick child or who needed to leave early for domestic reasons. These mechanisms are strictly contrary to the provisions of the Labour Code, but are quite common especially in rural areas, where the brigade will cover for members who wish to work on family plots at harvest and other peak periods of the agricultural year. Community mechanisms could, on occasion, also be created for those who were not members. Thus one brigade at Textiles had 'adopted' an orphan in the local community and made payments from the brigade fund for its welfare. The creation of an organic mechanism to resolve an issue of individual discipline is illustrated by an episode in a brigade at Heavy Engineering where an alcoholic worker was frequently absent and worked ineffectively. In the past it would have been the responsibility of the brigade leader or supervisor to initiate action. Now it was the brigade assembly which had to resolve the issue. (In the Yugoslav plants studied by Adizes discipline was the responsibility of an elected committee of the economic unit; it made recommendations to the council of the unit, which, not the assembly, took the final decision) (Adizes 1971: 169). The brigade council proposed that he should be disciplined according to the rules of the enterprise. The assembly was unhappy about the application of this mechanism and after lengthy discussion proposed a counter-mechanism. An agreement would be signed by the worker and all the other members of the brigade in which the worker committed himself to undergo treatment while the rest of the brigade pledged social support. However, the worker did not fulfil his obligation under the agreement and the brigade assembly then delegated the responsibility for action to the brigade council. The essential character of this, and all the preceding illustrations, lies in the application of social rather than immediate economic criteria: it was in the economic interests of the brigade to expel an ineffective worker, but the workers saw it as a human and social issue in which the social interests of the community should have priority. This case illustrates what may be termed an 'exchange or substitution of values': the design of the brigade and its routine operation were based on material values but in this episode social values prevailed.

Brigade responses to pressures from the top

The following episodes show brigades acting to defend their interests in response to actions initiated by top management. In preparation for a visit to the plant by a politician, the director at Heavy Engineering gave instructions for part of the factory to be painted while work was going on. (At some time in the past the plant had been visited by a politician from another socialist country who, on his return, had commented adversely in the press about the state of the paintwork in the plant.) The brigade protested to management and the trade union about the unsatisfactory conditions created by paint spraying but without success. The brigade then stopped work spontaneously. This can be seen essentially as a brief incident, but action by a dockers' brigade and a brigade at Components led to episodes with more complex sequences of action. The common trigger for action in both cases was a change in work which led top management to approve changes affecting the earnings of the brigades. The case of the dockers' brigade, investigated by Krastyn Petkov and one of the researchers, involved the brigade created by Miloushev which had been a prototype of the new type of brigade organisation in the 1970s (see Chapter 5). The researcher characterised it as a 'political' brigade because it contained an important core of party members. In its development as a community it had established the mechanism of an internal norm that it would not defend any member guilty of pilfering and this can be seen as an expression of its internal values (part of an internal moral code). This development reflected the strategy formulation and approach to redesign of Miloushev, who had been concerned to ensure that the criteria for the internal distribution of earnings and the mechanisms for implementation should both facilitate and maintain values that were shared by all its members. This process of redesign, initiated at the base, had been obstructed by management and criticised by other brigades, but under the strong leadership of its founder the brigade had established a high level of productivity and correspondingly high earnings. However, at this stage of its development it had more the character of collective than of community in that its actions depended to a large extent on the leadership of Miloushev rather than on the commitment of the whole membership. Thus Miloushev had on occasions sought to get the support of the collective to courses of action which he judged were in their interests, but without success even though he had used the threat of resignation as a mechanism for exerting pressure to secure the course of action he proposed.

The episode which showed the character of community action occurred after he had left the brigade. The challenge to the pattern of high earnings and productivity originated from a shift in the proportions of the kinds of cargo handled by the port – management wished to allocate them more often to lighter work which meant a fall in earnings. On one occasion, when they protested about the effects of diesel fumes, management used this as an opportunity to redeploy them to other work and said that they could only return to their usual work if they accepted a new contract. They were promised the next cargo, which was of the heavier kind, but this was actually given to another brigade. In protest they decided that they would stop work on a particular day, arranging for the brigade leader and his deputy to be absent in order to exclude them from the risk of discipline by line management. The assembly drew up a document setting out their grievance and the members signed it individually – another organic mechanism intended to promote internal cohesion and solidarity. Management, however, rejected the claim. The brigade then considered extending the action field by seeking media publicity, but rejected it in favour of asking the advice of a trade union official outside the plant. This was a complex episode in which the position of a leading brigade was threatened by managerial action and in which the site party and trade union organisations remained silent initially. However, when management proposed financial penalties the site trade union endorsed the proposal but at the same time decided to punish the production director for failing to provide full information to the brigade.

At Components, where the episode was investigated by one of the researchers, the brigade involved was an important one in the production process. In the past, relationships with the management had been considered good and the brigade had established a pattern of resolving production problems connected with the operation of the machines and supplies. The effectiveness of the brigade's organisation of production was reflected in the established pattern of high earnings and it had a high level of internal cohesion. Party members were not important in this brigade but external social relations and common social activities were judged by the researcher to supplement the internal cohesion of its members based on the labour process. The brigade leader was considered to have authority both inside the plant and in the community outside.

The origins of the episode derived from the introduction of a new component which required less work. For five months, however, the brigade were allowed to do the easier work, but with the old norms. Then the ratesetter altered the brigade's norms without consulting the brigade assembly well in advance, as required by the labour code. Management also took away one of the machines which the brigade argued was necessary for their work – the management argued that it was not fully utilised. The brigade appealed to higher management, who supported the ratesetter, and the new norms were then imposed. The brigade then appealed to the trade union and party organisations, who remained silent. The trade union is supposed to analyse such issues and to take a position. Its inaction eroded the mechanistic mechanism at one of its most important points – the criterion that it should operate in the interest of the primary collective. Other brigades in the plant advised against taking further action on the grounds that it could not be successful, but the brigade decided that they would act. The brigade came into the factory every day for a week and stood by their machines but did no work. The wife of the brigade leader acted as a spokeswoman for the brigade and information on the episode reached the press, who sent a reporter to investigate. Eventually, the norms were restored almost to their previous level. Subsequently the brigade was anxious to improve its relations with management, and to facilitate this process it decided that no member should talk about the episode with outsiders. This illustrates both the internal discipline that had been fostered by the episode and the ability of the collective/community to plan a sequence of actions to achieve its goals. After the episode the trade union committee's position was that while the action taken by the brigade was not right, the action taken by management was also incorrect. These cases illustrate the implementation of a mechanistic mechanism – norm revision – leading to a counteracting organic mechanism. In the first, it seems that the action was mobilised by consensus within the brigade; in the second, however, it was the researcher's impression that it was the leadership given by the brigade leader, although supported by the brigade, that was decisive.

Organic mechanisms by the main collective

The preceding episodes relate to single brigades; the following illustrate action in which the main collective became involved. The episodes, however, differ in their origins: at Textiles the origin was internal, whereas at Consumer Electronics it arose from an external decision. At Textiles the workers in several brigades wanted new machines which would improve both work and earnings. The issue had been taken to the plant council on a number of occasions, but although top management were sympathetic they were constrained by the regulations restricting the availability of the foreign currency needed to buy the machines and they had rejected the proposals as impracticable. Workers were dissatisfied with management's explanation and used a meeting of the general assembly of the plant as the mechanism for mobilisation of the issue on a wider base. Angry workers took notes from their pockets and shouted 'do you want our money to buy the machines?' Management then summoned the chief accountant of the plant to read out the regulation governing such purchases. The final sentence of the regulation ended with the words 'et cetera'. Workers then shouted that their demand should be covered by the 'et cetera' formula. Subsequently, management were able to find a way of securing the currency needed for the purchase of the machines. The significant feature of this episode is not the temporary tension between management and workers, but the way in which the collective used a series of different mechanisms to increase pressure in the promotion of their interests.

The next case, from Consumer Electronics, relates to an investigation conducted by Krastyn Petkov. At the beginning of 1987 the workers learned that the contract for one of the products was to be terminated as the result of a high-level decision taken above the enterprise. In anticipation of this impending event, the workers were concerned about a number of issues affecting their interests, such as alternative work, possibly with new norms and skill requirements and job security. They were opposed to the change particularly because they anticipated a loss of earnings and they asked for information from top management. The director explained the situation and promised that the enterprise leadership – the director, party secretary and trade union chairman – would take some steps to satisfy the workers' concerns. However, these steps were not taken and after approaching both the director and the trade union chairman without success, a group of workers eventually decided to use the provisions of the Labour Code as a mechanism and convene a meeting of the general assembly. Article 26 of the Labour Code provides that a meeting can be convened at the request of not less than one-quarter of its members. The intention was to use the assembly to elect a new director and trade union chairman and to take a decision about the impending loss of the contract and its ramifications. The workers secured the number of signatures needed, but the meeting was boycotted by top management, the trade union and the party. The party committee interviewed the workers individually and party members were asked to follow the party line of not taking action. However, although the plant trade union committee supported management and the party, the regional trade union committee met the workers and took a position on the basis of the collective's rights under the Labour Code. The episode was then reported in the Bulgarian press. It shows how the collective as a legal entity planned and took a series of steps, and then used its legal rights as a complementary mechanism to legitimate the action taken to defend its interests.

These episodes have shown sequences and the mobilisation of resources in response to incidents and events. However, it is also of interest to consider illustrations of limited or incomplete action in response to issues. At one level this can be seen as due to the failure to create sufficient organic mechanisms. At a different level this reflects a combination of insufficient community solidarity and the lack of leadership capable of devising effective mechanisms and a plan of effective action. Textiles provides an example of this, which is of interest because it contrasts with the effectiveness of the mechanisms and the mobilisation on the issue of new machines. The issue was the heating system in part of the plant which had been installed in such a way that it was difficult to control, so that at times the workplace became excessively hot. This was a common complaint by the brigade most affected. Rectification would have required considerable work by the installers and pressure to get them to work on this rather than another project. The brigade members complained about the conditions to a group of doctors who were visiting the plant (seeing them as a potential external resource). However, there was insufficient solidarity within the collective to secure additional internal mobilisation and the collective seems to have accepted management's explanation that the work involved would be put in hand when practicable.

The collective and the appointment of top management

Metals and Heavy Engineering provide interesting contrasts in the response of the base to changes in top management. As explained in previous chapters, top management at Metals had consciously formulated and implemented a strategy of developing the labour collective as *stopanin* since 1983. In July 1988, the leading managers responsible for this strategy were removed from their positions by the superior body. Their successors suspended the operation of most of the mechanisms introduced by their predecessors. Potentially, the creation of organic mechanisms as an active response from the plant community to this event might have been expected. However, the only clear response was a passive and silent one – there was a dramatic drop in production which was halved in the ensuing months. Given the complexity of organisational processes, any explanation of the absence of an active response can only be tentative. However, one way is to consider it in relation to the approach of the top in dealing with issues emerging at the base. In 1987 John Thirkell had a discussion with the trade union chairman about his conception of the organisational dynamics of the labour collective as *stopanin*. As a means of elucidating this, John Thirkell described the episode of the new machines at Textiles as an illustration of how the labour collective as subject might initiate a sequence of actions. The trade union chairman's reaction was very clear: at Metals such a sequence of organic mechanisms would not have been allowed to develop because the trade union and the party would have intervened at an early stage to resolve the issue identified by the collective. The researcher responsible for the fieldwork at Metals judged that, in general, the proactive approach of the top restricted the space at the base for the creation of organic mechanisms. Thus when top management was removed there was only a limited tradition of action on which the community could draw. Judged from the standpoint of the development of the collective, the absence of an episode at Metals can be interpreted as pessimistic. However, changes in top management at Heavy Engineering did produce some response from the collective. The director who had been responsible for formulating the strategy for the labour collective as *stopanin* (see Chapter 5), was promoted. Under his successor economic results deteriorated. This led to some pressure from the collective for the return of his predecessor. Details of the mechanisms by which pressure was applied are lacking, but the pressure was successful and his return was associated with an improvement in results.

CONCLUSIONS

The conclusions are devoted to four topics: (1) collective and community; (2) comments on the action sequences in the illustrations; (3) the relationship between the community inside the workplace and conditions outside; and (4) the relations between community and organisational design and self-management. Collective and community co-exist as different entities at the workplace which are convertible into each other: collective may become community and community may become collective. Collectives relate to units of organisational structure which are created externally (and hierarchically) as part of the operational structure. The functioning of the operational structure requires rules and mechanisms deriving from the environment, but also some additional rules and organic mechanisms which are generated internally. Patterns of action within the collective as part of the operational structure necessarily generate internal links based on interests and a process of exchange and reciprocity. The collective operates on the basis of mechanisms imposed from above such as the mechanisms for production plans and for the distribution of earnings, but the collective may also generate some organic mechanisms to cope with the operational process. The development in the direction of community is generally marked by actions involving organic mechanisms. Such mechanisms both express norms based on social linkages and criteria going beyond those required by the operational structure and contribute to the development of those norms. As explained earlier, some of these linkages and norms such as family brigades may be brought into the workplace from outside. However, organic mechanisms generated within the collective in response to incidents, episodes and events provide a basis for confirming and enhancing internal community norms and linkages. The outcome of the action process, if perceived as successful by the participants, may further confirm community, but so may failure – the solidarity of the defeated.

Organic mechanisms created for dealing with individual members of brigades are those that show most clearly the operation of social rather than collective norms. The episodes involving group rather than individual issues show a broad similarity in the sequence of actions and mechanisms: there was an appeal to the top, whether management, trade union or party for a resolution of the issue perceived as consistent with group interests and norms; when this was unsuccessful the group assessed its internal resources including its solidarity and often created mechanisms to protect its leadership. The process of planning and implementing a sequence of actions and the associated mechanisms can be seen as deriving from the collective but going beyond it in the direction of community through the strengthening of internal linkages. This leads to two general points about the development of community. The first is the significance of the operation of external threats or challenges. It can be argued that these are a frequent, if not always a necessary component of internal community development and maintenance. In this sense community within the workplace has some similarities with the processes outside the workplace.[1] The second is in relation to the theory of interests. Hethy points out in his study (1989: 149) that 'Interests came generally to the fore in conflict situations when the workers' positions were threatened i.e, when they were forced to think over their interests.' He further notes that in the negotiations he studied the:

> negotiating parties referred but rarely to their interests; instead they argued on the basis of their values. The workers repeatedly emphasized the aspects of safety, of keeping the regulations while the managers the necessity of common efforts aimed at common objectives.
>
> (Hethy 1989: 177)

Hethy sees values 'as far more permanent and far less flexible motives of action than interests' (1989: 151) which he sees as changing 'within a very short time and in very narrow sections of the society at a fast rate' (1989: 177). The important concept here, not used by Hethy, is that the mobilisation of interests in conflicts requires a basis of legitimation. In the illustrations of action by the community against the top it can be seen that there were problems of legitimation in relation to the conflict between 'official' norms and rules and the actions taken by the community. Thus the community could seek legitimation in the provisions of the Labour Code or by extending the action field to higher bodies outside the enterprise or to the press.

However, the inherent duality of incidents, episodes and events means that potentially the process of integration as collective or community may be enhanced or weakened by the response of the collective/community and no simple linear process of development can be expected. The process of establishing community norms and rules and their survival is one which necessarily takes time, and the existence of strong occupational groups, with their own interests, which may be in competition with each other, can make the integration of interests between them difficult. Shifts on the collective/community continuum may be expected to be reflected in the nature of authority and leadership within the unit. In the collective the authority of the leadership will derive from hierarchy and there may be informal as well as formal leadership. A shift towards community may be indicated by authority derived from the membership and the submergence of informal leadership. The process of internal decision making in community will be more by consensus than by other methods.

At a more general level the development of community from collective inside the workplace is partly dependent on conditions in the community outside the workplace and in the wider social and political environment. For much of the period covered by the research, conditions for community action outside the workplace were unfavourable and to some extent the episodes and illustrations used in this chapter are evidence that action was more feasible internally than externally. However, there were emerging changes in the external environment which, as the illustrations show, could offset the internal balance of forces and lead to the actual or contemplated extension of the action field by mobilising external resources such as media publicity. The cases of the docks and of Components show clearly not only community concern to protect the leadership to maintain internal solidarity at the base against the top but also the recognition that increasing *glasnost* in the external environment and legal standards that could secure external support, as at Consumer Electronics, made possible the extension of the action field in a way that would not have been feasible earlier. The July Plenum in 1987 recognised, at the political and theoretical level, both the concept of the labour collective as a self-managing community inside the workplace and the concept of the local self-managing community outside it. Thus it appeared to offer the potential for the development of processes in the local community to complement the emerging processes in enterprises, but no steps were taken to implement it in practice.

From the standpoint of organisational design, the essential requirement for the growth of the self-managing community inside the workplace is the creation of space so that organic mechanisms can flourish. Strategy formulation from 1981 to 1987 designed to establish the labour collective through a sequence of structural changes and imposed mechanisms created a base from which the self-regulating labour community could emerge. The creation of space permitting the emergence of organic social action in the community outside is equally a necessary condition for the growth of the self-managing local community.

NOTE

1   In July 1989 the Bulgarian Institute of Sociology carried out an investigation into the processes underlying the emigration of Turks from Bulgaria. This showed that until 1985 the Turks had not identified themselves as Turkish nationals but as Bulgarian citizens. The compulsory name change in 1985 (rescinded in 1989), as an external threat, changed the basis of their identification and they began to identify themselves as Turkish nationals.

11 Organisational design, the labour process and labour relations

In relation to the concepts of organisational design and labour relations as developed in this book, the labour process is seen as a product of a process of organisational design. Consequently any redesign of structures and mechanisms may lead to changes in the labour process and labour relations. A main concern of this chapter is, therefore, to consider the effects of redesign arising from the transition from the centralised model to the self-managed model. However, as explained in the Introduction, the concept of the labour process was elaborated by Braverman (1974) and since Braverman and some western writers have commented on the nature of the labour process in socialist countries these approaches are considered first and compared with some of the approaches adopted by social scientists in socialist countries. The labour process and the forms of organisation of work at the base are then discussed. The main comparison between the centralised and the self-management models is based on the core–periphery polarity, especially as developed by Burawoy (1985a) for his analysis of hierarchy and control. Here this polarity is used to compare the internal dynamics of mobilisation within the enterprise under the centralised and self-management models. Finally the issue of self-management, property relations and alienation is briefly considered.

APPROACHES TO THE LABOUR PROCESS IN SOCIALIST SOCIETIES

Braverman's analysis was centred on the labour process under capitalism but he briefly considered the question of whether the labour process under socialism was different and argued that it was not. He saw Taylor as the key theorist of scientific management (and the deskilling associated with it) and after noting Lenin's remarks on Taylorism he comments:

in practice Soviet industrialisation imitated the capitalist model, and as industrialisation proceeded the structure lost its provisional character and the Soviet Union settled down to an organisation of labour differing only in details from that of the capitalist countries, so that the Soviet working population bears all the stigmata of the western working class.

(Braverman 1974)

However, other western writers have argued that there are major differences between the two labour processes. Thus Thompson in *The nature of work* (1983) devoted some pages to a discussion of Eastern Europe. His principal conclusion was that:

while there is a common experience of hierarchical work organisation, mass production and some managerial techniques producing overlapping experiences among Eastern and Western workers, in other respects they are crucially different, and these differences relate to separate labour processes under separate modes of production.

(Thompson 1983: 223)

Lane, who also takes the position that the labour process under socialism differs from the capitalist labour process, describes his book as being concerned with the 'context of the labour process', and his main interest is with the consequences of the external dynamics of the centrally planned economy rather than the internal structures and mechanisms of the enterprise. He argues that in a centrally planned economy 'there is no effective propensity to increase profitability by reducing labour costs' (Lane 1987: 1). The dynamics of a centrally planned economy provide 'full employment and labour shortage. This affects the labour process by strengthening the position of labour *vis à vis* management and weakening the "control of management" ' (Lane 1987: 3).

To maintain a large and reliable workforce, enterprises seek to reward their employees with better facilities to earn wages and provide payments in kind. This gives rise to the differentiation of conditions and opportunities not as under capitalism as on the basis of a monopoly of skill or by bargaining position, but by the industry or enterprise in which the person works.

(Lane 1987: 2)

The essence of Lane's argument is that the basis of distribution is different and, although he does not use the term, there is a different 'mode of production'. While Lane's comments about the context of the labour process are valid, the actual labour process within the enterprise is rather more complex than he implies.

Burawoy on the other hand discussed the labour process itself as well as the economic environment. His analysis of the labour process under socialism derives from his experience of work in a Hungarian factory (Burawoy 1985b: 43–69) and from his interpretation of Haraszti's critical study (Haraszti 1977) of his experience as a pieceworker in a Hungarian factory exposed to the pressures generated by the New Economic Mechanism in 1969. Burawoy's analysis, like Lane's, deals with the external dynamics of plan bargaining under soft budget constraints, but he links this to internal relations at the base and to relations between the top and base of the enterprise. At the base, Burawoy sees the key mechanism as the individual piecework system without an adequate basic rate which creates income security, although there is job security. (He contrasts this with the income security but job insecurity which he found in the American factory where he worked (Burawoy 1985a: 171).) In the operation of the mechanisms of distribution, power is vested hierarchically in the head foreman: 'Everyone is dependent on the head foreman who fixes the level of pay, holiday, overtime, bonuses, awards' (1985a: 173). Burawoy also claims that auxiliary workers were in a hierarchical relationship to direct production workers: 'their interests lay with the bosses. Inspectors like setters and foremen were in a privileged position and obtained their jobs by the grace of the Party' (1985a: 176). Burawoy argues that irrespective of the Tayloristic approach to job design:

> supply constraints generate continual reorganization of the labour process. The fluidity of task structure and the continual need to redistribute workers among machines makes it very difficult to deskill production to separate conception and execution.
>
> (Burawoy 1985a: 163)

Burawoy's analysis of the nature of hierarchy at the base and the effects of irregular supplies are valid. However, in Bulgaria there was income security albeit at a low level.

The concept of the labour process is not one that has been used by Soviet (or Bulgarian) writers on the organisation of work. In part this reflected the dominance of the scientific organisation of work as a school of thought and practice, a dominance which was challenged only with the emergence of sociological studies of work from the late 1960s onwards. The problems of the labour process were touched on indirectly and did not use Braverman's terminology or approach. Thus in the late 1960s Zdravomyslov, Rozhin and Iadov (1967) studied the relationship between job content and attitudes to work in the context of the need to enrich the content of routine industrial jobs and so overcome the contradiction between the expectations of workers, especially young ones, and the actual content of jobs. In the 1960s worker participation in management prompted a number of studies which considered how workers might exercise some control over the managerial apparatus or how routine manual tasks might be combined with some creative managerial functions. The work of Hethy and Mako (1989) on worker behaviour in response to managerial changes in mechanisms has been mentioned in earlier chapters, and in Hungary the concept of the labour process has been used (Mako 1989).

The labour process and work organisation

Despite Burawoy's comments on the way in which the vicissitudes of the shortage economy require workers to deploy a range of skills to overcome them, it is clear that the dynamic of the individual system of payment and the approach to task allocation and norm setting associated with the scientific organisation of work operated to separate conception from execution as Braverman argued. However, by the end of the 1970s, this approach was beginning to break down and give place to collective forms of work organisation of which the brigade system was the most common. This process was associated with the expansion of skill profiles – there were official mechanisms to encourage workers to acquire more than one skill. At a different level, the conception of the self-managing brigade with the final authority resting in the brigade assembly, can be validly seen as integrating conception and execution in so far as the planning and allocation of tasks is concerned. It is, however, worth noting that this is not a necessary result of adopting the concept of self-management. Rus (1984: 382) has commented of the Yugoslav enterprise (which does not have brigades): 'Since the old Tayloristic system of task distribution and task co-ordination has not been changed, the power of executive hierarchy remains very high.'

The design of the self-managing brigade and its introduction have been discussed in earlier chapters. In essence, the conception was that of transferring a large measure of control over the labour process at the point of production to the brigade. To show the operation of the labour process at the base, the study of brigades and self-management at Heavy Engineering is used. This was undertaken in the spring of 1987 by the researcher who covered the enterprise. The researcher interviewed 20 brigade leaders and 20 workers about their perceptions of what self-management meant in practice. The replies of the brigade leaders emphasised the independence of the brigade in deciding, without involvement from above, mainly operational issues relating to the organisation of work, cadres, discipline, the maintenance and repair of machines and the distribution of supplies – 90 per cent of their responses referred to these operational issues. The preponderance of worker responses (70 per cent) emphasised the right to decide issues related to work loads, earnings, working time and the distribution of income. The researcher concluded that, at that time, it was the mechanism of the co-efficient of participation that was at the heart of the dynamic of self-management at the level of the brigade.

The researcher studied the operation of the institutions of self-management – brigade leaders, brigade councils and the general assemblies of the brigade – and the relationships between them. All of the 54 brigade leaders were workers, the majority being setters. Brigade leaders were asked to list the issues that were decided within the brigade by the brigade council and the brigade assembly. The list included production problems, discipline, payment, admission of workers to the brigade and release from it, training of young workers, qualifications and issues arising from the reconstruction of the plant. The researcher was concerned to investigate any differences in the roles of the brigade council and the brigade assembly. Of the brigade leaders interviewed 40 per cent said there was no difference in role. On disciplinary issues, for example the exclusion of members, the decision of the general assembly was sometimes to accept the recommendation of the brigade council, but on occasions to reject it.

The labour process and core–periphery relations

Burawoy introduces the concept of core and periphery in discussing hierarchical relationships between top and base. He sees these relationships deriving from the dynamics of the shortage economy.

> The need to respond frequently and rapidly to changing requirements gives a great deal of power to the skilled and experienced worker, who over time develop a monopoly of knowledge essential to the running of the enterprise. From the management side penetration of external uncertainties onto the shopfloor elicits two strategies. On the one hand management can seek to reward co-operation, particularly of the core workers; on the other it can intensify surveillance and control, particularly over the more peripheral workers.
>
> (Burawoy 1985a: 163)

Categorising sections of the workforce of a factory in terms of core and periphery has recently figured in the British debate on the 'flexible firms', in which Atkinson (1984) has argued that employers are increasingly separating their workforce into a 'core' of full-time workers and a 'periphery' of part-time, temporary and sub-contracted workers. In essence the criterion for this categorisation is based on status, that is, the distinction between full-time employment status and part-time employment status. In the debate on the 'flexible firm' Pollert (1988) has criticised 'the vagueness of the model's key variables "core" and "periphery"'. However, this criticism fails to take account of the conditions for which core–periphery is an effective concept for the analysis of organisational dynamics. First, core–periphery has to be used in relation to particular organisations or units of organisation of specified structural characteristics. Organisations with different structures will have different core–periphery relations. While the members of any organisation or unit of organisational structure may have a core and a periphery, the actual basis of the categorisation will be contingent upon the functions of the organisation and its environment. Second, the identification of core–periphery in an organisation cannot be derived from quantitative data alone, but requires interpretation by key informants from within the organisation who are able to analyse its dynamics. Experience shows that key position holders in organisations can use core–periphery to analyse the dynamics of action in their organisations. Thus John Thirkell has found that trade union conveners in British factories can easily divide their members into 'trade unionists' (the core) and 'cardholders' (the periphery) and apply this categorisation to provide insights into the operation of the union organisation. If the size of the core in a unit of trade union organisation is small in relation to the periphery, the pattern of mobilisation of the trade union membership around issues is likely to be different from that in a unit with a larger core. In the same way, when a senior plant sociologist in a very large Bulgarian plant was asked, as a key informant, to apply the core–periphery categorisation to his enterprise he had little difficulty, although the concept was new to him, in categorising the workforce in this way and using it to analyse patterns of action and labour relations at the base of the enterprise. He defined the core as the established older long-service workers and the periphery as the younger, short-service workers, many of whom were working there as an alternative to military service. The sociologist judged that in this structure (not typical in Bulgaria) much of the action focused on the relations deriving from the interdependence of core and management to the relative exclusion of the periphery. He thus confirmed the proposition that core–periphery analysis provides insights into organisational dynamics.

The essence of the case for core–periphery lies in its relationship to the classical concept of the division of labour which is used horizontally to describe the structure of jobs and tasks at the base and vertically to describe the division of functions between top and base. The limitation of the division of labour as a concept is that it may easily lead to a rather static description of occupations rather than an analysis of organisational dynamics. As used here, core–periphery is intended to illustrate the dynamics of action processes. The basic criteria for core and periphery are those of status and action. Status is relative to the structure of the organisation and means that the core is characterised by the holding of positions or a status which is recognised internally within the organisation. Action means that the core is distinguished by pattern of action in relation to issues. Thus at the level of the brigade the brigade leader and the elected brigade council may constitute the core (this is formal status relative both to the rest of the brigade and the enterprise) and they will normally take the lead on issues. (Core–periphery at brigade level is discussed below.)

Core and periphery under the centralised and self-management models

The concept of core–periphery is applied to analyse the patterns of mobilisation in top–base relations and at the base itself. Applying the concept to the centralised model as it operated in the 1960s and 1970s in Bulgaria, it is clear that the method of work organisation and payment provided only a weak basis for collectivity at the base and consequently for the development of core–periphery relations at the horizontal level. As Burawoy argued in relation to Hungary, core–periphery relations developed primarily on a vertical line linking management at the top with core workers important for the production process. A fundamental feature of this model was that the linkage between the top and the base through the core was essentially through individuals and only weakly collective. The mobilisation of and through the core was based on the movements for socialist emulation etc.

Top–base relations under the centralised model in Bulgaria have to be set in the dynamics of mobilisation at enterprise level arising not only from coping with the uncertainties deriving from irregular and short supplies, or other problems arising at the base, but also from the imposed revision of plan targets by the superior bodies. Two collective institutions were normally used in these processes. The first was the *operativka* composed of leading position-holders at the top – the senior managers and the party and trade union leaders. This was convened by the director and he (and subordinate managers in the operational structure) could, through the trade union, convene production meetings. However, on important issues the *aktiv* was a major instrument of mobilisation. Authority for convening the *aktiv* rested with the party secretary. Its significance was that it would normally comprise position-holders in the management hierarchy and others such as party and trade union activists, specialists and leading workers drawn from different levels of the enterprise. Its function was to mobilise support, by leading and by explaining, from the top downward on an issue identified at the top. Although its membership was not constituted formally and participation was by invitation, the workforce would generally be aware of who was or was not a member of the *aktiv* so that there was recognition of status. It therefore operated as a core which linked vertically different levels of the enterprise and horizontally the operating and social–political structures.

The redesign of structures and mechanisms to establish the emerging self-managing model can be seen as presenting a challenge to both the composition and the operation of the traditional *aktiv*. Elected brigade leaders accountable to the base became the key position holders whose support was necessary in the processes of internal mobilisation which required co-operation between top and base. Consequently, they emerged as a main element in the emerging self-management core. The process of transition from one pattern to another would, of necessity, be a gradual one. Thus the sociologist cited above judged that although the *aktivs* still operated they were losing their effectiveness in mobilisation from top to base because they had lost a measure of credibility with the collective at the base as a result of the redesign of structures.

Under the self-management model core–periphery relations at the base can be considered from two aspects. First, in relation to the conception of the brigade leader and the brigade council as the formal core with the remainder of the workers as the periphery. Second, in relation to the party members as a core with the non-party members as the periphery. On the first aspect, at Textiles the researcher judged that in production brigades the brigade leader and the council were in practice a core which took the lead in the processes of mobilisation. However, the researcher covering Heavy Engineering found that while this was clearly so in some brigades in others the differentiation was much less apparent. The pattern of core–periphery relations would depend in part on the structure of interests within the brigade and their representation. Thus researchers noted that on occasion informal leaders would emerge at the assembly meetings to act as spokesmen for some interests within the brigade which in their view had not been adequately represented in the council. The issue of the party members as a core has to be set in the context of the official formulation of the relationship between the party organisation and the labour collective: 'party members represent the party organisation in the labour collective and the party members represent the collective in the party organisation'. This formulation has a strong top–base element. Associated with this was the conception of the vanguard role of the party and its members and the practice of the party organisation at the base to give an opinion on issues faced by the collective. This meant that although it did not claim the right to decide the collective view of the party members as a core of activists and leading workers it could be extremely influential. It was suggested above that the brigade council may, though not necessarily, constitute the core of the self-managing brigade and there was a tendency for party members to be disproportionately represented on them. Thus at Heavy Engineering the researcher found that there was a total of 295 brigade council members for the 54 brigades. Of this total 101 were members of the party and 53 were members of the Komsomol. However, the distribution of party members was not even, and 11 brigade councils had no party members. Of the brigade leaders 28 were party members. The general conclusion of the researchers in relation to the five plants was that in the routine processes there was no difference between the actions of party and non-party workers. However, illustrations from the five plants show that it was especially in relation to incidents that the party members acted as a core. At Metals the researcher noted that it was frequently the party members who were most active in putting pressure on management when work was interrupted by lack of supplies or other problems. At Chemicals when a brigade leader was asked to describe the position of the party members in his brigade, he emphasised their importance in promoting a good psychological climate within the collective and gave an illustration of an incident. He explained that the machinery required an annual maintenance overhaul. When it had been introduced, the party members had volunteered to undertake this task, which was regarded as difficult and uncertain. This precedent had now become established practice – party members undertook the annual maintenance, while the non-party members of the brigade took a holiday. Party members were expected to set an example in 'rush' or weekend work to catch up with plan targets. At Textiles the brigade party organiser explained that the party members were expected to volunteer and she commented 'when we stop work, everybody stops work'. On the other hand, an incident from Heavy Engineering shows how party members could mobilise against line management and weekend work. The brigade was instructed to work on a number of weekends to catch up with plan targets. However, the brigade was not convinced that there would be sufficient supplies for them to work effectively on a particular weekend, and they judged that their attendance would be a waste of time. Their appeal to the director to withdraw the instruction was rejected. The brigade party members then put the brigade's case to the party secretary, who supported them and got the director to withdraw his instructions. This illustrates the party members representing the interests of the collective through the party organisation.

THE LABOUR PROCESS, ALIENATION AND PROPERTY RELATIONS

The wider frame of Braverman's critique of the labour process was that of the classic Marxist concern with the alienation of the worker under capitalism, of which the separation of conception from execution was but one aspect. For Braverman, analysing monopoly capitalism in which private ownership of the means of production was the dominant form, it was logical to take as given the alienation deriving from private ownership. For Marx himself ownership of the means of production was a central feature of alienation under capitalism. Marx, however, saw private property, the division of labour and alienation from work as a historically and logically determined triad, developing in a defined historical sequence: alienation occurs in parallel with the division of labour, which contributes to the strengthening of private property. In Marxist logic private property from being an effect of the division of labour and alienation then becomes a cause of both. In socialist countries it has been taken as axiomatic that the starting-point for the reduction of alienation is to reverse the historical sequence, beginning with the abolition of private property. Apart from Yugoslavia, where the introduction of self-management was closely associated with the redefinition of enterprise as social property, state ownership of the means of production has been seen as the precondition for the reduction of alienation. The theory has been that in principle every worker is an equal co-owner, but only as a single member of the whole people. As such a member, the worker delegates legal and economic power to the state as the supreme co-owner. Until recently it has been assumed, at least theoretically, that under socialism the fundamental basis of alienation has been eliminated and negative behavioural phenomena are the result of specific rather than general conditions. During the 1980s this assumption has come to be questioned on both empirical and theoretical grounds. In the 1970s in Bulgaria the phenomena of high labour turnover, absenteeism, low labour discipline and a widespread passivity among workers at the base became recognised through research studies as well as everyday experience. At higher levels there was a parallel in the various forms of corruption, mismanagement and fraud.

Theoretically, the roots of alienation can be interpreted as deriving from the nature of the interrelationships between two main levels of economic structure: first, between the workers at the base of the enterprise and the management at the top, and second, between the enterprise and the higher levels of the administrative command structure. At the base of the enterprise the worker knows that it is his status in relation to the division of labour rather than his status as a co-owner that is the determining factor of his actual economic and labour status. Within the enterprise, where the worker relates directly to state property, his status derives from his occupational and educational qualifications and not from his relationship with the means of production – the materials and the equipment which are the instruments of labour. Within the enterprise the traditional hierarchical structure of management differentiates the 'equal co-owners' into two large groups: managers and subordinates, and this provides the basis of the 'us and them' perception of the relationship between the two groups. In its external relations the enterprise had limited autonomy because initiative was the prerogative of the centre, so that the producers in the enterprise were largely confined to the execution of plans imposed in the name of the state through the agency of a special stratum of administrators. They exercised external power over the enterprise, so that the internal division into managers and managed was paralleled by an external division between the administrators and the administered. These divisions and the symptoms of alienation arising from them can be seen as rooted in the concentration of ownership in the state.

In relation to the organisational design of the labour process, it can be argued that a strategy for alleviating alienation which can be derived from Marxist theory is to restructure ownership relations by altering the relations of workers to the means of production. The attempts in 1987 and 1988 to introduce the transfer of the means of production to the main collective (enterprise level) and the primary collective (brigade) were an expression of this strategy. In relation to the concentration of ownership under the control of the state, the importance of Decree 56 of January 1989 was that it recognised a plurality of forms of property which can be developed alongside state property – co-operative, group, family, individual, local authority and joint ventures with foreign participation. The intention was to create the conditions for competition between these different forms of property and so to foster the establishment of direct economic links between the individual and the means of production.

CONCLUSIONS

As used here the labour process acts as a concept which integrates key aspects of labour relations which arise from the division of labour at the point of production and between top and base, that is between the managers and the managed, and at a more fundamental level the relations of labour to the means of production. Within both aspects of the division of labour the concept of the core–periphery polarity provides insights into organisational dynamics which cannot be derived from the study of the division of labour alone. However, organisational design is directly connected with the structures and mechanisms which affect the division of labour. Although it is sometimes assumed that the division of labour at the point of production is determined by technology, the argument here is that there is evidence from socialist countries that suggests that while a given technology may condition the division of labour there is considerable scope for choice in the forms of work organisation at the base. Thus the brigade organisation of work in Bulgaria and in some other countries, differed very significantly from the operational pattern adopted in Yugoslavia. In the same way the Hungarian VGMK (vállalati gazdasági munkaközösség: enterprise work partnership) (discussed in Chapter 12) was not designed in relation to technology. Brigades and the VGMKs provide significant elements of autonomy which integrate conception and execution and modify the basis of control over the labour process. Core–periphery relations at the base and in relations between top and base were a significant feature of the Bulgarian enterprise as it operated under the centralised model. Redesign of structures and mechanisms altered, although not consciously, the nature of core–periphery relations at the base and between top and base. At the base the brigade council operated as the main core, though sometimes the party members assumed a special function in relation to incidents. In top–base relations the structure of the self-managing brigade reduced the significance of the *aktiv* in its traditional form and required recognition of the key position of the brigade leader in top–base relations. Occasionally, the conscious creation of a core can be recognised as a design issue, although it will normally derive from what are seen as operational needs. Thus at Metals the trade union *aktiv* was developed by the trade union chairman as an essential agent in the process of restructuring.

Finally, it has been argued that the relations of workers to the means of production should be seen as a cause of the symptoms of alienation which have become apparent in Bulgaria and that the remedy for this should come from a redesign of ownership and property relations. Ownership is, of course, related to power and in this context particularly to economic power. Implicit in the conception of the transfer of property and the provisions of Decree 56 was a significant shift in the exercise of economic power. However, in relation to the transfer of power to firms, as provided in Decree 56, it has been argued that: 'there is a need for mechanisms of control from below and for the executives being accountable to the elected bodies' (Petkov 1989: 52) to overcome alienation at the point of production. It has been further argued that the concentration of ownership and power in the state 'produces political alienation from government and from public affairs' (Petkov 1989: 51).

12 Alternative models of enterprise management – a historical and comparative analysis

The general aim of this chapter is to analyse on a historical and comparative basis the process by which alternatives have been created to the centralised model of enterprise management developed in the Soviet Union in the 1930s and transferred to other countries after the war. (As in Chapter 2, the unit of analysis is the enterprise, its internal structures and some of its mechanisms.) The assumption is that since the Soviet model was transferred to other socialist countries as well as Bulgaria, the evidence on the development of the Bulgarian alternative presented in the preceding chapters needs to be compared with developments in some other countries and in the Soviet Union in order to show the significance of the similarities and differences in the various models. The previous chapters on Bulgaria have shown how attempts were made to increase enterprise autonomy and to redesign the structures and mechanisms of management and labour relations from the late 1970s. The process of decentralisation which was attempted was intended to establish a self-management model. In comparing the processes in different countries it is argued that there are two basic alternatives to the centralised model: a managerial model and a labour-managed model. In both models there is some increase in enterprise economic autonomy, so that there is a shift in the pressures which provide the external source of its dynamics from those of the central planners towards some pressures from the market. Internally the essential difference between the two models is in the basis of power and authority in the enterprise. Thus, as explained in Chapter 3, the model established in Bulgaria from 1982 to 1988 was a labour-managed model whereas the model introduced in 1989 was a managerial model. In practice, neither is a pure model, but in the labour-managed model there is a clear concept of accountability to the general assembly at the base as well as upwards to the higher bodies whereas in the managerial model power is explicitly conferred on management and the role of the general assembly is primarily consultative or advisory. The two models imply different models of the labour process and labour relations. It is an aim of this chapter to show the processes by which such alternative models came to be designed since 1950.

The design of alternative models derives from the process of strategy formulation at the national level. In this chapter strategy formulation is discussed from two standpoints. The first is the dynamics of the political process which leads to strategy formulation. As explained in Chapter 3, strategy formulation in Bulgaria from 1978 to 1988 was developed at the political level by groups of specialists and endorsed by the political leadership without pressure from below. However, at particular periods in some other countries, for example, Poland, the process of strategy formulation at the political level has been influenced by pressure from the base, so that the dynamics of the process are different from the one which is essentially from the top down. This approach to the process of strategy formulation leads to some consideration of the relationship between changes in economic and labour relations and changes in the political structures. The second aspect from which strategy formulation is discussed is whether it follows the synoptic or incremental models. As explained in Chapter 3, strategy formulation frequently proceeds incrementally but occasionally a synoptic model is followed. Thus in Chapter 3 it was shown that the redesign of labour relations in Bulgaria in the period from 1981 followed the synoptic model in two respects: first, that design was derived from a primary concept – the labour collective as *stopanin*; and, second, that the redesign of labour relations was closely and consciously interwoven with economic reform. In this chapter, one aim is to consider whether the model of strategy formulation for the redesign of the enterprise and its external relations has tended towards the synoptic or the incremental model. This means considering the relationship between changes in economic organisation and changes in the enterprise structures and mechanisms governing labour relations. In relation to the latter it is hypothesized that:

1 Changes in economic structures and mechanisms necessarily lead to some changes in the structures and mechanisms of labour relations.
2 Changes in the structures and mechanisms of labour relations alone can only have limited effects.
3 The most significant changes in labour relations occur when there is conscious redesign of the structures and mechanisms of labour relations and of the structures and mechanisms of economic organisation. This means that the integration of labour relations and economic strategy proceeds synoptically rather than incrementally.

In terms of organisational design a central concern is the relationship between the base of the enterprise, where labour relations predominate, and the top, where labour relations and management are intermingled. This requires discussion, first, of the levels within the enterprise at which redesign takes place, that is at the top, the middle or the base; and, second, of the extent to which redesign affects the first and second vertical structures, that is, the operational structure and the social–political structure.

The presentation of the empirical material follows a mainly historical sequence. It starts with Yugoslavia as the prototype from the 1950s, and then discusses the emergence of other alternatives to the Soviet model in the 1950s and 1960s. Hungary, where radical economic restructuring began in 1968 is then considered. This is followed by a brief summary of developments in Poland since the Solidarity crisis, of the changes in the Soviet Union mainly since 1983 and in Czechoslovakia. Although Yugoslavia and Hungary are given more attention this does not mean that this chapter seeks to deal with the totality of the different models in these countries. Nor does it mean that the processes, especially in the Soviet Union, or in Poland and Czechoslovakia, are considered less important – this is simply the result of constraints on the time available to conduct research.

YUGOSLAVIA

Yugoslavia was the first country to adopt the concept of self-management, to undertake the consequent redesign of the socialist enterprise and so to provide the prototype of an alternative to the Soviet model. The process of organisational development has continued for forty years, so that the design sequence and its consequences can be considered in a broader perspective than in those countries where adoption of the concept of self-management has occurred more recently. In Yugoslavia three stages are of special significance in terms of strategy formulation at the political level with consequences for enterprise design: the late 1940s and early 1950s; the mid 1960s; and the early 1970s. Outside these periods decisions at the political level are not of primary importance. However, there is evidence of autonomous design of structures and mechanisms in specific enterprises and sectors which in some cases become prototypes for decisions at the political level.

In the immediate post-war period Yugoslavia set out to follow the Soviet model of industrialisation based on centralised planning. In the process of industrialisation the Soviet labour-relations structures of shock brigades and frontrankers with the mechanisms of socialist emulation were transferred to Yugoslavia. The break with the Soviet Union in 1949 and the atmosphere of political crisis opened the way for consideration of alternative models of socialist development in the leadership group. Djilas

(1972: 157–8) describes how in 1950 his rereading of Marx prompted by the crises led him to the concept of the free association of producers and from this to the concept of self-management. He then discussed this with Kardelj and Kidrič. Djilas had identified the concept; Kardelj linked the concept to the structure of workers' councils established as advisory bodies on an experimental basis in some enterprises in 1949. Kardelj and Djilas then presented the proposal to Tito, using political criteria:

> The most important part of our case was that this would be the beginnings of democracy, something that socialism had not yet achieved; further it could be plainly seen by the whole world and the international workers' movement as a radical departure from Stalinism. Tito paced up and down, as though completely wrapped in his own thoughts. Suddenly he stopped and exclaimed 'Factories belonging to the workers – something that has never yet been achieved!'
>
> (Djilas 1972: 158)

The Basic Law on the Management of Enterprise by Labour Collectives was passed in 1950. It made the enterprise a three-structure model – the third structure comprising the workers' council at the top of the enterprise, elected by and generally, though not legally, accountable to the general assembly of the labour collective at the base. The workers' council became the body responsible for policy decisions, and in theory the function of the managerial/operational structure was to carry out the policy decisions of the workers' council. However, the director, although elected by the workers' council, remained legally the representative of the state in the enterprise, and he retained control over individual labour-relations questions, which thus remained within the operational structure. The 1950 Act provided for a board of management as a permanent executive organ of the workers' council and elected by it (three-quarters of its members had to be engaged in production, although the director was an ex officio member). Although the workers' council had the power to approve plans and other policy questions at this stage, there is no evidence of the creation or redesign of internal structures or mechanisms. More importantly, during the 1950s the external structures and mechanisms of central planning continued to operate to a significant extent. The enterprise had some say in product mix, but investment and prices were controlled by external bodies. Consequently, the economic autonomy of the enterprise was restricted and therefore the scope of the decisions to be made by the workers' council. Thus at this stage a third structure had been created but with only minor changes in internal and external mechanisms.

The concept of self-management is often seen as salient in Yugoslav theory, but in the ideological debate with the Soviet Union the Yugoslavs criticised the Soviet model of bureaucratic centralisation and advocated and argued for an alternative, based on the classical theory of 'the withering away of the state'. This had important consequences for the elaboration of self-management in theory and practice. At the heart of Soviet theory was the state ownership of property and the development of production relations were seen as decisive in shaping social relations in employment. However, in Yugoslavia the passing of the Law on Management was accompanied by Tito's declaration that 'state ownership of the means of production . . . will become transformed into a high form of socialist ownership. State ownership is the lowest form of social ownership and not the highest' (Boskovic and Dasic 1980: 77). Legally, therefore, the enterprise was given the status of 'social property' and was no longer state property. (The complete transfer of the management of fixed assets to the labour collective took place early in 1954.) Another early departure from the Soviet model was the creation in 1952–3 of an external link for the internal third structure through the chambers of producers as territorial organs (district organisations) of producers and collective representatives of enterprises.

The key features of strategy formulation in Yugoslavia in the first stage were the political crisis, the adoption of self-management and social property according to political rather than economic criteria and concepts drawn from classical Marxist theory in contrast to those of Soviet Marxism–Leninism of the 1920s and 1930s. Strategy formulation was, as explained above, created entirely within the close circle of the top leadership without pressure from below. At the same time, although the main emphasis was on industrial self-management, there was recognition of the need to reduce the power of the state and in this way provide an embryonic basis for a model of societal development. In the second main stage of strategy formulation, from the late 1950s till 1965, increased economic autonomy for enterprise was the central political and economic issue. During the first period the centrally imposed plan had been the dominant mechanism; the issue now became how far this should be replaced by the mechanism of market pressure. In contrast to the first stage of strategy formulation, there was now pressure from below from collectives and enterprises. In the political arena the trade unions under the leadership of Vukmanovic-Tempo became for the first time a significant force in strategy formulation at the national level, articulating pressures for the rights of enterprises to determine their own patterns of income distribution. The terms of the debate were partly about the criteria for distribution: should it be according to the traditional criteria of work done or according to the criteria of the overall results of work done? The outcome of the debate was a major change in the powers of the external state structures in relation to those of the enterprise, which now achieved substantial economic autonomy. The principal mechanism now became that of income distribution by the enterprise determined by the workers' council.

The development of the economic mechanism of income distribution led to the issue of the relationship of internal structures within the enterprise to the self-management structure at the top. In their study based on research in 1959 the International Labour Office (ILO) found that there were departmental councils in some enterprises, that is, at the intermediate level. These were often advisory and the ILO noted that:

> it is generally held that councils at the department level are unlikely to develop satisfactorily as long as they have no economic responsibilities of their own. Attempts are therefore being made . . . to decentralise financial and accounting procedures so that councils at department level can be given actual powers of management.
>
> (ILO 1962: 81)

Thus an aim of the process of enterprise redesign was to take self-management to a lower level of the enterprise, but this required a change in the internal economic mechanisms. The ILO case study on the TOZ pencil factory in Zagreb (Pasić *et al.* 1982: 115) illustrates the relatively close relationship between the structure of internal self-management and income distribution: 'As early as 1958 self-managing economic units were formed within the organisation and by 1961 income was computed and distributed at the level of these units.' The two textile plants studied by Adizes in 1966 show the operation of self-management at the level of the economic unit (department). At one plant the assemblies of the units had to approve the annual plans for their unit and this involved them in a bargaining process with the planners: 'The Units try to suggest higher cost norms while the planner tries to reduce them' (Adizes 1971: 135). They also had a say in transfer prices. The outcome was of course the annual plan (not strictly an agreement). At the other plant the assemblies 'did not have the right to make their own plans but could only comment on plans prepared for them by the administrators' (Adizes 1971: 140–1). These cases point to the interrelationship of structures and mechanisms and to the logic of design development. The economic unit as a self managing unit, rather than as a purely operational unit, required the mechanisms of income distribution; equally, the mechanism of income distribution generated pressures for the constitution of economic units as units of self-management. However, Drulović quotes official statistics of 1970 showing that of 8,114 enterprises 'in only 1, 458 had certain rights of the enterprise been transferred to parts of the enterprise and smaller units' (Drulović 1978: 64). This suggests that while changes in economic mechanisms could create pressure for structural changes in some enterprises which could occur autonomously, in the majority of enterprises in the absence of a specific normative regulation, economic and institutional constraints would prevent the economic units becoming a self-management unit as well as an operational unit. This indicates the limits of economic pressure separated from strategy formulation at the political level.

The main structures and mechanisms of the 1960s model of self-management, centred on the workers' council elected by the collective as the only internal body for policy making, were all designed and imposed externally. Adizes' case studies of plants at this time provide some evidence on how organic structures and mechanisms developed in plants. At the top of the plant the principal organic structures were the political *activ* and the collegium. These were non-elected bodies and were 'not mentioned in the federal laws or company by-laws' (Adizes 1971: 47). The political *activ* was an integrating institution bringing together the three structures: director and departmental heads from the operational structure; the president of the workers' councils from the different levels of the plant (the self-managing structure); and the secretaries of the party and trade union committees (the socio-political organisations). The collegium was a meeting of heads of departments presided over by the director. The function of both bodies was to consider alternatives and issues to be put to the workers' council. Adizes concludes that:

> these groups are convened by the administrators and invariably exist in every company with almost the same membership composition. Their existence and operation seem to be directed by organisational necessities; a central, unifying group is needed as a centripetal force when the organisation's authority and power are highly segmented – 'and when there is extensive decentralisation'.
>
> (Adizes 1971: 47)

Adizes' evidence also suggests how the structures of self-management tend to create organic mechanisms for the mobilisation and resolution of issues. Thus he shows that, for example, on the issue of plant modernisation (new machines) it was necessary to secure consensus in the various sections of the collective and in management by establishing a 'ripple effect' – spreading the idea through various groups. 'We discussed the matter until they were convinced . . . '; 'discussion always continued in each group until a unanimous vote developed' (Adizes 1971: 97) and consensus was achieved. The general conclusion was that such issues were not contested in the workers' council because they were only put to it when such consensus had been established.

The dynamics of the 1960s model of the enterprise combined increased external pressure from market forces with a tendency to decentralise management within the enterprise. This led to pressure to enhance the powers of management and professionals in decision making. As a result, in 1968 the management board was replaced by a business board of managerial specialists. The period of economic and political crisis at the end of the 1960s triggered a new stage of strategy formulation. In part, the process of strategy formulation was the result of pressure from the base to the political level for the reduction of market pressures and their replacement by greater political control. The various pressures were translated into structuring through the Constitutional Amendment of 1971, the Constitution of 1974 and the Associated Labour Act of 1976. The political issue of the relationship between the federation and the republics accompanied the process of enterprise redesign and was linked to the issue of restoring the status of planning mechanisms in a self-management framework. The concept of associated labour was adopted as the primary concept in the process of strategy formulation and this facilitated a synoptic model of strategy formulation rather than the incremental model which had been followed in the 1950s and the 1960s. The redesign of enterprise structure (since 1963 legally the term enterprise had been replaced by 'work organisation') centred on the creation of the Basic Organisation of Associated Labour in the 1974 Constitution. According to Rusinow (1977: 328–9) the:

> new Statute in effect destroyed the enterprise as it had existed since 1950 completing the gradual evolution of 'work units', created in the late 1950s and since 1971 called BOALs, with the central legal entity of the economics system. The enterprise remained as the form in which a contractually integrated cluster of BOALs would normally appear on the market or be represented in other external relations, but only on the basis of powers delegated by the otherwise independent BOALs. Most important of all, net income from economic activities was now BOAL income, its distribution with few restrictions under each BOAL's control; the enterprise had no income of its own.

The design criteria for the BOAL were interdependent work, independent calculation of income and the ability to manage the unit and its income. The establishment of the BOAL meant that in productive industry the department now became the basic unit, with the relationships between BOALs and the enterprise governed by agreements which included transfer prices. In the process of strategy formulation at the political level an explicit goal was to reverse the trend towards increased technocratic power associated with the market economy. In addition to the creation of the BOAL, there was a general strategy of replacing the mechanisms of representation by the mechanisms of delegation (in the political system as well as with enterprises). There was also conscious redesign of the management structure – now placed in their own structure (termed a work community) – and the development of the concept that specialists should provide a service function for the workers' organisations.

Although redesign began at the top of the enterprise with the workers' council and extended as far as the department, Horvat, as a theorist of self-management, is clear that in theory the labour-managed enterprise should be designed from the base upwards: the first organisational principle is that:

> the basic organisational unit is not the enterprise but the work group (or work unit) . . . Whenever the decisions of a work unit affect substantially the interest of other work units, the right to decision making ought to be delegated to the next higher level. This is the justification of establishing a working council as the second level decision making body.
>
> (Horvat 1982b: 240–1)

This is clearly design from the base upwards and conceives the enterprise as a federation with relations governed by the mechanisms of agreements. However, Horvat criticises the establishment of the BOAL (the department) as the basic unit as a 'poorly designed institutional reform that established the so-called basic organisation of associated labour' (Horvat 1982b: 258) because it leads to fragmentation and conflicts. Equally, Horvat takes the view that work teams should have strictly limited functions and quoted the conclusion of Rus on the basis of Slovenian research that teams:

> should be limited to those functions only which could not be performed by any other body in the work organisation . . . autonomous work groups should not decide about hiring or firing and also not about promotion and education of these members. In this way autonomous work groups will be unifunctional and partial, and not multifunctional and total.
>
> (Horvat 1982b: 586–7)

In essence, therefore, Horvat criticises the conflict arising from making the department the basic unit of self-management but rejects brigades as the basic unit.

Alternatives to the Soviet model of the enterprise in other European socialist countries

The existence of the Yugoslav model as the only prototype of an alternative to the Soviet model influenced the challenges which emerged in the 1950s and 1960s in other countries. The first challenges occurred in 1956 in Hungary and Poland. In the Hungarian uprising factory councils were established (it is suggested that the Yugoslav model had some influence on this) and radical changes were made in the position of the trade union. In Hungary these changes did not outlive the crisis, but in Poland in response to the Posznan riots the concept of self-management was officially recognised and with it the creation of a council at the top of the enterprise which survived as a structure although with changes in its position over the years. Workers' councils were created spontaneously (organically) in some Polish factories in the summer of 1956, and in November 1956 the law provided for their establishment in all factories. These councils were created without redesign of the other internal structures of the enterprise and without changes in the external mechanisms of central planning, although a small factory fund for distribution by the council was established. As Kolaja (1960: 8) noted, in contrast to Yugoslavia there was no attempt to redefine the property status of the enterprise. However, the issue of the relationship of the council to other bodies soon emerged and in May 1957 the council was placed under the trade union. The conception of the 1956 law was one of co-management by the director and the council. However, this situation did not survive for long. In December 1958 it was decided that co-management was to be exercised by the Conference of Self-management composed of representatives of the council, and the plant party and trade union organisations plus the director, thus weakening the direct influence from workers at the base.

In the 1960s reform of economic mechanisms emerged as a strategic issue in the Soviet Union and other countries. In the Soviet Union attention was concentrated on the planning mechanisms and on the redesign of structures above the enterprise, especially the association and the trust, which was conceived as the main unit of planning. The internal structure of the enterprise remained unchanged. However, in the debate about new approaches the idea of the mechanism of elections of managers was floated and a few experiments were made (Kapeliush 1979). In 1965 Volkov wrote a book on self-management both within enterprises and in the wider society. He saw industrial self-management as developing in two stages. In the transitional stage, management would be constituted as a special apparatus under the control of the workers, while the social aspects would be carried out by the workers themselves. Under full self-management:

the workers, the immediate producers of material and cultural wealth will not simply control, through various forms, the managerial apparatus determined by them and will not simply participate in the performing of its functions but will entirely take upon themselves the management.

(Volkov 1965: 158)

Such an optimistic projection is an indicator of the kind of thinking that the Khrushchev period could facilitate; shortly after publication the book was withdrawn from circulation.

However, it was in Czechoslovakia that the concept of self-management emerged most strongly. The redesign of economic mechanisms to improve economic performance had been at the centre of the political agenda since 1962–3, and this was accompanied by the emergence of debates about the place of market mechanisms and even of the role of trade unions and of participatory mechanisms. In 1965 the Labour Code removed important restrictions on the movement of labour and in the same year the strategy of devolving responsibility from ministries to trusts and associations was adopted. (This strategy was similar to that of the Soviet Union, Bulgaria and other countries.) In terms of the hierarchy of power in state economic organisation, this was, in general, a strategy of strengthening the power of the middle at the expense of both the top (the ministry) and the base (the enterprise). However, in Czechoslovakia the Principles of Enterprise Management of January 1967, which were aimed at shifting from the administrative command system of planning to one with a stronger economic base, focused more strongly on the enterprise as the basic economic unit. Following the party's change in leadership, the action programme of April 1968 placed special emphasis on ensuring the independence of enterprises from state bodies. The greater economic independence of enterprises was recognised as requiring a redesign of enterprise structure:

> The economic reforms will increasingly place the working communities of socialist enterprises in the position of bearing the direct consequence of good or bad management. The Party therefore considers it as essential that those who bear the consequences should exert an influence. There is a need for democratic bodies in the enterprise with well defined powers in relation to management. The directors and top executives should be responsible to those bodies for overall performance and be appointed by them.

(Vitak 1971: 280)

In the debates accompanying the action programme a series of theoretical and strategic issues emerged. Thus the issue of enterprises as self-governing units led to the issue of whether, as in Yugoslavia, there should be a change in the ownership status of enterprises. Sik commented that: 'the working people, who were supposed by law to be the co-owners of socialist property, in fact lost this sense of ownership' (Vitak 1971: 274). But although the Yugoslav model was very much in the minds of those involved in strategy formulation, the Yugoslav approach to property was rejected: 'The reform could encourage elements of group ownership . . . but the economy should not be split into separate units of enterprise ownership' (Vitak 1971: 281). The issue of a democratic or managerial model of enterprise management was intensively debated, especially in relation to the composition of the workers' council and its powers. The issue of composition was about the relative proportions of workers' representatives, management representatives and representatives of external state bodies or banks. The basic structure envisaged in the provisional guidelines on the Democratisation of Enterprise Management of June 1968, was that of a workers' council with the majority of its members elected by the collective with provision for outside representatives, a director appointed by the council and a management board, with members nominated by the director but not normally members of the workers' council. The trade union structure remained unchanged and the mechanism of the collective agreement signed by the director and the trade union was to continue. The party organisation, according to one participant in the process of strategy formulation, was conceived as being 'in the background'.

Overall, the process of strategy formulation, halted by the Soviet invasion, was one in which economic reform was primary. However, economic reform was recognised as requiring redesign of management structures at the top of the enterprise and the issue of the place of the second structure was beginning to emerge. But within the enterprise the operational structure remained untouched, so that labour relations at the base were not redesigned. Essentially, the internal structure of the Czechoslovak enterprise was one derived from the prototype established by the Bata company in the period between the two world wars. Its main features were internal divisionalisation and a Tayloristic approach to the organisation of work.

HUNGARY

The new Economic Mechanism of 1968, universally acknowledged as a turning point in the development of socialist economic organisation, was the product of a process of strategy formulation which had begun in 1964. The essence of the reform was to combine central control of the socialist economy with the introduction of self-regulating market mechanisms. Although the concept of 'enterprise autonomy' was central to the reform, this has to be set in the context of the centralisation of organisational structures that preceded the reform:

In the middle of the 1960s . . . a great wave of centralisation took place in Hungarian Industry. Large enterprises were formed by fusing several formerly independent enterprises, and so-called trusts were set up amalgamating, in many cases, whole industrial branches into a single horizontally integrated trust – almost into a single enterprise.

(Szakolczai and Meszaros 1988: 23)

Thus 'enterprise autonomy' meant autonomy for these corporations and not for individual plants. In terms of mechanisms it meant the abolition of annual plan targets centrally imposed on enterprises, and greater scope for contractual (rather than allocational) mechanisms in securing supplies and in the distribution of the products. The main mechanisms of central control were the fiscal ones of credit and taxation, and regulation of the wage fund (the tariff wage scales and average wages per head also remained under central control). The internal structure of the enterprise remained unchanged, and the principal new internal enterprise mechanism was related to the distribution of profits: a proportion of profits could be distributed (differentially) to managers, staff and workers. The theory was that this would create incentives for greater economic efficiency and a basis for identity of interests between top and base. As presented by Kadar in his speech to the Central Committee in November 1967, the concept of the reform was, in organisational terms, essentially managerialist:

The nature of economic management is such that aside from the two to three hundred thousand executives, the working millions will not be able to exercise a direct influence on it . . . the workers working at the machines, the peasants working in the fields, or the mass of professional and office workers engaged in simpler jobs, because of their very positions, cannot be involved operationally in the actual realisation of the reform, in its implementation and in the arrangements. That depends on these two to three hundred thousand executives.

(Kadar 1984: 254)

In fact, 'the main beneficiaries were the managers or rather the enterprise directors – a rather narrow group after all, since there were fewer than 1000 enterprises in the whole of the manufacturing and mining sectors' (Szakolczai and Meszaros 1988: 24). The power of directors increased vertically in relation to the ministries (through the relaxation of some controls), horizontally (through the end of supply allocation and the greater freedom to buy, sell and contract) and internally (through the relaxation of some central restrictions). The reform was, therefore, imposed on established plant structures and mechanisms which at this time conformed to the general model of those in centrally planned socialist economies, that is to say, a three-level hierarchical operational structure – factory, shop and work group operating on the principle of one-man management and with the parallel structures of party, trade union and Komsomol. At the level of theory, however, there was some recognition that the new economic model had implications for labour relations and that some reassessment of the assumptions of the centralised model of labour relations was required. As Hethy (forthcoming) points out, this assumed that the:

State ownership of the means of production, the rule of the party representing the 'working class' were suppose to lead to one prevailing common social interest, accepted and followed by all individuals, social groups and organisations – and therefore no conflict of interests existed among people.

By 1969, a Hungarian party document drawn up with the central committee of trade unions, recognised the divergence of interests and suggested that participation, in which the trade union should have an important place, was a mechanism for resolving conflicts (Hethy forthcoming). In 1970 the 10th Party Congress recognised that objective conflicts of interest could emerge in a socialist society, for example, over wages and prices (previously conflicts were regarded as subjective). In the process of strategy formulation at the national level in the period 1966–8, there was conscious consideration of the role of the trade unions. In the Labour Code of 1967, the trade unions were given the right of consent (strengthened in 1973) in wages, remuneration and social benefits. But this did not extend to operational matters. At this stage there were no new structures or mechanisms for drawing workers into management apart from the production conference and the collective agreement, the traditional ones of the centralised model.

The changes in economic structures and mechanisms were designed to generate pressures on enterprises and to create new patterns of behaviour by enterprise top management and also at the base. The logic of such pressures was to foster the development of individual, group and managerial mechanisms. In turn these generated pressures for some redesign of structure (the trade union) and of the imposed mechanisms. At the base there was some differentiation between the responses of core workers (the more skilled) and peripheral workers (less skilled). The former could press for money; the latter could not bargain, but could leave the enterprise more easily as individuals, because the Labour Code permitted the movement of labour (a labour market), and this led to pressure which the trade union and party organisations took up as 'the policy of grievances'. The 'policy of grievances' was mobilised externally in the political arena and led the party to recentralise some economic mechanisms in 1969, and further recentralisation in 1972.

Two well-known case studies illustrated the pressures generated by the new economic mechanism. Haraszti's 'Piece-rates' (Haraszti 1977) based on his experience as a worker at the Red Star tractor factory, showed the intensification of work deriving from external economic pressures, and the salience of the operational structure – the operational mechanisms worked in a downward direction and evoked little collective response; the trade union organisation at the top was separated from the worker at the base. Hethy and Mako's study of the Raba carriage works (Hethy and Mako 1989; 1970–71: 541–53) showed the consequences of a managerial decision to change the mechanism of wage distribution and to decentralise it in one shop. Managerial intentions were frustrated by the organic structure of the collective of skilled workers, who were able to alter the direction in which the mechanism was designed to operate. Hethy and Mako pointed to the discrepancy between the recognised model and the reality in the plant. The recognised model assumed two structures of interests and power: the management, concerned to safeguard the interests of the enterprise and its own power; and the trade union at the top of the enterprise, concerned to represent the interests of all employees. Hethy and Mako argued that in reality there were multiple centres of interests and hence of power, mainly based on the operational units of workers at the base. It appears that external mobilisation – 'the policy of grievances' – was easier for the trade unions than the resolution of conflicts of interests within the plant (Soos 1987: 434–51). Analysis of experience in the period after 1968, and social science research was to lead to recognition of the need to strengthen the role of the trade unions in the enterprise and its links between top and base.

From the standpoint of economic organisation and mechanisms, this period appears as one of relatively little change; on the other hand, it is characterised by incremental changes in the structure and mechanisms of direct and representative democracy. Managerial autonomy in the design of work organisation and payment systems meant that direct (job-centred) democracy depended on top managerial initiatives in particular enterprises – such as Rada, Taurus, and the Budapest Chemical Works (Hethy and Mako 1977: 9–21). But the policy of enterprise autonomy precluded any attempt to develop more general models from these prototypes. At the same time, the process of technological change (often using western technology) was often accompanied by a Taylorist approach to job design. At the base of the enterprise a common feature was wage/work bargaining between work groups and management representatives, with little trade union involvement.

In contrast to direct (job-centred) democracy, development in the structures and mechanisms of representative democracy was centrally directed and centred on increasing the role of the shop steward. In 1976 they were given increased powers in relation to the work groups which they represented. Research by Hethy and Mako (Hethy 1980: 491–503) showed that as a result of this change, workers at the base with individual grievances were now more likely to use trade union channels than those of the party or management, which formally were often more effective. More recently, Hethy (forthcoming) cites a case study of a factory where only 1 per cent of the workers sought the aid of the plant trade unions in dealing with piece-rate problems. This is in line with Burawoy's account of the problems of resolving a personal grievance about non-payment for work done which probably indicates the existence of differential access to the top between the 'core' and other workers (Burawoy 1985b). In 1977, there was a change in structure designed to create a new link between base and top. The shop stewards elected as work-group representatives now participated with the trade union council (elected by the whole workforce) in a number of mechanisms for distribution at enterprise level – annual wage increases, distribution of profits, adoption of the collective agreement, the social plan, and the distribution of social and cultural funds. (In 1980 the shop stewards' body replaced the trade union council.) These changes and the changes in structures enhanced the place of the collective agreement, negotiated by the trade union, as a mechanism for the resolution of plant issues. At a theoretical level these changes can be seen as expressing the need for the representation of interests and the reconciliation of conflicts of interests.

The co-ordination of interests requires negotiation and bargaining between the two groups (Management and workers) . . . it requires continuous bargaining with workers and the reconciliation of interests.

(Mako 1978: 31)

At the political level, recognition was now given to the concept of 'the mediation of interests', primarily through the agency of the trade unions.

In 1981 a new stage of strategy formulation began with a new round of economic reforms, the introduction of new forms of work organisation and the redesign of structures at the top of the enterprise. The main changes in economic organisation and mechanisms came in 1985, but as in 1968, the changes were preceded by a lengthy process of strategy formulation in the political arena which began in 1981, and by important changes in work organisation (enterprise work partnerships – VGMKs) in 1982. Increased enterprise autonomy was recognised as necessary for improving economic performance, but in contrast to 1968, it was also recognised that autonomy required the conscious redesign of enterprise structures to extend participation. Consequently, the changes in economic mechanisms and structures were closely interwoven with changes in the structures and mechanisms of participation in 1984–5. However, the introduction of the law permitting VGMKs in 1982 – which spread rapidly, especially in heavy industry – was a contested issue in the political arena. As a temporary autonomous work organisation at the base of the operational structure of the enterprise governed by a contract negotiated with management, the VGMK was outside the control of the trade union. (The dynamics of VGMKs are analysed in the studies by Ternovszky and Neumann (Ternovszky 1989; Neumann 1989).) The trade unions responded by seeking to revive the socialist brigade movement for which they were responsible and which co-existed with VGMKs. The paradox of this is that both are secondary rather than primary units of work organisation: the VGMK because it is on a temporary contractual basis intended to overcome the problems of labour shortage and monetary incentives; and the socialist brigade, because in the manufacturing industry, brigade organisation is only weakly linked to the primary operational units, often comprising workers from more than one shop, and often focusing on activities outside work. (In mining and construction, there is a closer correspondence between brigades and operational units.) Both the VGMK and the socialist brigade are structures fostered by central regulations; the primary operational units are at the base and their structures, mechanisms and boundaries are determined solely by enterprise management. There was thus a contrast at the base of Hungarian plants between the traditional 'value-orientated' socialist brigades and the new 'interest based' collective forms of work organisation (essentially the VGMK), co-existing at the same time in many plants. ('Collectivity' in normal time working depends on local production technology and payment systems and not on normative regulation by central authorities on the brigade organisation of work (Csuhaj *et al.* 1989).)

In 1985 a major redesign of enterprise structures was put into operation. Enterprises were placed into three groups (essentially a new form of categorisation for enterprises in European socialist countries). The first group comprised enterprises regarded as of strategic importance for the national economy. In this group the structures of management remained unchanged. There was strong central control by state directives, and some supplies were allocated centrally. In the second, and most numerous group (about 60 per cent of enterprises), the enterprise had greater autonomy, bearing the main economic responsibility for its activities. There was an enterprise council at the top of this enterprise which elected the director. The third group comprised small enterprises (of between 100 and 500 employees), with a managerial structure based on the model of the co-operative with a general assembly which elected managers and directors. The theory underlying the new structures of the second group was that while the enterprise remained state property:

> the state cedes the right of administration permanently and irreversibly, to the community of workers and employees of the enterprise. Thus inducing the community to feel that their financial situation depends on their own activity.

> (Szakolczai and Meszaros 1988)

Collective management responsibility rested with the enterprise council which made the main strategic decisions relating to the plans and development of the enterprise. The council elected the director, after competition, by secret ballot for a term of five years, but his appointment was subject to ratification by the appropriate ministry. The theory was that the council decides on policy while the director was responsible for implementation of day-to-day operations. The council itself had three categories of members: half were elected as worker/employee delegates by the general assembly, while the other half were management representatives, the majority *ex officio* as heads of organisational councils and a minority as nominees of the directors. (Party and trade union representatives formally participated only as observers.) The creation of the enterprise council represented the introduction of the third structure at the top of enterprise. Its composition reflects a compromise between different interests and the enterprise model can be seen as a hybrid composed of two co-existing models – the 1970s trade union and shop steward model derived from the position of the worker as wage earner, and the 1980s model which is related theoretically to the worker as a co-owner. The relative balance between these two models and the interrelationship between enterprise council, director and trade union is an open question. Preliminary research cited by Hethy (forthcoming) on the composition of councils of thirteen industrial enterprises showed that only 21 per cent were manual workers (and of these 72 per cent were supervisors) the remainder being drawn from different managerial strata but especially from top management (49 per cent). Seventy per cent were party members, while 60 per cent had held trade union positions in the past, about 40 per cent as shop stewards. The council thus provided opportunities for participation in strategic decision making by a wider group of managers rather than by workers from the base, though the significance of this, in practice, will depend on whether there is strong pressure from the base on certain issues. The duality of this structure, that is, whether it serves the interests of management or workers, has been discussed by Mako (1987).

The predominant design criteria in the successive Hungarian models can be characterised as follows: the 1960s model was dominated by economic criteria with partial recognition of the consequences for labour relations;

changes in the mid- to late-1970s model was dominated by labour relations criteria; and the early 1980s model was designed to combine both economic and labour relations criteria. The first two models were essentially managerial. Successive redesign of the Hungarian enterprise has now produced a model which differs substantially from that which operated under the centrally planned economy and which now incorporates elements of 'the third structure', that is, a labour-managed model. However, the operational structure remains essentially unchanged, except for the special, temporary contractual unit of the VGMK. At a theoretical level, Hungary provides an example of redesign derived from 'the autonomous enterprise' as the primary concept, within which other concepts, notably representation of collective interests by the trade union and direct participation by work groups at the base, have been elaborated. 'Self-management', though used as a concept, is not recognised at the political level and the enterprise remains state property. The concept of 'labour collective' has no place in Hungarian theory.

POLAND, 1980–1988

The developments in the redesign of enterprise structures and labour relations since 1980 are a product of a crisis in which labour relations became the focus of a struggle for solutions to the economic crisis and for political power. There is no space here to discuss the details of events in Poland the aim is only to consider some aspects of developments there which relate to the general themes of this chapter. At a general level the obvious point is that in the history of socialist societies this was the most serious crisis in which labour relations were initially the main focus of action. Solidarity as a mass trade union movement from below challenged both the traditional form of the second structure and the structure at the top of the enterprise in its demands for a workers' council and for control over the appointment of directors through the mechanism of elections. The demands of Solidarity were made within the concept of self-management, and the increased autonomy of enterprises was seen as a conscious challenge to centralised planning and with it to the direct powers and detailed control of the state and party over the activities of enterprises.

In 1981 laws on state enterprises and self-management were passed, but their implementation was retarded by martial law. The key features of these laws was that there were three institutions of self-management: the general assembly of the labour collective, legally the highest body; the council of the labour collective elected by secret ballot; and the director, either elected by secret ballot or, in the case of enterprises classed as strategic by the sponsoring ministry. The council had a dual status as a forum of the labour collective and as a forum of the enterprise, and was envisaged as the manager, though not the owner, of state property, and as the employer of the workforce. The director represented the interests of the state.

The dynamic of trade union pressure from below which promoted the redesign of enterprise structures resulted in the co-existence of self-management structures with, at that period, a novel redefinition of trade union functions. The self-managing structures were conceived as representing the economic and employer interests of the collective, while the trade union represented the interests of the collective as wage-earners and in terms of protection, that is in the fields of social provision, working conditions and health and safety. The traditional trade union function of production atrophied and was assumed, in a broader economic context, by the structures of self-management. The model can, therefore, be seen as a hybrid, combining the structures of the labour-managed model with an enhanced role for the trade union in a form of collective bargaining. The division of powers within the enterprise was regulated through the mechanism of internal agreements between the different parties: between the director and the trade union, particularly on wages; between the trade union and the council; and between the trade union and the party organisation. Agreements on wages and conditions were the subject of negotiations between the state and the trade union at regional and sectoral levels (Petkov 1987: 47–9). The right to strike as a trade union mechanism was granted by the 1982 Trade Union Act.

In terms of the design of self-management structures, the most important structure that was absent was the brigade as a generic form of work organisation with the potential, as in Bulgaria from 1978, to become a self-managing structure at the base of the enterprise. Brigades in the centralised model had been part of the movement for socialist emulation and were not constituted as economic units. Although there were some attempts to introduce collective forms of work organisation, there was no strong central strategy for this and where they existed the link between them and the councils was weak (Janowska *et al.* 1989). It does not appear that there was any significant redesign of other internal levels of the operational structure such as the department. Whereas in the period from 1980 the issue of state property was essentially one of how control over it was to be exercised, since 1988–9 the importance of developing a plurality of ownership forms as an alternative to state ownership has been recognised. At present the forms that will be created are unclear but it seems likely that they will be combined with forms of participation (Wolnicki 1989).

THE SOVIET UNION

As in Bulgaria, structural redesign in the Soviet enterprise began at the base with the introduction of new-type brigades. An important prototype was the Kaluga turbine plant, where the director decided in the late 1960s to establish brigades with brigade councils and at the enterprise level a council of brigade leaders which met with the director and made decisions on the operational management of the plant. Another important prototype was the Volga automobile plant (Slider 1987: 388–405). In the late 1970s these prototypes were widely publicised and in 1979 a political decision was taken by the central committee that the brigade system should be adopted as the generic form of work organisation for the 1981–5 Five-Year Plan. At this stage brigade organisation was defined as improving the economic mechanism although it could also be linked to the concept of participation in management which was widespread in the 1970s. However, the 1977 Constitution had given recognition to the concept of the labour collective (Article 8) which meant that at some stage its position in the enterprise would require more detailed legal regulation. The draft of the Law on Labour Collectives was published in April 1983 and after widespread discussion was presented in its final form in June. Although the introduction referred to 'participation . . . in the management of enterprises' this was linked in the final version (though not in the draft) to 'genuine socialist self-management' – a concept which had hitherto been excluded from political discourse. (The concept of self-management was mentioned, and therefore legitimated, by Andropov for the first time in 1983 (Andropov 1983).) The law gave legal recognition to the brigade as a structural unit for the first time and established the base of the third structure in the form of the general assembly of all members of the enterprise. The law provided that the general assembly had to approve any changes in the plan proposed by management and the collective agreement, and had the right to put forward proposals for the improvement of work organisation through mechanisation and automation. The collectives were also given powers in relation to issues of labour discipline. In terms of strategy formulation, this was an attempt to change labour relations without changing the mechanisms of economic organisation and in this sense its effects on labour relations were limited.

In 1984 the model regulations on production brigades first issued in 1980 were updated and amended. They provided for a brigade council, and specified the rights and duties of the brigade leader and of the council of brigade leaders. The latter was established at the levels of the enterprise, production unit or department and was defined as a consultative body for the manager concerned. However, it represented a new structure within the operational structure. Integration of redesign of economic mechanisms with those of labour relations came with the Law on State Enterprises (Amalgamations) of July 1987. The economic conception was that enterprises should have greater autonomy operating on the principle of full *khozraschet* and self-financing. Profit or income, rather than plan fulfilment was to become the main indicator of enterprise performance. The labour collective was defined as master (*khozain*) of state property and the principle of self-management of the labour collective was endorsed. The main structural change was the establishment of the council of the labour collective at the top of the enterprise, that is, a third structure at the top to complement the general assembly which was already established as the third structure at the base. The design sequence was, therefore, from the base to the top, that is, brigades first, then general assembly and finally the council. The law also provided for the mechanisms of elections (of the director) and of collective agreements between the management and internal units, whether sections or departments. The prototypes of agreements between managements and departments had been developed, particularly in the Novosibirsk experiment in the period 1984–5 (Nikitin 1989). Initial research into the operation of councils (Gerchikov forthcoming) showed that there were three main categories: in the first category (80 per cent of the surveyed enterprises) the council operated as a consultative forum; in the second (5 per cent), the council made decisions which were then implemented by management; and in the third, decisions were made jointly with management.

CZECHOSLOVAKIA

As in Bulgaria and the Soviet Union the first redesign of enterprise structure began at the base with the introduction of brigades in 1982 (Cziria 1989). This collective form of work organisation involving payment to the collective rather than the individual worker, required the consent of the workers as collective payment was contrary to the Labour Code. In 1988, following the Soviet Law on Enterprises, a State Enterprise Act was passed which established the third structure with a council at the top of the enterprise elected by and accountable to the general assembly, which also elected the director. However, although some experiments in a limited number of enterprises with changes in the external economic mechanisms were initiated there was no general programme of economic reform associated with the act. Consequently, the process of redesign was one of changing labour relations at the base and between top and base within the enterprise without major changes in the economic environment.

THE CONSEQUENCES OF REDESIGN FOR THE SECOND STRUCTURE

The focus on redesign in the preceding sections of this chapter has been on the creation of the third structure. The creation of such a structure in whatever form has implications for the functions of the second structure, that is, of the trade union and the party organisations. The purpose of this section is to discuss the consequences for the second structure at enterprise level; first, of the labour-managed model; and, second, of the managerial model.

The labour-managed model

The evidence for the effects of the labour-managed model on the role of the trade union is taken partly from Yugoslavia but mainly from Bulgaria. However, to understand the changes it is necessary to recall that in the centralised model the classical conception of the trade unions was that their functions were those of production, promoted especially through socialist emulation and production conferences, protection, based on securing the implementation of the provisions of the Labour Code and other normative regulations, and on the provision of welfare and social and cultural facilities. The establishment of self-management in Yugoslavia largely displaced the production function and replaced it with the responsibility for the development and implementation of self-management in the enterprises. This was similar to the model created in Bulgaria in 1982. The primary function of the trade unions was designated as that of 'organiser of the labour collective', a function centrally concerned with the promotion and introduction of changes in structures and mechanisms. There the shift from central planning to a more decentralised model with stronger economic incentives significantly reduced the function of direct involvement in the promotion of production.

Coalescence between the second and third structures

For Bulgaria empirical research by the Georgi Dimitrov Institute revealed an unintended consequence of the operation of the third structure in relation to the other two structures. Studies showed that the redesign of enterprise structures resulted in some coalescence of self-management and trade union forums and even of self-management and trade union positions. Thus, in practice, the brigade assembly and the brigade trade union meeting often operated as a single forum, and without – in the minds of participants – a clear division between their functions. The brigade leader was sometimes elected as chairman of the brigade trade union and was often elected to represent the brigade at the general assembly of delegates, which, since his job was to represent the brigade's interest there, was not inappropriate. However, there was also evidence that the conference of trade union representatives and the general assembly of delegates often had largely similar memberships. This was generally explained by the fact that insufficient organisational activists had emerged. The trade union chairman was sometimes asked to preside over the general assembly of delegates. At the top of the enterprise the functions of the plant council and the trade union committee often became closely interwoven. It was common for them to hold joint meetings and to discuss issues together and to take joint decisions even on issues which were formally the responsibility of the council or the trade union committee alone. In the same way, it was common for a trade union chairman to be elected as a member of the plant council and for senior managers to be elected to the trade union committee.

The phenomenon of lateral coalescence between levels of what are formally separate vertical structures has occurred in the past with the consultative structure designed to encourage worker participation in management. Initially, these were independent of the trade union, although the trade union convened them. However, gradually, the structures for participation were assimilated into the trade union structure which was organisationally stronger. It can be argued that under self-management the reverse process of assimilation was taking place and that the trade union structure was gradually dissolving into the self-management structure. There was also evidence that the third structure was sometimes used to resolve routine issues such as overalls, the allocation of holidays, working conditions, grading and supplies, all of which should have been resolved within the first or second structures. Quite frequently these issues were taken out of the enterprise to the district trade union council. (Similar problems of overlapping functions and duplication between the trade union and the third structure were reported from the Soviet Union (Gerchikov forthcoming).)

The managerial model

The evidence from Hungary in the 1970s shows that the adoption of a managerial model of enterprise autonomy was recognised as requiring a redefinition of trade union functions so that the representation of the interests of workers was seen as central. This was the first time in socialist countries that representation was given primacy. In Bulgaria the adoption of a managerial model at the beginning of 1989 was soon acknowledged as requiring the recognition of the primacy of the representative function and with it the development of collective bargaining and the negotiation of collective agreements. In late 1989 it was reported that in Yugoslavia the economic crisis was seen to require a law of enterprises to replace the laws on associated labour, and thus to replace the labour-managed model with a managerial model. This was seen to require the establishment of the representative function for the trade unions.

The party

Historically, in the centralised model, it was the accountability of the enterprise party organisation for plan fulfilment that determined its function in the enterprise. However, decentralisation and increased economic autonomy does not, in itself, appear to diminish the party's role. The experience of Yugoslavia suggests that until very recently the party's role was important in two main respects: first, in relation to its control over the selection of directors; and, second, through its representation in institutions above the enterprise such as local authorities and banks which are important in investment decisions. However, the enhancement of the third structure and especially the mechanism of elections of directors and other operational managers could significantly diminish the influence of the party in the enterprise. Thus, in the view of a Hungarian specialist, it was the changes introduced in 1985, with the enterprise council and the election of directors, that really reduced the party's power in the enterprise. In Bulgaria the elections of 1986 and 1988 had a similar effect. In 1988 Krastyn Petkov had a meeting with a member of the Politburo. The latter expressed his concern about the enhancement of the power of the labour collective and asserted that the party could not contemplate sharing power in the enterprise with the labour collective.

CONCLUSIONS

Organisational design: the labour-managed and managerial models – sequence of internal redesign and choice of internal levels

Horvat's view that the labour managed model should, at least in theory, be designed from the base upwards was quoted in the section on Yugoslavia, although historically it began there at the top with the workers' council. The general point, however, is valid that the fully labour-managed enterprise requires restructuring of the internal levels of the enterprise as well as at the top. Essentially, there are two internal levels at which redesign and restructuring may take place – the level of the department and the level of the work group. The evidence presented in this chapter shows that in Yugoslavia design and the internal pressures tended to make the department the unit of distribution and democracy, while the work group was not redesigned and remained under hierarchical control. On the other hand, in Bulgaria, the Soviet Union and Czechoslovakia, redesign began at the base with the creation of the brigade organisation, which restructured the labour process at the base and altered the functioning of the operational structure. In theory, there is a choice in redesigning these structures between giving salience to the department or to the work group, and this choice is a central strategic issue in the redesign of the self-managed enterprise (Petkov and Thirkell 1988b: 28–33). The choice depends on the design criteria – especially the extent to which an attempt is made to make the internal unit, whether department or work group, a unit of *khozraschet* – and also the technological criterion. In many cases the technological and *khozraschet* criteria will tend to strengthen the importance of the department. In practice there is a range of options but the significance of redesign of structures at the base and at the middle is that it means a change in labour relations at these levels and that it affects the relations between top and base. Relations between top and base, with or without a council at the top will be different when there has been significant internal redesign affecting these levels. The attempt in Bulgaria in the mid 1980s to make the department a level of co-ordination rather than a level of hierarchy has not been followed elsewhere.

In contrast to Bulgaria, the Soviet Union and Czechoslovakia, the significance of the Hungarian and Polish models is that there was no general strategy of introducing collective forms of work organisation. In Hungary there was no significant redesign of the internal operational structure apart from the VGMKs which co-existed with the operational structure. This has so far been generally true in Poland, where the dynamic was for redesign of the second structure and at the top of the enterprise rather than in the operational structure. Consequently, the scope for a labour-managed model has been restricted. In practice neither the labour-managed nor the managerial model is a pure type, and, as the evidence presented shows, several variations are possible. Thus it is, in practice, possible to have labour management at the top of the enterprise without labour management at the base and it is also possible to have labour management at the base without labour management at the top, though the dynamics of this model may lead to pressures for further redesign.

Strategy formulation and the labour-managed and managerial models

In Chapter 3 it was explained that in the late 1980s there was a debate in Bulgaria about the sequence of societal development and the interrelationship between developments in the fields of politics, economics and labour relations. Here the main aim is to review the evidence set out in this chapter on the processes of strategy formulation and to see whether it followed the synoptic model consciously linking the redesign of economic mechanisms and structures with those of labour relations, or the incremental model. At the same time the dynamics of the process of strategy formulation at the political level is considered, especially in terms of the sequence and linkage of changes in economic organisation and labour relations and also of the relationship to political change. Such processes of strategy formulation can be analysed in terms of the origins of the sources of pressure for change. In all cases strategy is formulated at the top, that is at the political level. However, there are, in practice, differences in the dynamics deriving from the different sources of pressure. Thus, as explained in Chapter 3, strategy formulation in Bulgaria from 1978 was initiated from the top by specialists without any significant pressure from below, that is, from enterprises or workers. This contrasts with Poland, where mass pressure from workers at the base provided the dynamic for changes in labour relations and economic organisation.

Strategy formulation in Yugoslavia in 1949–50 was distinguished by the political leadership's conception of the necessity of creating an alternative to the Soviet model of socialist society in which the concentration of power and ownership in the state needed to be restructured and reduced. It, therefore, used some of Marx's and Lenin's writings to develop and legitimate self-management as a primary concept. This led to the creation of the third structure, with a workers' council at the top of the enterprise elected by the general assembly of the labour collective. However, this strategy was designed to change labour relations without, at this stage, changing significantly the centralised model of economic organisation. The model of strategy formulation was, therefore, incremental although the reduction of state power and state property was seen as providing the basis for a model of societal development, as well as for the organisation of enterprises. Historically, the importance of the Yugoslav model in the 1950s and 1960s was that its appearance constituted an alternative to the Soviet model which could be used as a reference prototype in other socialist countries where restructuring emerged as a political issue. Thus in 1956 the model which had been created from the top in Yugoslavia was used in Hungary and Poland by movements from the base seeking an alternative to the Soviet model. In Hungary the movement was, however, against the political system as a whole, while in Poland the challenge, where the concept of self-management was adopted, was against the system of economic management.

In the 1960s there were two major trends in economic restructuring. The first was the strategy of economic reform adopted in the Soviet Union, Bulgaria, Czechoslovakia and other countries. In all these countries this was the result of strategy formulation at the top without, initially, significant pressure from the base. The essential characteristic was that at the top this was conceived as essentially a change in economic mechanisms and in changes in the structures of economic organisation above the enterprise, the structures of which remained largely intact. In strategy formulation there was no recognition at the political level that economic reform should be accompanied by significant changes in labour relations (although the concept of participation in management on a consultative basis emerged during this period). The model of strategy formulation was therefore incremental. In Czechoslovakia there was significant pressure from the intelligentsia for economic reform, which was seen by some as requiring political change. The pressure from the intelligentsia was followed by extensive pressure from the base for political reform. In both the Soviet Union and Czechoslovakia the termination of economic reform precluded the possibility of any significant change in labour relations.

The second trend in the 1960s was of pressure from the base for economic reform in Yugoslavia and in Poland. In Yugoslavia in the 1960s there was pressure from enterprises and collectives against the constraints of central planning which led in 1965 to the formulation of a strategy for a significant decentralisation of the economy and a greater degree of market pressure. In Poland in 1968, as in 1956, there was significant pressure from the base for improved economic rewards and this led to a revival of enterprise redesign, with the third structure and the concept of self-management.

Significant strategy formulation and restructuring for most of the 1970s occurred only in Hungary and Yugoslavia. The significance of Hungary is that it was the only country to carry through at the end of the 1960s important changes in economic organisation, associated with the primary concept of 'enterprise autonomy'. The model was explicitly managerial and labour relations were only consciously redesigned after a time lag, during the 1970s, in part as a result of pressure from the base. In Yugoslavia in the early 1970s strategy formulation, which had hitherto been mainly incremental, moved to the synoptic model with the adoption of the concept of associated labour as the primary concept which was used to integrate both economic organisation and labour relations. This led to a major redesign of internal enterprise structures. The pressures which led to this process of strategy formulation were complex, reflecting pressures from different republics as well as from collectives.

At the end of the 1970s strategy formulation in Poland derived from mass pressure from the base in the form of the Solidarity movement, which sought self-management and this pressure was transferred from the industrial to the political sphere. In other countries through the early and mid 1980s strategy formulation was initiated from the top without significant pressure from below. As explained in Chapter 3, in the process of strategy formulation in Bulgaria during the 1980s the restructuring of labour relations was closely interwoven with changes in economic organisation and the adoption of the labour collective as *stopanin* made possible a synoptic model of strategy formulation. Reform of labour relations was seen as a way forward at a time when political change was not practicable. In the Soviet Union the model of the early 1980s was unusual in that it started with labour relations – the law on worker collectives – without any significant changes in economic organisation and mechanisms. In 1987, however, the law on state enterprises, combining changes in economic organisation and the redesign of enterprise structure, marked a shift to the synoptic model of strategy formulation. In Czechoslovakia the law on enterprises of 1988 restructured the enterprise, although it was not accompanied by radical change in economic mechanisms and organisation. Many specialists there considered that radical economic change could not be introduced without political changes and an alternative model of societal development from that favoured by the government then in power.

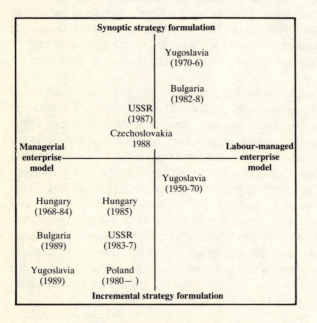

Figure 12.1 Models of strategy formulation

Figure 12.1 is designed to provide a summary of the alternatives to the centralised model in terms of the model of strategy formulation and of whether the model of the enterprise was managerial or labour-managed. It should be noted that this categorisation cannot be precise on either axis – in reality models are never pure.

The location of the entries on the managerial–labour-managed axis is intended to provide a rough approximation of the degree to which the model was managerial or labour-managed. Thus those in the middle – for example, 'Hungary 1985' – are seen as being of a mixed type. The categorisation in this table suggests that the synoptic model of strategy formulation has not so far been applied to create the decentralised managerial model.

13 Conclusions

The aim here is to draw together the main themes of the book, to offer some conclusions on the process of organisational design and the labour process and to discuss the prospects for strategy formulation.

Chapter 2 explained the development of the model of the Soviet enterprise. It was a model designed to operate according to the principles of the administrative command system, democratic centralism and central planning, and its internal structures and mechanisms were designed to comply with these principles. The primary source of pressure for its dynamics were imposed pressures from above. Its transfer to Bulgaria and other countries after the war meant that it became a type of universal model for industrial organisation in socialist societies. In retrospect it appears as a model of remarkable durability and alternatives to this model, except in Yugoslavia, were only established after a long period of time. Chapter 3 explained the process of strategy formulation in Bulgaria which sought to replace the Soviet model of enterprise organisation and to alter its internal dynamics with some designed internal pressure from below.

A general feature of socialist societies has been that the most important decisions on organisational design are taken at the national level, although initially prototypes may be developed locally and subsequently there may be space for local adaptations of the national model. It has been argued here that in a national system the critical decision in the process of strategy formulation for enterprise redesign is the choice of a primary concept which shapes the subsequent choice of structures and imposed mechanisms. At certain stages in strategy formulation there may be competing concepts, but it is essential that eventually a clear choice of primary concept should be made as otherwise contradictions will inevitably emerge. Examples of such primary concepts are: 'enterprise autonomy' (Hungary); 'associated labour' (Yugoslavia); and the 'labour collective as *stopanin*' (Bulgaria). In reality the redesign of models of existing organisations is always a process involving a number of steps – this is clearly shown by the example of

Bulgaria and in the Soviet Union since 1979. Implementation of each step requires normative regulation. Theoretically normative regulation can be of two types: either specifying the criteria in detail or offering only broad general guidelines. It is argued that the first type, used in Bulgaria, is necessary when the strategy is to redesign a standard model which has shaped patterns of behaviour over many years.

The central purpose of any process of redesign is to change the patterns of behaviour and action of the people in the organisation at different levels: the top, the middle and the base. Changes in habits occur gradually. It is argued here that such changes arise principally through the operation of mechanisms rather than from changes in structure alone. At each stage of the implementation of a process of redesign it becomes important to assess the responses of people at different levels in the organisation in terms of behaviour and action. Otherwise the timing, implementation and redesign of structures and mechanisms for the next stage cannot effectively be decided. As the experience of Bulgaria shows, the environment in different organisations is crucial to the effectiveness of restructuring and this is determined by the approach of the agencies in the organisation. In the introduction of brigade organisation operational management were generally passive rather than creative except in those organisations where key managerial personnel had recognised a need for new structures and mechanisms and used the process of national redesign as an opportunity for local action. The patterns of behaviour fostered by the mechanisms of the centralised model did not facilitate organisational innovation at enterprise level which was further constrained by the economic environment. The trade unions participated in the process as an active and generally effective agency of redesign. On the other hand several of the episodes involving the creation of mechanisms by the labour collective, described in Chapter 10, showed that trade union officials at the top of enterprises failed to take action of the kind provided for in the Labour Code. This indicates some of the problems of an organisation adapting to new functions.

Clearly each step in the process of redesign requires monitoring by the organisations responsible for strategy formulation and implementation. Monitoring has two main purposes: first, to secure information on the actual implementation of change; and, second, to detect shifts in the patterns of action, and especially in the directions in which mechanisms operate and whether they are blocked or impeded in their operation. This information is necessary to determine both the timing of the next step and its precise form. This leads to the question of the kinds of research method which are most appropriate for detecting shifts in the internal dynamics of units of structure and between units and levels. Although statistical data and data based on questionnaires administered to samples of individual respondents can provide useful indications of shifts in action, they are constrained in the indications they provide about units of structure and the qualitative changes that are manifested within them. The authors consider that the method of the extended case study based on the periodic collection of information about the emerging patterns of action in selected structural units is an essential, though not an exclusive method, for monitoring processes of change.

Organisational design – the integration of structures and mechanisms

Chapters 5 to 10 explained the pattern and sequence of organisational redesign in Bulgaria which extended from 1978, when the structure of the brigade organisation was introduced, to 1986–7 when the Labour Code and the Regulation on Economic Activity completed the process of normative regulation required to establish the model as an entity. The paradigm of organisational design is centred on the relationship of structures and mechanisms. Structures require appropriate mechanisms to make them work effectively as units of organisation, that is, to provide their internal dynamics. At the same time the design process is concerned to provide mechanisms that link levels of structure and generate the dynamics between these levels. An issue of concern is the way in which the different imposed mechanisms are linked together as components of the model, and this is partly about the sequence in which they are introduced.

In assessing the design process in Bulgaria in the period under review, it is necessary to recognise that at no time were the four mechanisms of counterplanning, distribution (the co-efficient), agreements and elections in operation simultaneously. However, attempts were made to synchronise mechanisms in order to make the design process more effective. Thus the first round of brigade elections in 1984 was designed to be related to the mechanism of counterplanning and to strengthen its operation. However, there was a combination of old mechanisms, for example counterplanning and worker proposals, and new ones such as agreements; moreover, there were some contradictions arising from the interrelationship between mechanisms. Although, as explained in Chapter 3, the model of strategy formulation was synoptic, it did not follow from this that the design sequence at the national level, which was influenced by pressures from different sources, followed an ideal design logic. In this respect strategy formulation at Metals was a better example of the logical redesign of structures and the implementation of a set of mechanisms.

The brigade as a structure was introduced in 1978 in association with the internal mechanism of the coefficient of participation and the criterion, only partially implemented, that it should operate as a unit on internal accounting. From the standpoint of organisational design it is especially important to note the integration between the structure and the mechanism of the co-efficient. Experiments with the co-efficient in the 1960s failed because an appropriate structure had not been designed. It is clear that the 'set' of brigade organisation and the co-efficient was an effective design in that it made the brigade work as a collective. Chapter 7 showed that the co-efficient could operate in different directions: sometimes to differentiate the structure of earnings within the brigade, but more often to create the solidarity of *uravnilovka* or to maintain traditional skill or effort stratification. Irrespective of the outcome, the central importance of the co-efficient was that its operation provided the main dynamic of the monthly meeting of the brigade assembly and a focus for action by the collective around which patterns of behaviour were created, modified and maintained, and which necessarily led to the creation of some internal organic mechanisms to complement that of the imposed mechanistic one. It also led to an element of internal and partially autonomous normative regulation in that the brigade could draw up its own internal rules for the operation of the co-efficient. In this sense the co-efficient was the mechanism that corresponded most nearly to the dictum that 'good mechanisms are self-regulating' (McQueeney personal communication 1987).

Establishment of the brigade as a stronger unit made possible the adaptation and redesign of the older mechanism of counterplanning to link the new structure at the base to the higher levels of the enterprise in a way which was intended to create some pressure from below. The linkage of counterplanning to the traditional mechanism of worker proposals (a secondary mechanism) to operate initially within the brigade, though often with the assistance of some specialists from the higher levels, was frequently blocked by constraints of various external kinds. However, as the evidence from some plants shows, it was possible to detect shifts in the pattern of proposals from social and welfare to more technical and economically significant ones, and thus to consolidate a differently based pattern of action.

The second external mechanism, that of agreements, introduced in the Regulation of 1982, was intended to operate vertically between brigades and the higher levels of management, and horizontally between brigades. This mechanism was designed as the next stage in the development of the internal dynamics of the enterprise and the internal action field. As a mechanism it should have operated in different directions: from base to top, from top to base and laterally. This means that by engaging the interests of both the brigade and the top management it should have generated opposing pressures from the parties which were reconciled in the terms of the agreement. However, as explained in Chapter 8, the parties generally did not see it as practicable or in their interests to seek to enforce the agreements which they had signed. Consequently, it had relatively little effect on patterns of action. In part, this was due to the constraints imposed by the shortage economy. However, as with counterplanning, the limitations of the mechanism were also related to the central controls over funds. As explained in Chapter 7, the mechanisms of distribution were subject to less redesign than any other although the organic upward pressure on funds was more significant than any pressures deriving from designed mechanisms.

At a different level of analysis the failure of agreements as a mechanism can be seen as a design failure in that no other complementary mechanism relating to the operation of the brigade as an economic unit could be designed at that stage. Consequently, there was a 'break' in the sequence of the series of mechanisms. In retrospect, therefore, the introduction of agreements should have been delayed until some complementary mechanism had been designed. In the same way agreements for the transfer of property would have required the design of associated mechanisms to have become effective.

Elections, the last mechanism to be introduced, were intended to complete the model of the brigade as a self-managing unit with internal and some measure of external autonomy. As such, the significance of elections in the design process cannot be separated from the operation of the previously established structures and mechanisms. The evidence from Chapter 9 shows that the elections could lead to significant mobilisation of resources in the action field and that elections as a mechanism led more frequently than other mechanisms to episodes as sequences of action. In the context of self-management, elections have a special significance in relation to organisational design because there is some evidence of the labour collective emerging as a subject. One of the essential attributes of management as a subject is that it has the power to create and modify organisational structures. The creation and modification of organisational structures is the essential feature of organisational strategy. It follows from this that an essential attribute of self-management must be that self-managing bodies exercise the right to change structures. The evidence shows that, although not typical, examples of such structural change could emerge from the base in the context of the elections.

Since the concept of interests is used extensively in this book, it is desirable to relate interests to the operation of mechanisms. Conceptually, the significance of mechanisms relates to the engagement of interests: a strong mechanism is one which engages interests, or has sufficient space to engage interests. The strongest mechanism is that of wage payment but this was the one which was least redesigned, so that the latent dynamic of the mechanism was unfulfilled. Subject to this qualification, it appears that the stronger mechanisms were the co-efficient and elections, though in the case of elections, the engagement was most apparent when latent conflicts became manifested. In terms of practice, the mechanism of counter-planning was stronger than the mechanism of agreements, because it could operate, although within considerable constraints. Agreements, on the other hand, could not operate generally because their potential strength to engage interests was greater than the interests that either management or the collective could sustain: disengagement was simpler and safer.

A further point, of significance for the theory of organisational design, relates to the atrophy of mechanisms when they are not maintained by external normative regulation. Thus the mechanism of counterplanning was officially terminated in 1988 but no decision was made on the secondary mechanism of worker proposals. Whether it continued to operate was not systematically investigated, but it seems to have continued to operate in some enterprises in a weaker form. In the same way the institution of frontrankers who were strongly linked to socialist emulation appears to have survived in some sectors, such as mining. On the other hand, the establishment of self-managing brigades undoubtedly displaced the traditional structure of production conferences as a mechanism at the base. However, the historical approach to the study of organisational design adopted in this book provides several examples of the way in which mechanisms which operated for a time at an earlier period were later revived in new contexts. Thus later redesign might revive worker proposals in a new form.

A distinctive feature of strategy formulation in Bulgaria was the aim of creating opportunities for people in organisations to become integrated as communities with sufficient organisational space to regulate their own relations. In Chapter 10 it was argued that the emergence of organic mechanisms indicated shifts in the direction of self-regulation. Such organic mechanisms were created especially in response to external challenges from above, often through imposed mechanisms. Organic mechanisms could, however, also be created to complement an imposed mechanism such as elections.

The labour process

From 1917, as explained in Chapter 2, socialist theory has seen state ownership of the means of production as a fundamental basis of socialist society and condemned forms of 'group' ownership. In the process of developing alternative models, as shown in Chapter 12, property has emerged as an issue at periods of major redesign as with the creation of the concept of 'social property' in Yugoslavia in the 1950s and, although alternative concepts were rejected then, in Czechoslovakia in 1968. In the mid 1970s the problem of preventing 'self-management from perverting "social property" into "group property" through appropriation of effective ownership rights by the professional cadres or even the workers who managed it' was an issue in Yugoslavia (Rusinow 1977: 328). During the 1980s the issue of ownership of property emerged again. Thus in Bulgaria Zhivkov is reported to have said that the concept of *stopanin*, explained in Chapter 3, was a solution to the problem of property. In the Soviet Union the concept of the labour collective as *khozain*, set out in the 1987 Law of Enterprises, was seen in the same way.

Although in the west the concept of the labour process is usually related to the organisation of work, it has been argued here that the ownership of economic organisations is a fundamental determinant of the labour process. Thus Braverman discussed the capitalist labour process in which there is a separation of functions because property divides society into owners and non owners. The division of labour, and the organisation of work and labour relations function within the structure of ownership. Sociologically, the ownership of the means of production is about the distribution of power and, as argued in Chapter 11, the concentration of power in the state contributes to the alienation of the worker. One of the aims of the strategies for designing the labour-managed self-managing organisation in Bulgaria and in some other socialist countries, as described in this book, has been to effect a redistribution of power within the enterprise. In this context it is worth noting that although Burawoy, as a theorist of the labour process, analyses factory regimes in different kinds of society – 'early capitalism', 'advanced capitalism', and 'state socialism' – he does not discuss the labour-managed enterprise in Yugoslavia. He does, however, refer to 'collective self-management, species of which have only been realized for fleeting moments under very unusual circumstances' (Burawoy 1985a: 19). Here it is argued that restructuring in Bulgaria to establish the labour-managed enterprise was intended to lead to a different type of labour process which could go beyond the 'politics of production'.

Prospects and pressures for strategy formulation

The processes of strategy formulation in Bulgaria analysed in this book were the product of central design, without pressure from below, imposing structures and mechanisms on enterprises through normative regulation. This process leads to conflicts (latent) and to turbulence. The result of the process is the emergence of new pressures from below which require further redesign, which in many cases cannot be imposed by central normative regulation. Consequently, the process of strategy formulation at the national level is more likely in future to follow the incremental rather than the synoptic model of organisational design. (Whether the pressures from below which led to the adoption of the synoptic model in Yugoslavia at the beginning of the 1970s can be repeated in the changed political conditions of the 1990s is an open question.) In general, the dynamics of strategy formulation change with the decentralisation arising from the establishment of the self-managed model. However, for individual organisations the scope for adopting the synoptic model remains and indeed the opportunities for its adoption are enhanced.

Strategy formulation for the redesign of industrial organisations is also related to politics at the national level and to societal development. Looking back over the past forty years it is clear that when the possibility of political change is excluded societal development can only occur through changes in economic organisation and labour relations. However, changes in economic organisation can be constrained, as in Czechoslovakia in 1968, by the lack of political change. In times of political crisis, as in Yugoslavia in 1950 and in Poland in 1980, labour relations can be linked to political change, though the pressure in the former came from the top and in the latter from the base. At the end of 1989 the rapid pace of political change in Eastern Europe attracted the greatest attention both inside these countries and in the rest of the world. It is, however, widely recognised that economic reform is a precondition for successful societal development. The necessity of such reform, usually associated with a greater emphasis on market forces, has understandably tended to divert attention from the future development of labour relations. Economic restructuring, however, inevitably has major implications for employment and labour relations. The prospects now are for both a greater plurality of forms of property and political pluralism. Such conditions which imply a greater diversity of sources of pressure from the base through different structures will tend, at the societal level, to result in the adoption of the incremental rather than the synoptic model of organisational design. However, it is the conviction of both authors that when political changes have been established together with changes in economic organisation, it is essential that labour relations should be consciously recognised in strategy formulation as an essential component of strategies for societal development.

Postscript
Redesign of the second structure

In late October 1989 the authors met in Paris to discuss the last stages of completing the text. In the course of these discussions the question emerged of the historical and practical significance of the labour-managed model of self-management as it had been developed in Bulgaria from 1982 to 1988. The principal issue was the significance of historical experience: specifically whether the experience and activity of the labour collectives in this period, associated with the establishment of the third structure and its mechanisms, could have any future influence on patterns of action. There were some unexpectedly quick answers to this question following the political events in November. A special plenary session of the Central Council of the Bulgarian Trade Unions with representatives from many labour collectives was held on 24 November to respond to the situation and to formulate trade union strategy. A delegate from one factory took the floor and demanded to know 'Why did Zhivkov take workers' self-management away from us?' This was not an isolated case as the majority of letters sent to *Trud*, the trade union newspaper, at this time were concerned with that very question. At the same time enterprises which had been concentrated in large corporations, which controlled the funds, as a result of the provisions of Decree 56 began to secede from the larger units using the third structure of the general assembly to legitimate their action. In such episodes the initiative came from the top of the enterprise but there were frequent examples of initiatives from workers themselves. Thus workers used the third structure to legitimate strike decisions and to get rid of directors or to express lack of confidence in them, especially in the spring of 1990. This emergence of organic mechanisms provided some confirmation that labour-managed self-management had established certain roots and that the concept had engaged workers at the base. The wave of strikes in enterprises in different parts of the country was, however, mainly related to issues of distribution, employment, and health and safety. These strikes were essentiallly organic mechanisms rather than the result of external mobilisation. Thus Dr K. Trenchev, President of Podkrepa estimated that 5 per cent of these strikes were organised by representatives of the established trade unions and 10 per cent by representatives of Podkrepa, while the remainder were spontaneous (interview with John Thirkell in July 1990). The political crisis thus brought issues of labour relations to the centre of the political arena.

DYNAMICS AND ORGANISATIONAL DESIGN IN POST-REVOLUTIONARY CONDITIONS

The general aim of this postscript is to analyse the dynamics of post-revolutionary conditions up to the beginning of July 1990 by examining the opportunities for the redesign of organisational structures and the processes of strategy formulation at the national level. In earlier chapters it was shown that the process of strategy formulation at the national level in Bulgaria was initiated at the top without significant organisational pressure from below. This was also broadly true, as shown in Chapter 12, of Czechoslovakia in the 1970s and 1980s and of Hungary but not, of course, of Poland where the Solidarity movement was the major agency of pressure from the base, operating as a parallel structure to that of the official trade unions. The dynamics in post-revolutionary conditions derived from political pluralism which widened the sources and centres of organisational pressure operating at the national level and provided space for the mobilisation of both political and industrial pressures from the base through strikes and demonstrations. Although the initial interest of the authors was in the significance of episodes involving the use of the third structure it immediately became clear that in these conditions the redesign of the second structure, that is, of the party and trade union structure, was now the central strategic issue for labour relations. For the established trade unions there was a duality in the situation: on one side, the prospect of the diminution or elimination of the enterprise party structure meant the creation of organisational space into which trade unions could potentially expand and develop their organisation; on the other side, the nature of pressures from the base provided opportunities for the creation of new union organisations. A key issue, therefore, was whether the established unions could be effectively redesigned as organisations appropriate for the new conditions.

After analysing the pressures and processes of strategy formulation in Bulgaria some comparisons are made with the parallel processes in Czechoslovakia and Hungary. This derives from the approach followed in Chapter 12 which postulates that the significance of what happens in one country in Eastern Europe is only fully intelligible when compared with what happens or does not happen in others. At the same time, the influence of history on the pattern and outcomes of organisational redesign, which has been a theme of the book, is also examined. It is hypothesised that the previous history and operation of established organisations has an influence on the extent to which they can survive and operate as effective agencies in new conditions, and also that the basis on which new organisations are created partly reflects the imprint of past policies. However, the actual outcomes in terms of organisational structures is also dependent on the balance of organisational forces in the political arena at specific moments and on the extent of political consensus. Both of these can shift significantly over time as the result of actions and events in conditions of political flux.

TRADE UNION STRATEGY – STRATEGY FORMULATION IN CRISIS

The aim here is to show the processes by which trade union design and redesign took place. The case of Podkrepa ('Support') is discussed first. Its organising members had been in existence as a small group before the revolution and some had been in prison. Activities began in September 1989 and were initially confined to contacts with the western mass media. After 10 November, Podkrepa was able to operate openly. Its immediate strategy was to create a membership base. Essentially its approach was to offer advice and assistance to individuals or to workplaces where labour-relations issues had emerged. However, the leadership's demands at this time were primarily political, calling for the overthrow of the Communist Party. Initially, it recruited individuals especially in the social sector, such as health and education. Its tactic was then to try to hold a meeting of the collective and to persuade them to declare for Podkrepa. Generally, this did not occur in production industries, apart from mining where affiliation was linked to the miners' strike over conditions and in some industries where particular factories joined as collectives. The emergence of Podkrepa preceded the creation of the Union of Democratic Forces as a political opposition to the Communist Party. Pressures from the new political organisations were brought from the political arena into the employment situation in some regions and sectors. Thus in Blagoevgrad, where the Union of Democratic Forces was well established, many managers were replaced as a result of external political pressure. However, this replacement of position holders was in no way comparable with what happened in Czechoslovakia (see p. 216). In March 1990 Podkrepa held its congress to establish its organisational structure as a confederation with representatives from districts and unions. Over half the delegates had higher education. At that time it claimed a membership of 100,000.

For the leadership of the established trade unions organised by the Central Council the key issue was to create the basis for survival as an organisation and a movement. This required strategy formulation to resolve a series of strategic issues related to both external and internal relationships. Thus there was the issue of the future relationship of the trade unions to the party and the state organisations with which they had hitherto been closely integrated. This emerged very rapidly at the top in the Central Council and there was a division between those who considered that independence was essential for survival and those who hoped for the continuation of the existing relationship with the party. The principle of independence was publicly declared at the end of December, together with the position that, in future, the party should no longer operate as an organisation within enterprises. However, in addition to the direct external challenge from Podkrepa, the existing trade unions faced internal pressures both from striking plants and from important sectoral unions – for example, light industry and the airline pilots which declared their autonomy from the Central Council. There was the possibility that such organisations could affiliate to Podkrepa. The strategy for resolving the issue of internal structure was to redesign and transform it from an organisation operating according to the principles of democratic centralism, with authority concentrated at the top, to one operating as a confederation with authority derived from the base. (The redistribution of control over trade union funds from the top to the base was part of this process.) The dynamics of the process of organisational redesign of the new confederation were fundamentally different from those faced by Podkrepa. For the leadership of the latter, the creation of a membership base was the first stage, but the second was to create effective organisational cadres at the intermediate level between workplaces and the leadership. For the confederation leadership a main constraint was the position of some established trade union cadres, especially at the intermediate level, who stood to lose by the restructuring. These intermediate levels were subject to pressure from the base from the strike committees set up in many enterprises, and this led to the replacement of many position holders when elections for the congress were held at the beginning of February. Thus the dynamics were those of alliance between the base and the top against the middle.

The Confederation of Independent Bulgarian Trade Unions was formally inaugurated at the extraordinary congress held on 16–17 February with delegates representing 3.5 million workers. The main tensions were between the emerging radicals supporting redesign and the established position holders opposing it. The congress confirmed the basic principles of trade union organisation elaborated by the leadership: (1) independence of political parties and management; (2) the rejection of democratic centralism as an operational principle and of the *nomenklatura* mechanism for the appointment of trade union officials; and (3) the creation of a confederal structure. The general position of the confederation in politics and society was defined as that of 'constructive opposition'.

The Confederation's strategy for the conduct of labour relations and for the organisation of the economy was developed in parallel with the redesign of its internal structure. At the special plenum on 26 December in addition to the principle of independence of party and state, the representation of the interests of workers in discussions and negotiations with the state and with employers was defined as the primary function. At the beginning of January the trade unions drew up a list of proposals for a general agreement with the government. The list included the right to work, fair labour remuneration (including an increase in the minimum wage), guaranteed social security (including the indexation of wages and pensions), safety and hygienic working conditions, and provisions for democratisation of enterprise management. The draft was published for discussion and comment by workers through the trade union organisation and was then submitted to the government in the round table discussions which continued through January and February. (The round table consisted of representatives of the government, political organisations and the trade unions.) In March these discussions were joined by representatives of employers in the state sector whose organisation had been encouraged by the confederation as necessary for the establishment of the structures of tripartism at the national level. Meanwhile, to test and mobilise support from the base, the Confederation used the mechanism of a referendum of trade union members at the end of January. The issues put to the membership were those of the market economy, the privatisation of state property and whether the Confederation should have its own platform in the political elections to be held in June. Some two million workers voted in secret ballots held at their place of employment and there were large majorities in favour of the market economy, for equality of forms of property, and for a trade union platform. The political significance of the referendum was that the Confederation, as a mass organisation, had secured support and legitimation from its base on the strategic issues of the organisation of the economy and the place of the trade unions in politics.

The political organisations and Podkrepa lacked comparable endorsement from their bases on these issues. The Confederation now had a basis of support for developing its strategy at the political level and participation in the round table discussions with the government. The Confederation's position was that economic strategy should be created on the basis of tripartite discussions between the government, trade unions and employers. The mechanism for this was a national collective agreement negotiated with the government, the trade unions and the employers' organisation which was signed on 15 March and provided for a national minimum wage increase and rises in pensions. The second mechanism for labour relations was the law on strikes and the collective settlement of disputes which set out procedures for arbitration. Preparations for this had begun in December and, following advice from the ILO on content, the Confederation exercised its constitutional right to put the legislation to the National Assembly for approval. Although this mechanism created a legal basis for strike action the operation of the procedures had the effect of reducing the number of strikes which at that time were widespread in many sectors. The top leadership of the Confederation participated in mediation in many of these disputes which were between the first and second structures.

At its congress at the end of January, which coincided with the fall of the government, the Communist Party abandoned democratic centralism and became the Socialist Party. The congress facilitated the process of separating the trade unions from the party, but party organisations in enterprises did not immediately disappear. However, in March an agreement was signed by the parties represented at the round table discussions that party organisations should no longer operate within enterprises, although members could meet outside. The relations of the Confederation with Podkrepa went through different phases. The initial phase, until the Plenum of 26 December, was one of confrontation and competition. Subsequently, there were contacts but the Confederation took the position that it could not co-operate so long as Podkrepa remained both a political and a trade union organisation. Later a number of joint working groups were established to formulate trade union strategy on a number of issues such as indexation, and proposals for a law on trade unions and revision of the Labour Code.

In preparation for the June elections the Confederation set out its platform for economic and social strategy. The initial premiss was that the way forward lay in a regulated market economy. A market economy was recognised as requiring legal equality for all forms of property – co-operative, private, state, shareholders, local authority, foreign and mixed. However, the essential trade union condition for the restructuring of the economy was that it should be accompanied by measures for social protection covering income distribution, retraining and a regional plan of labour supply. Within a protective framework the level of pay should be determined by collective agreements at national and local levels. As a mechanism the platform had some similarities with the past annual economic reviews of the British TUC, but whereas the latter were designed to influence budgetary decisions by governments the former were designed to offer members criteria for assessing the programmes of parties (and individual candidates) in the election.

CZECHOSLOVAKIA

The outstanding effect on labour relations of the political changes in Czechoslovakia in November–December 1989 was the demise of the plant party organisations and of the official trade union organisation and the replacement of many senior position holders in enterprises (and in other institutions) who held their positions as members of the *nomenklatura*. Typically, representatives of Civic Forum and the new political movements organised meetings in enterprises which called for the replacement of directors and trade officials by new people. Until the elections of 1990 the dominant feature of Czechoslovak society was the establishment of new patterns of political behaviour and the debate on future economic strategy centred on the pace of movement towards a market economy: in this period the main change in the internal structure of enterprises was the dissolution of the party organisation and the recomposition of the trade unions from the base. The latter process saw the emergence of some occupationally based unions but also the continuation of others on the traditional basis of branch structure. There were some industrial strikes, mainly triggered by threats of plant closure, for example, in the arms industry, or fears about the future of plants such as at the car plant in Bratislava. There were also a few cases of attempts to change enterprise structures. Some new directors, as in Bulgaria, sought to separate their plants from the larger units of which they were a part. It was generally true, however, that the concentration on the processes of political change in the wider society displaced issues of enterprise structure and labour relations – pressures operated in the political rather than the industrial arena – and there was less space for the development of trade unions. Although a new independent trade union centre CSKOS had been established claiming the affiliation of six million members the extent to which the government would recognise it was unclear and the structures and mechanisms of tripartism had not been established.

HUNGARY

In Hungary, change in the institutions of labour relations began with the emergence of new trade unions in 1989. This was closely associated with the strategy for the development of political pluralism initiated by the party in the autumn of 1988 through the mechanism of the draft law on associations which permitted the formation of trade unions as well as political organisations. These unions and their membership were concentrated in the government and service sectors rather than in those of production, and their declared aim was the protection of occupational interests – for example, the trade unions of teachers, scientific workers, and artists. These organisations formed the Democratic League of Independent Unions and became allied in the political sphere with the Free Democrats. In response to these and political pressures SZOT (the National Council of Hungarian Trade Unions) initiated its own programme of redesign. This was intended to establish its independence from the state and to make it more responsive to demands from the membership at the base, though it did not declare its independence of political parties until September 1989. The function of protecting workers' interests became central, and the production function, exercised through the promotion of socialist emulation, was abandoned in 1988. SZOT changed its name to MSZOSC to reflect a looser federal structure. In the middle of 1990 MSZOSC enjoyed numerical predominance (despite the independence of the chemical workers) with a membership of some 3.5 millions compared with some 60–80,000 in the trade unions affiliated to the league.

In October 1988 a National Council for the Co-ordination of Interests was set up on the initiative of the government, with representation from the state, the trade unions and employing organisations. This was seen as necessary for the adoption of new mechanisms of wage determination introduced in 1989, replacing the traditional mechanisms of state wage determination (see Chapter 7). These mechanisms were

> 'in line with the logic of a market economy, based on the functioning of the labour market on the one hand and on the bargaining and agreements among the major social partners interested in wage determination (i.e. workers, employers and the state) on the other hand.'
>
> (Hethy and Csuhaj 1990: 32)

Its competence includes decisions on minimum wages, pay determination in budget-dependent institutions, and exemptions from tax on wage increases.

In March 1989 the law on strikes was passed after lengthy debate between the trade unions and the government, while an amendment to the Labour Code established procedures for conciliation in labour disputes, though the trade union aim of securing a law on collective bargaining has not been achieved so far. Analysis of the dozen or so strikes in the period July 1988–July 1989 (Hethy and Csuhaj 1990: 70–74) concluded that the participants fell into three main groups. The first were those such as miners whose position and prospects had been undermined in the 1980s, and the second were in the education sector where wages had been restricted relative to those of less-qualified workers. The third group is of particular interest in relation to one pattern of organic mechanisms in Bulgaria: these were strikes related to the appointment or dismissal of directors and/or to promote the secession of plants from their enterprises. Action in such cases can be seen as reflecting the experience of the third structure of enterprise councils established in 1984. There were also a few cases where workers declared that the enterprise council should register as an 'association', assuming trade union functions independently of the established unions (Hethy and Csuhaj 1990: 92).

CONCLUSIONS

The influence of history

The influence of history on post-revolutionary developments in the three countries is most clearly seen in relation to the trade unions. In Czechoslovakia the political revolution and the rapid eclipse of the Communist Party from its leading place in political life was accompanied by the equally rapid eclipse of the established trade unions whose close association with the party and pattern of action excluded them from any role in the reform process. In Hungary, on the other hand, the decline of the party was not accompanied by a parallel decline in the established trade unions. The survival of SZOT can be partly explained by the nature of the incremental process of political reform initiated from within the party which allowed SZOT to formulate a new strategy parallel with the reform process within the party. However, SZOT's ability to reformulate its strategy has to be seen in the context of its operation from the late 1970s when the trade unions were officially conceptualised as 'autonomous' organisations. 'Autonomy' was not synonymous with 'independence' but the pattern of trade union activity in the pre-revolutionary period made the transition much easier to establish. In contrast, the process of political change in Czechoslovakia, which was associated with the disintegration of the established unions and the reconstruction of unions on a new basis, inevitably created problems of reconstruction which weakened their coherence in relation to the new government and as institutions for bargaining with employers.

In Bulgaria, post-revolutionary politics have been dominated by the political division between the (reformed) party and the opposition, which was not resolved by the elections in June 1990. This has inhibited the establishment of the political consensus needed for economic and societal development. In the conditions of political flux in the first half of 1990 the maintenance of the organisational cohesion of the confederation as a mass organisation and its elaboration of strategy on economic policy and labour relations, endorsed by the base, meant that it was able to establish a pivotal position among the organisations operating in the political arena. The publication of the confederation platform challenged political parties to develop their own positions on these issues. As in Hungary, the process of strategy formulation in the immediate post-revolutionary situation was of great significance for the establishment of trade union independence. But also as in Hungary, the operation of the trade unions in the 1980s was a facilitating condition for the transition. The function of the trade union as organiser of the labour collective from 1982 had given it experience of direct action in the redesign of enterprise organisation and of trade union organisation, while the adoption of interest protection through collective bargaining made necessary by the firm organisation required by Decree 56 was an intermediate step which facilitated the change of function.

The pattern of alternative trade unionism in both Bulgaria and Hungary reflects, to a considerable extent, the imprint of history. In both countries the support for alternative unions was concentrated in the non-productive sphere especially among teachers, scientific workers and employees in parts of the health service – although membership was not limited to these sectors. Underlying this pattern of action was the pre-revolutionary wage policy which gave priority to heavy manual work in productive industry rather than to the qualifications held by many workers in service sectors. The discontent of the technical intelligentsia had been identified by the Central Council of the Bulgarian Trade Unions in the mid 1980s from survey research, and in 1987 a proposal to create an occupational union for scientific workers had been approved by the Congress. However, it was not proceeded with, although a wage increase was obtained for this category. An example of the transmission of experience at a different level from within the first structure comes from the Hungarian VGMK (see Chapter 12). Although the VGMKs have now been terminated, the workers' experience of internal entrepreneurship provided training for their subsequent participation in the creation and running of small businesses (C. Mako, personal communication, December 1989).

Emerging models of labour relations

In Bulgaria, as in Hungary, the structures of collective bargaining are being established and the collective agreement is set to become a dominant mechanism of labour relations. Some decentralisation of control over wages has been introduced providing space for local negotiations.

However, in Dr Trenchev's view (interview July 1990), the main constraint on collective bargaining was the lack of employers with the power to negotiate, a situation especially true of the social sector. A further issue is the levels of collective bargaining above the enterprise. As Hethy and Csuhaj point out for Hungary (1990: 39) if there is collective bargaining at the level of the enterprise and tripartism at the level of the national economy there is a potential void at the middle level of the industry or sector.

The creation of the third structure has been a central theme of earlier chapters. In Chapter 12 it was shown that one of the unintended consequences of the creation of a strong third structure in Bulgaria was the displacement and coalescence of the second and third structures. If a strong and redesigned second union structure is established to represent the interests of workers through the mechanisms of collective bargaining, can a third structure continue to exist or will it be displaced by the second structure? One of the questions most frequently put to Krastyn Petkov by activists and workers is 'What is the future of self-management?' The answer to this question is not, at present, clear, as it depends on the significance of a number of factors, especially the structure of ownership (discussed below), the size of employing organisations and their internal structures. Brigades, which were the strategic unit of change in the previous period, still exist, but their status as 'primary collective' (see Chapter 3) was removed by Decree 56, and it is likely that the trade union structure will have primacy. However, it is possible that the trade unions may use the forums of the third structure to legitimate their positions on some issues. In Hungary, where the structures of participation have a long history, there may be scope for their maintenance in some of the new organisations.

The issue of core–periphery relations within enterprises has been discussed, particularly in Chapter 11, where it was argued that the redesign of structures to establish the labour collective had eroded the pattern of core–periphery relations between top and base which was characteristic of the centralised model. It is plausible to hypothesise that the post-revolutionary structural changes will create a new pattern of core–periphery relations. Although the empirical research to investigate this has yet to be undertaken it seems likely that management will need to create a new core for the operational structure while in the second structure the trade unions (and strike committees) will develop their own cores distinct from those of the operational structure.

In the immediate post-revolutionary period the dynamic of organisational redesign has centred on the second structure through the elimination of the party organisation in enterprises and the restructuring of the trade unions. In terms of organisational design, the concept of the market economy, widely accepted in Eastern Europe, has become associated with the concept of privatisation which has the potential to operate as a primary design concept (see Chapter 3). The dynamic of the next stage of organisational design will therefore derive from changes in the structure of ownership, that is, of the transfer from state ownership to alternative forms of ownership, whether joint stock companies, joint ventures with foreign investors, co-operatives or other forms. This will entail, in some sectors, the break-up of the large units which have been characteristic of both the productive and non-productive sectors. In Hungary, the privatisation of 70 per cent of state firms has been declared as a government aim though the rate and feasibility of change are at present unclear. In Bulgaria, a similar trend is anticipated and structural changes have already been made in the tourist industry and are expected to follow in food processing. Such changes will have varying consequences for the structures and mechanisms of labour relations, but a plurality of models is inevitable in a mixed economy.

Trade unions and societal development

A theme of earlier chapters was the dynamics of societal development and its relationship to changes in models of economic organisation and labour relations. In the early 1980s in Bulgaria, as shown in Chapter 3, the establishment of self-management from above was conceived as a means of taking society forward at a period when alternative strategies were excluded. In Poland, on the other hand, at the beginning of the 1980s, Solidarity was the driving force and the leading agency of societal development. In post-revolutionary conditions driving forces and effective agencies to exert pressure for societal development are essential. The usual agency for societal development are political parties, and in Eastern Europe as a whole the process of forming and reforming political parties and establishing coalitions is of critical importance for securing effective societal consent. When, as in Bulgaria at the time of writing, the political divisions constrain the effectiveness of parties as agencies of societal development effective pressure depends on the capacity of the trade unions to mobilise as a driving force in the political arena.

Where, on the other hand, there is an effective political structure with wide popular support the role of the trade unions at national level may be exercised more through the structures and mechanisms of tripartism or in direct discussions with the government. In Bulgaria the establishment of tripartite structures at the national level and the mechanism of the General Agreement has already established a pattern of action – the implementation of the agreement has required continuing discussion and negotiation. The structures, though not the mechanism, have also been established in Hungary, though the extent of support from the government elected in 1990 is not clear, but in Czechoslovakia the structures do not yet exist. The prospects for tripartism depend partly on the effectiveness and strength of trade union organisation at the base and partly on the organisation of employers but also on the dynamic of economic change and the response of workers to its consequences. The social costs associated with economic change may be severe and it is possible for political consensus to be eroded by industrial and social conflicts deriving from such changes. In such circumstances, effective trade union organisation is essential to negotiate consent between state and workers and by securing the maximum social protection.

The relationship of the new and restructured trade unions to the new and reformed parties may shift in response to the dynamics of political and economic change. Thus, in Bulgaria, Podkrepa's primary objectives in the immediate post-revolutionary period were explicitly political in that it sought the overthrow of the Communist Party. In July 1990 Dr Trenchev's view was that it was necessary for Podkrepa to avoid the mistake of Solidarity, which had begun as trade union but then moved directly into the political arena as a party taking direct political responsibility and then losing membership. In July 1990, however, the confederation and Podkrepa were in broad agreement on the need to exercise direct trade union pressure on the National Assembly to undertake action on the economic crisis. It seems likely that a wider range of structures and mechanisms for the relations between trade unions, governments and political parties will need to be developed. It is the view of the authors that the new models of democracy in Eastern Europe require trade unions as well as a plurality of political parties.

Bibliography

Adizes, I. (1971) *Industrial democracy: Yugoslav style*, Free Press, New York, Collier-Macmillan, London .

Andors, S. (1977) *China's industrial revolution, politics, planning and management 1949 to the present*, Martin Robertson, London.

Andropov, Yu. (1983) 'Uchenie Karla Marksa i nekotorie vopros sotsialisticheskogo stroitelstva v SSSR', *Kommunist*, no. 9.

Aroyo, Y. (1987) 'Opit ot provedeni otcheti izbori na samoupravlenie', *Sotsiologicheski Problemi*, no. 4.

Atkinson, J. (1984) *Flexibility, uncertainty and manpower management*, report no. 89, Institute of Manpower Studies, Brighton.

Bailes, K. E. (1977) 'Alexei Gastev and the Soviet controversy over Taylorism, 1918-24', *Soviet Studies*, vol. XXIX, no. 3.

Bailey, F. G. (1960) *Tribe, caste and nation*, Manchester University Press, Manchester.

—— (1969) *Strategems and spoils: a social anthropology of politics*, Basil Blackwell, Oxford.

Baum, A. T. (1987) *Komsomol participation in the Soviet first five year plan*, St Martins Press, New York.

Baykov, A. (1950) *The development of the Soviet economic system*, Cambridge University Press, Cambridge.

Bell, D. (1956) 'Three technologies: size, measurement, hierarchy', in L. E. Davis and S. C. Taylor (eds) (1972) *Design of jobs*, Penguin Books, Harmondsworth.

Bertsch, G. (1978) *Power and policy in communist systems*, John Wiley & Sons, New York.

Bettelheim, C. (1978) *Class struggles in the USSR, second period 1923–1930*, Harvester Press, Hassocks.

Boev, V., Markov, M., Minchev, M., and Karatanchev, S. (forthcoming) *Sotsialism i samoupravleneto*.

Boskovic, B. and Dasic, D. (eds) (1980) *Socialist self-management in Yugoslavia 1950–80*, Socialist Thought and Practice, Belgrade.

Botev, B. (1987) 'Empirichno izuchavane na problemite situatsii v trudoviya kolektiv; metodika, protsedura, instrumentarium', *Sotsiologicheski Problemi*, no. 1.

Braverman, H. (1974) *Labour and monopoly capital*, Free Press, New York.

Burawoy, M. (1985a) *The politics of production*, Verso, London.

—— (1985b) 'Piece rates, Hungarian style', *Socialist Review*, vol. 15, February, reprinted in Pahl, R. E. (ed.) (1988) *On Work*, Basil Blackwell, Oxford.

Butenko, G. A. (1982) 'Protivorechiya razvitiya sotsializma kak obshtestvennogo stroya', *Voprosi philosophii*, (Moscow).

—— (1987) *O novom teoreticheskom videnii sotsializma.*

Carr, E. H. and Davies, R. W. (1969) *Foundations of a planned economy 1926–29*, Macmillan, London.

Chandler, A. D. (1962) *Strategy and structure*, MIT Press, Cambridge, Massachusetts.

—— (1977) *The visible hand, the managerial revolution in American business*, Harvard University Press, Cambridge, Massachusetts.

Cocks, P. (1976) 'The policy process and bureaucratic politics', in Paul Cocks, Robert V. Daniels and Nancy Whittier Heer (eds) *The dynamics of Soviet politics*, Harvard University Press, Cambridge, Massachusetts.

Cohen, S. (1988) 'Nepovskaya al 'ternativa', *Nauka i zhizn*, vol. 10.

Comisso, E. T. (1979) *Workers' control under plan and market*, Yale University Press, New Haven and London.

Crenson, M. A. (1971) *The un-politics of air pollution*, Johns Hopkins University Press, Baltimore.

Csuhaj, I., Lado, M. and Toth, F. (1989) 'Collectivity and collective work organizations in Hungary', in L. Hethy, M. Lado and J. E. M. Thirkell (eds) *New collective forms of work organization in Eastern Europe*, Institute of Labour Research, Budapest.

Cziria, L. (1989) 'The application of new collective forms of work organisation in Czechoslovakia', in L. Hethy, M. Lado and J. E. M. Thirkell (eds) *New collective forms of work organization in Eastern Europe*, Institute of Labour Research, Budapest.

Davidov, P. (1987) *Self-management and manager*, Profizdat, Sofia.

Deutscher, I. (1950) *Soviet trade unions*, Royal Institute of International Affairs, London.

—— (1954) *The prophet armed. Trotsky 1879–1921*, Oxford University Press, London and New York.

Djilas, M. (1972) *The unperfect society*, Methuen, London.

Drzhaven vestnik (1982) 'Pravilnik na ikonomicheskiya mechanism', 2 February.

Drulovič, M. (1978) *Self-management on trial*, Spokesman, Nottingham.

Engels, F. (1962) 'Origin of the family, private property and the state', in Karl Marx and Friedrich Engels *Selected works*, Foreign Language Publishing House, Moscow.

Flanders, A. (1975) *Management and unions*, Faber & Faber, London.

Fox, A. (1971) *A sociology of work in industry*, Collier-Macmillan, London.

Galbraith, J. (1977) *Organisation design*, Addison-Wesley, London.

Galbraith, J. and Nathanson, D.A., (1978) *Strategy implementation: the role of structure and process*, West Publishing Co., St Paul, Minnesota.

Gerchikov, V. I. (forthcoming) 'Business democracy: work collective councils and trade unions', in G. Szell (ed.) *Labour relations in transition in Eastern Europe*, Walter de Gruyter & Co., Berlin and New York.

Giddens, A. (1979) *Central problems in social theory*, Macmillan, London.

Granick, D. (1954) *Management of the industrial firm in the USSR*, Columbia University Press, New York.

Gustavsen, B. (1986) 'Evolving patterns of enterprise organisation: the move towards greater flexibility', *International Labour Review*, vol. 125, no. 4, July–August.

Haraszti, M. (1977) *A worker in a workers' state*, Penguin, London.

Harris, C. C. (1980) *Fundamental concepts and the sociological enterprise*, Croom Helm, London.

Hethy, L. (1980) 'Trade unions, shop stewards and participation in Hungary', *International Labour Review*, vol. 120. no. 4.

—— (1989) *Organisational conflict and cooperation*, Akademiai Kiado, Budapest.

—— (forthcoming) 'Participation in planning in Eastern Europe', in *Reference Book on Workers' Participation*, vol. 2, International Institute for Labour Studies, Geneva.

Hethy and Csuhaj, I.V. (1990) *Labour relations in Hungary*, Institute of Labour Research, Budapest.

Hethy, L. and Mako, C. (1970–71) 'Obstacles to the introduction of efficient money incentives in a Hungarian factory', *Industrial and Labour Relations Review*, vol. 24.

—— (1974) 'Work performance, interests, powers and environment', *European Economic Review*, no. 5.

—— (1977) 'Workers' direct participation in decisions in Hungarian factories', *International Labour Review*, vol. 116, no. 1.

—— (1989) *Patterns of worker behaviour and the business enterprise*, Institute of Sociology of the Hungarian Academy of Sciences and Institute of Labour Research Hungarian State Office for Labour and Wages, Budapest.

Hethy, L., Lado, M. and Thirkell, J. E. M. (eds) (1989) *New collective forms of work organization in Eastern Europe*, Institute of Labour Research, Budapest.

Holmes, L. (1986) *Politics in the communist world*, Oxford University Press, Oxford.

Horvat, B. (1982a) 'Dvije masovne ideoloshke devijacje u suvremenom Jugoslovenskom drushtvu', *Sociologija*.

—— (1982b) *The political economy of socialism*, Martin Robertson, Oxford.

—— (1983) 'The organisational theory of workers' management', in *International Yearbook of Organisational Democracy, Vol. 1, Organisational Democracy and Political Processes*, C. Crouch and F. A. Heller (eds) John Wiley & Sons, Chichester and New York.

Ianchev, B. (1984) *Novo Vreme*, Sofia, no. 11, (in Bulgarian).

ILO (1962) *Workers' management in Yugoslavia*, International Labour Office, Geneva.

Jackson-Cox, J., McQueeney, J. and Thirkell, J. E. M. (1987) *Strategies, issues and events in industrial relations*, Routledge & Kegan Paul, London.

Janowska, Z., Kulpinska, J. and Strzeminska, H. (1989) 'New collective forms of work organization in Poland' in L. Hethy, M. Lado, and J. E. M. Thirkell, (eds) *New collective forms of work organization in Eastern Europe*, Institute of Labour Research, Budapest.

Kadar, J. (1984) *Socialism and democracy in Hungary*, Speeches, Articles, Interviews 1957–82, Corvino Kiado, Budapest.

Kapeliush, I. S. (1979) 'Public opinion on electing managers', in M. Yanowitch (ed.) *Soviet work attitudes*, Sharp, New York, and Martin Robertson, Oxford.

Kapferer, B. (1972) *Strategy and transaction in an African factory*, Manchester University Press, Manchester.

Kaplan, F. I. (1969) *Bolshevik ideology and the ethics of Soviet labour*, Peter Owen, London.

Kolaja, J. (1960) *A Polish factory*, University of Kentucky Press.

Kornai, J. (1980) *Economics of shortage*, North Holland Publishing Co., Amsterdam.

Kuromiya, H. (1984) 'Edinonachalie and the Soviet industrial manager 1928-37' *Soviet Studies*, vol. XXXVI, no. 2, April.

Kyuranov, C. (1980) 'Organizatsiyata na truda kato organizatsiyata na interesi', Sotsiologicheski problemi, no. 3.

—— (1982) *Choveshkite obshtnosti*, Nauka i izkustvo, Sofia.

Labour Code (1986) Sofia Press, Sofia (English translation, 1987).

Laky, T. (1979) 'Enterprises in bargaining position', *Acta Oeconomica*, vol. 22.

Lane, D. (1987) *Soviet labour and the ethics of communism, full employment and the labour process in the USSR*, Wheatsheaf Books.

Lawrence, P. R. and Lorsch, J. W. (1967) *Organisation and environment*, Harvard Business School, Cambridge, Massachusetts.

—— (1969) *Developing organisations: diagnosis and actions*, Addison-Wesley, Reading, Massachusetts.

—— (eds) (1970) *Organisational structure and design*, Irwin-Dorsey, Homeword, Illinois.

Lee, D. J. and Newby, H. (1983) *The problems of sociology*, Hutchinson, London.

Lenin, V. I. (1967) *On socialist economic organisation*, Progress Publishers, Moscow.

Literaturnaya gazeta (1988) 12 October.

Makarenko, A. (1986) *Sochineniya*, Moscow, vol. 7.

Mako, C. (1978) *Shopfloor democracy and the socialist enterprise* University of Turku, Turku.

—— (1987) 'Enterprise councils in Hungary: tools of management or tools of workers?' in Kosmas, Pittsburgh University Press, Pittsburgh.

—— (1989) 'The importance of creating social consensus in the labour process', paper presented at the University of Kent conference on 'The economic and social effects of restructuring in socialist societies'.

Malle, S. (1985) *The economic organisation of war communism 1918–1921*, Cambridge University Press, Cambridge.

Marinov, A. (1987) 'Teoretiko – metodologicheski orientiri Empirichnoto izledvane na problemite situatsii v trudoviya kolektiv', *Sotsiolgicheski problemi*, no. 1.

Marx, K. (1975) *Early writing*, Penguin Books, Harmondsworth.

—— (1981) *Capital*, vol. 3, Penguin Books, Harmondsworth.

Marx, K. and Engels, F. (1973) 'The civil war in France', *Selected works*, vol. 2, Progress Publishers, Moscow.

Masterman, M. (1970) 'The nature of a paradigm', in I. Latakos and A. Musgrave (eds) *Criticism and the growth of knowledge*, Cambridge University Press, Cambridge.

Mateev, E. (1987) *Struktura i upravlenie na narodnoto stopanstvo*, Nauka i izkustvo, Sofia.

Mikhailov, S. (1978) *Promishlenoto predpriyatia-sotsiologicheska sistema i trudova aktivnost*, Bulgarskata Akademiya Nauka, Sofia.

Miloshevski, A. (1963) 'Km vprosite za zasilvane na materialnata zainteresovanst v ikonomikata' *Novo vremae*, no. 2.

Mitchell, J. C. (1983) 'Cases and situation analysis', *Sociological Review*, new series, vol. 3.

Mrachkov, V. (1987) *The new labour code and the construction of the developed socialist society in the P.R.B.*, Profizdat, Sofia (in Bulgarian).

—— (1988) *Profsiosite i Samonpravlenieito*, Sofia, no. 1.

Naisbitt, J. H. and Aburdene, P. (1972) *Re-inventing the corporation*, Warner Books, New York.

Neumann, L. (1989) 'Modification of work organisation and wage bargaining in enterprise work partnerships (vgmks)' in L. Hethy, M. Lado, and J. E. M. Thirkell, (eds) *New collective forms of work organization in Eastern Europe*, Institute of Labour Research, Budapest.

Nikitin, V. A. (1989) 'The development of the brigade form of work organisation and the collective contract in the USSR' in L. Hethy, M. Lado, and J. E. M. Thirkell, (eds) *New collective forms of work organization in Eastern Europe*, Institute of Labour Research, Budapest.

Nikolayev, A. (1932) *A business accounting brigade*, Co-operative Publishing Society of Foreign Workers, Moscow (in Marx Memorial Library).

Nisbet, R. A. (1966) *The sociological tradition*, Basic Books, New York.

Nosach, V. (1976) *Borba proletarskih organizatsiya za sotsialisticheskoi trudovoi ditsiplina 1918–20*, Moscow.

Nove, A. (1977) *The soviet economic system*, George Allen & Unwin, London.

Pasić, N., Grozdanić, S. and Radević, M. (eds) (1982) *Workers' management in Yugoslavia – recent developments and trends*, Geneva, International Labour Office.

Petkov, K. (1985) *Sotsiologiya na truda*, Profizdat, Sofia.

—— (1987) *The Transition to self-management in the socialist countries*, Georgi Dimitrov Research Institute, Sofia.

—— (1989) 'The causes of alienation', *World Marxist Review*, vol. 32, no. 10, October.

Petkov, K. and Kolev, B. (1982) *Sotsiologiya na trudoviya kolektiv*, Profizdat, Sofia.

Petkov, K. and Thirkell, J. E. M. (1987) *La organizacion del trabajo por brigados en Bulgaria*, Georgi Dimitrov Trade Union Research Institute, Sofia.

——(1988a) 'Managerial elections in Bulgaria: interests, conflicts and representation', *Labour and Society*, vol. 13, no. 3, pp. 306–18.

—— (1988b) 'Redesigning the self-managed enterprise', *Uchast Pracujucich na riadeni – suchasnost a perspektivy*, Dom techniku, Bratislava.

—— (1988c) *Brigadnaya organizatsiya truda: Bolgarskii opit*, Sofia Press, Sofia.

—— (1988d) *The brigade organization of work in Bulgaria*, Sofia Press, Sofia.

Petrochenko, P. F. and Kuznetsova, K. (1974) *Organizatsiy i normirovanie tryda v promishlenosti SSR*, Moscow.

Petrov, T.S. (1975) 'The programme of the Bulgarian communist party for the building of a communist society', in M. Isusov (ed.) *Problems of the transition from capitalism to socialism*, Bulgarian Academy of Sciences, Sofia.

—— (1987) 'Pojava i ytvrzhdavane na brigadnata organizatsiya na trud v blgariya, (1944-49g)', *Istoricheski pregled*, no. 9.

Pollert A. (1988) 'The flexible firm: fixation or fact?', *Work, Employment and Society*, vol. 2, no. 3, September.

Pravda (1988) 'Vremya trudnykh voprossov-Istoriya 20-30-kh godov i sovremennya obschestvennaya mysl, *Pravda*, Moscow, 30 September.

Pretsenka otnosno provedenie otcheti i izbori na organite na samoupravlenie (1986) Sofia.

Prodanov, V. (1988) *Personality and politics*, Partizdat, Sofia.

Profsiosite i samoupraveneto (1988) Sofia, no. 5.

Rus, V. (1984) 'Yugoslav self-management – 30 years later', in B. Wilpert and A. Sorge (eds) *International perspectives on organisational democracy*, John Wiley & Sons, Chichester.

Rusinow, D. (1977) *The Yugoslav experiment 1948–1974*, C. Hurst, London.

Russky yazik (1987) *Russian–English dictionary of socio-political terms*, Russky yazik, Moscow.

Rutland, P. (1986) 'Productivity campaigns in Soviet industry' in D. Lane (ed.) *Labour and employment in the USSR*, Harvester Press, Brighton.

Shkaratan, O. I. (1978) *Promishlenoe predpriatie*, Misl, Moscow.

Siegelbaum, L. H. (1982) 'Socialist competition and socialist construction in the USSR, the experience of the first 5 year plan (1928–32)', *Thesis Eleven*, vol. 4.

—— (1986) 'Production collectives and communes and the "Imperatives" of Soviet industrialisation 1929–31', *Slavic Review*, vol. 45.

—— (1988) *Stakhanovism and the politics of productivity in the USSR 1935–1941*, Cambridge University Press., Cambridge.

Slider, D. (1987) 'The brigade system in Soviet industry: an effort to restructure the labour force', *Soviet Studies*, vol. XXXIX, no. 3, July.

Solokov, K. (1931) *Socialist Competition*, Centrizdat, Moscow.

Soos, K. A. (1987) 'Wage bargaining and the policy of grievances: a contribution to the explanation of the first halt in the reform of the Hungarian economic mechanism 1969', *Soviet Studies*, vol. XXXIX, no. 3, July.

Sotsiologicheski problemi (1983) 'Sotsiologiya i upravlenie' (razgovor okolo kraglata masa), Sofia, no. 4.

Szakolczai, G. and Meszaros, J. (1988) 'Changes in the role of the trade unions in Hungary', *Labour and Society*, vol. 13, no. 1, January.

Tadjer, V. (1983) 'Legal problems of the labour collective', *Socialist Law*, 5, (in Bulgarian).

Ternovszky, F. (1989) 'Wage and performance bargaining in economic work partnerships within enterprises', in L. Hethy, M. Lado, and J. E. M. Thirkell, (eds) *New collective forms of work organization in Eastern Europe*, Institute of Labour Research, Budapest.

Thirkell, J. E. M. (1985) 'Brigade organisation and industrial relations strategy in Bulgaria, 1978–83', *Industrial Relations Journal*, vol. 16, no. 1.

Thompson, J. D. (1967) *Organisations in action*, McGraw-Hill Book Company, New York.

Thompson, P. (1983) *The nature of work: an introduction to debates on the labour process*, Macmillan, London.

Tilkidzhiev, N. (1989) *Sotsialni grupi*, Nauka i Izkustvo, Sofia.

Tito, J. B. (1980) Address in June 1950, quoted in B. Boskovic and D. Dasić (eds) *Socialist self-management in Yugoslavia 1950-80*, Socialist Thought and Practice, Belgrade.

Tomov, A. (1987) *Socialisation and democratic centralism*, Partizdat, Sofia.

Tremblay, M. A. (1982) 'The key informant technique: a non-ethnographic application' in R. G. Burgess (ed.) *Field research: a source book and field manual*, George Allen & Unwin, London.

Trocsanyi, L. (1986) *Fundamental problems of labour relations in the law of the European socialist countries*, Akademiai Kiado, Budapest.

Trudovijat Kolektiv – Stopanin na Sotsialisticheskata Sobstvenost (1987), Partizdat, Sofia.

Tsonev, N. (1982) *Konkurst i ozborit pri izdiganeto na stopanskite kadri*, Partizdat, Sofia.

Tyagay, Y. (1956) *Ekonomika promyshlennosti SSR*, Moscow.

Van Velsen, J. (1964) *The politics of kinship among the Tonga of central Africa*, Manchester University Press.

—— (1967) 'The extended case method of situational analysis' in A. L. Epstein, (ed.) *The craft of social anthropology*, Tavistock, London.

Vitak, R. (1971) 'Workers' control in Czechoslovakia' in J. Vanek (ed.) (1975) *Self-management: economic liberation of man*, Penguin, Harmondsworth.

Volkov, Yu. E. (1965) *Kak rozhdaetsya kommunisticheskoe samoupravlenie*, Misl, Moscow.

Voprosi istorii (1988), no. 3.

Vrtiak, V. (1989) 'Collective forms of work organisation in Czechoslovakia' in L. Hethy, M. Lado, and J. E. M. Thirkell, (eds) *New collective forms of work organization in Eastern Europe*, Institute of Labour Research, Budapest.

Wolnicki, M. (1989) 'Self-government and ownership in Poland' *Telos*, no. 80.

Yanchev, B. (1984) 'Sebektite na proizvodstvenite otnosheniya pri sotsialisma', *Novo vreme*, Sofia, no. 11, p. 30.

Zaslavskaya, T. (1986) 'Cheloecheskii faktor razvitiya ekonomiki i sotsialnaya spravedlivost', *Kommunist*, no. 13.

Zdravomyslov, A. G., Rozhin, V. P. and Iadov, V. A. (1967) *Chelovek i ego rabota*, Moscow.

Zhivkov, T. (1975) *Izbrani sachineyiya*, Partizdat, Sofia, vol. 9.

—— (1976a) 'Osnovi nasoki za pro-natatashnoto razvitie na sistemata na upravlenie na nasheto obshtestvo', *Izbrani sachineniya*, Partizdat, Sofia, vol. 15.

—— (1976b) *Izbrani sachineniya*, vol. III, Partizdat, Sofia, vol. 20.

—— (1977) 'Za usvrshenstuvane na planovoto rukovodstovo na ikonomikata na socialisticheskata organizatiya na trud', *Ikonomichkata politika na Bulgarskata kommunistichka partija*', vol. III, Partizdat, Sofia.

—— (1981a) *Report of the Central Committee of the Bulgarian Communist Party*, Sofia Press, Sofia.

—— (1981b) *Report of the CC of BTU to the 12th party congress and the forthcoming tasks of the party*, Partizdat, Sofia.

—— (1982) *A new conception of labour and labour relations in socialist Bulgaria*, Sofia Press, Sofia.

—— (1984) 'Osnovni polozheniya na partiynata kontseptsiya', *Izbrani sachineniya*, Partizdat, Sofia.

—— (1987a) *The cause we have taken up is a revolutionary cause*, Sofia Press, Sofia.

—— (1987b) *The work collectives – sovereign masters*, Sofia Press, Sofia.

—— (1987c) *Some practical methods and approaches for further implementation of decisions of the July 1987 Plenum of the CC of BCP*, Sofia Press, Sofia.

Znanie-sila (1982) 'Uroki samoupravleniya', Moscow, no. 6.

Index

Aburdene, P., on middle management 81
action field, concept of 66–7
administrative command system 15
Adizes, I. 150, 177, 178
agreements 123–31 *passim*; at Baltic shipyard 26–8; as mechanism 205–6; under NEP 20
aktiv 166–7; political *aktiv* in Yugoslavia 178
Andors, S., on middle level of management in Cultural Revolution 82
Andropov, Yu, and, self-management 192
alienation 5, 168–71
Aroyo, Y. 143–4
assembly enterprise 68–9; counterplanning 97–8; elections 137, 141; introduction of brigade organisation 78
Assessment and Conflict Commission, 20
associated labour 44, 179
association of producers 44, 175
Atkinson, J., and core and periphery 164

Bailey, F. G., and concept of 'field' 66
Bailes, K. E. 20–1
Baltic shipyard, Leningrad 26–8, 73, 91
Basic Organisation of Associated Labour (BOAL) 179–80
Baum, A. T. 24
Baykov, A. C., on *khozraschet* 38

Bell, D. 74
Bertsch, G. 40
Bettelheim, C. 20
Boev, V. 32
Bogdanov, A. A. on 'proletarian collective' 20–1
Bosković, B. 176
Botev, B., and 'problem situations' 61
Braverman, H., and the labour process 4–5, 160–1, 168–9
brigade organisation in Bulgaria: brigade as primary collective 51–2; complex brigades 77; design criteria 74–6; introduction of brigade organisation 72–81; Party Conference of 1978 42; responses of management 84–8; responses of workers 86; specialist brigades 77; *see also under* enterprises
brigade organisation in Czechoslovakia 193
brigade organisation in Soviet Union: in War Communism 18; in 1928–31 25–8; in 1970s and 1980s 192–3
Bukharin, N., and gradual transition to socialism 19
Burawoy, M., and the labour process 5, 27, 160–2, 164, 187, 208
Butenko, G. A. 18, 46

Carr, E. H., on centralised planning 22
Chndler, A. D. 10, 13
Chemicals combine, 69; agreements 125; counterplanning 98–9; director's salary 117–18; elections

135–6, 141; introduction of brigade organisation 78; party members in brigade 168

clothes hanger model of enterprise structure 83

Cocks, P. 74

co-efficient of labour participation 112–14

Cohen, S. 19

collective agreements *see* agreements

collective bargaining 219

collective labour relations *see* labour relations

Comisso, E. T. 63

community: and collective 146–9; and organic mechanisms 156–9

Components enterprise 152–3

Confederation of Independent Bulgarian Trade Unions 213–15, 218–9

Consumer Electronics enterprise 154, 158

core and core–periphery relations 164–8, 220; frontrankers as core 92–3; Stakhanovites as core 30

counterplanning 88–102 *passim*; at Karl Marx factory 25–6; as a mechanism 205

Cziria, L. 193

Crenson, M. A. 62

Csuhaj, I. 188, 217, 218, 220

Czechoslovakia: brigades 193; concept of self-management 182; factory councils 32; post-revolutionary developments 216, 221; State Enterprise Act (1988) 193

Danube river docks and elections 142

Dasić, D. 176

Davies, R. W., on centralised planning 22

Decree 56 60, 171, 210

democratic centralism in industrial organisation 22–3

department level in Bulgarian enterprise 141–5

design criteria *see* brigade organisation

Deutscher, I. 16, 17

division of labour 5; and core–periphery 165; and hierarchy 169–70; and technology 171

Djilas, M. I. and concept of self-management in Yugoslavia 174–5

Drulović, M. 177

duality of structures 7

dynamics of the enterprise *see* organisational dynamics

Dyulgerov, P. 43

edinonachalie 17–18, 23–4, 33–4

elections 132–45 *passim* 206; in Hungary 189; in Soviet Union 181

Engels, F., on authority 144

episodes: concept of 66; examples of 151–4

events, concept of 66

extended case study method 61–7, 204

factory committees in Soviet Union 16–17, 18

factory Councils: in Bulgaria 32; in Soviet Union 14

Flanders, A. 146

Fox, A., on collectivity 148, 149

frontrankers 30, 92, 94–5, 207

functional foremanship 29

Galbraith, J. R. 7; on organisational design 5–6

Gastev, A., and Taylorism 20–1

Gerchikov, V. I. 193, 195

Giddens, A. 7

Granick, D. 22–3

group ownership of property *see* property

Grozdanić, S. 177

Gustavsen, B. 81, 83

Haraszti, M. 162, 186

Harris, C. C., on interests 10

Heavy Engineering enterprise 69; agreements 127; brigade organisation and the labour process 163–4; core–periphery relations 167; counterplanning 98; elections 140–1; managerial strategy and brigade organisation 78–9; organic mechanisms 150–1, 156; party membership in brigades 168; restructuring of intermediate level 82

Hethy, L. 217, 218, 220: and assertion of interests 10; on strategic informers 64; and study of construction industry 63, 65; and study of the Raba factory 63, 65, 104, 108, 186; on values and interests 157

Holmes, L.T., and synoptic and incremental models 40–1

Horvat, B., and self-management 147, 180

hot spot, concept of 90, 91, 93, 95, 100

Hungary: enterprise autonomy 183–4, 199; enterprise councils 188–9; post-revolutionary developments 216–18; strategy formulation 199; VGMKs 187–8

Iadov, V. A. 162

incidents, concept of 66; and organic mechanisms 151

incremental model of strategy formulation *see* strategy formulation

individual labour relations *see* labour relations

International Labour Office (ILO) 177

interests: administrative command model 37; and community 51; concept of 10–11; hot spots 90; levels of in the enterprise 81; theory of distribution 121–2

Jackson-Cox, J. i, 40

Janowska, Z. 191

Kadar, J. 184

Kaluga Turbine Plant 192

Kapeliush, I. S., on elections 181

Kapferer, B., defining concept of action field 66

Kaplan, F. I. 16

Karatanchev, S. 32

Kardelj, E. 175

Karl Marx factory, Leningrad 25–6

Kerzhentsev, P. 40

key informants, concept of 64, 67, 68, 165

khozain 47, 193

khozraschet 19, 38–9 n1

Kidrić, B. 175

Kolaja, J. 181

Kolev, B. i, 147

Komsomol and First Five-Year Plan 24–5

Kornai, J. 90, 103, 116, 119

Kuibyshev, V., 42

Kulpinska, J. 191

Kuromiya, H., on *edinonachalie* 24

Kuznetsova, K. Kh. 20

Kyuranov, Ch. 11, 46

Labour Code, Bulgaria: (1951) 33, 104; (1986), agreements 126–7, criteria for brigade organisation 74–6, distinction between primary and main collective 51, drafting of 54–6, elections 134

Labour Code, Czechoslovakia 193

Labour Code, Hungary 185

labour collective in Bulgaria: concept of 43–7; distinction between primary and main collective 50–2; and labour community 146–9, 156–9; as *stopanin* 47–50

labour community 51; collective and 146–9, 156–9

labour process: and alienation 168–71; concept of 4–5, 160; core-periphery relations 164–6; labour process in socialist societies 160–3; and ownership 207–8

labour relations: in the administrative command model 37; in Bulgaria 49–50; collective 2–3; concept of 2–3; individual 2; socialist 3–4; in the Soviet Union First and Second Five-Year Plan models 30

Lado, M. 188

Laky, T. 90

Lane, D., on the labour process 161

Lawrence, P. R. 5

Lee, D. J., on community 146

Lenin, V. I., and competition 24; and differentials 119; and *edinonachalie* 17; on Taylorism

20; and trade unions 17; and worker's control 16

Lorsch, J. W. 5

Lozovsky, S. A., on workers' control 16

McQueeney, J. i 40; and self-regulating mechanisms 205

main collective 51–2; and organic mechanisms 153–5

majstor 37, 92

Makarenko, P., defining labour collective 44–5

Mako, C.: and enterprise councils 189; and influence of VGMK 219; on interests 11, 187; and the labour process 163; and study of the Raba factory 63, 65, 104, 108, 186

Malle, S. 17, 18

Markov, M. 32

Marinov, A. and 'problem situations' 61

Marx, K., and alienation 169; and associated labour 44; and the division of labour 3; and labour relations 1; and ownership 4

Masterman, M., on paradigms 13n

Mateev, E. 109

Materials enterprise 127, 144–6, 151

mechanisms: atrophy of 24, 125, 211; imposed mechanisms, concept of 7; sequence and timing of 89t; and interests 11, 206–7; mechanisms and structures 87, 204–7; organic mechanisms 150–6, concept of 7–8; self-regulating mechanisms 205; *see also* agreements; co-efficient of labour participation; counterplanning and elections

Meszaros, J. 184, 189

Metals combine 69; absence of organic mechanisms 155–6; agreements 126; counterplanning 100–10, 176; elections 136–7, 142; introduction of brigade organisation 140; managerial strategy 79–81, synoptic approach 204; trade union *aktiv* 171; transfer of property 130–1

Mikhailov, G 45

Miloshevski, A. 34

Miloushev, Z. (brigade leader) 51, 128–9, 151

Minchev, M. 32

Mitchell, J. C. on extended case study method 63, 65

model, concept of 11–12

Mrachkov, V. 56, 130

MSZOSC 217

multifactor wage system 108

nachalnik 37, 92, 94–5

Naisbitt, J. H., on middle management 81

Nathanson, D. A. 7

Neumann, L. and VGMKs 188

New conception of labour and labour relations in socialist Bulgaria 2, 42, 59

New Economic Mechanism 43

New Economic Policy (NEP) 18–21, 23, 31, 36–41, 44, 57, 60, 70

Newby, H., on community 146

Nikolayev, A. (brigade leader) 26–8, 73

Nikitin, V. A. 193

Nisbet, R. A., on community 146

nomenklatura, and elections 133–4

normative regulation: concept of 8; at national level in Bulgaria 53–7, 203

Nosach, B. 18

Nove, A. 38

operativka 35–6, 144, 166

organisational design 5–9; initial level of redesign 42, 174; and primary concept 41, 43, 60, 202; and organisational space 158

organisational dynamics: and agreements 130; in centralised model 34–5; concept of 20–3; core–periphery relations 165–6; and mechanisms 88; pressure from below 88–91, 117–19

Party organisation: in centralised model 35–6, 92; counterplanning 94; elections 133–4, 144; introduction of brigade

organisation 84–5; and labour relations 49; party members and core 168; and self-management 196
periphery *see* core–periphery
Pasic, N. 177
Petkov, K., i, 125, 142, 147,151, 154 171, 197
Petrov, T. S., 32
Petrochenko, P. F. 20
piece-work 29, 105
plan bargaining 90; *see also* hot spots
Podkrepa 211, 212–15, 222
Poland: absence of brigades 191; self-management 181, 190–1; Solidarity 190, 199, 222
Pollert, A. 165
Popov, G. and 'administrative system' 15
pressure from below *see* organisational dynamics
primary collective 51–2
primary concept *see* organisational design
privatisation as primary design concept 220
Prodanov, V. 58
production communes 25
Production Conference 20, 35, 37
production relations 7–9
prototypes, concept of 12
property: group ownership of 16, 46, 109, 183, 208; Social 128, 176; Transfer of 54, 127–30, 169–71

Regulation on Economic Activity 53–4, 56
Rodevic, M. 177
Rozhin, V. P. 162
Rus, V. on collective and community 147–8, 163; on work teams 180
Ruse experiment, in elections 133–4
Rusinow, D. 179, 208
Rutland, P. 61

scientific organisation of work 21, 53, 105, 130, 162–3
self-management: Bulgaria, self-managed brigades 75–6, self-managed society and community 40, 158, structure of

self-managed enterprise 51–2; Czechoslovakia 182–3; labour-managed and Managerial models 172, 194–6, 200f; Poland 181, 190–1; Soviet Union 181, 192–3
Shkaratan, O. I. 45
shock work 17–18, 24
Siegelbaum, L. H. 29
Sik, O. 182
situational analysis 70–1
Slider, D. 192
social property *see* property
socialist emulation: in Bulgaria 32–3, 37; in Soviet Union 24, 27
socialist labour relations *see* labour relations
socialist organisation of work 42
socialist property *see* property
Solidarity 190, 199, 222
Solokov, K., on Counterplanning at Karl Marx factory 25–6
Soos, K. A. 186
space, organisational *see* organisational design
Stakhanov, A. G. 29, 32
Stakhanovites, as core 30
Stalin J. V. on planning 22
stopanin, concept of 47; *see also under* labour collective
stopanska smetka 38n, 129
strategy, concept of 6–7
strategy formulation: concept of 6, 40; integration or separation of economic organisation and labour relations in strategy formulation 15, 21, 30, 31; labour-managed and managerial models 197–200; models of societal development 31, 58–60; at national level in Bulgaria 41–6; at enterprise level 78–81; synoptic and incremental models of 41, 58, 198–201; trade union strategy formulation in post-revolutionary conditions 212–16
Streziminska, H. 191
Strumilin, S., on planning 22
subbotniks 12, 17, 31
synoptic model of strategy formulation *see* strategy

formulation
Szakolczai, G. 184, 189
SZOT 217

Tadjer, V. 46
tariff scales 104
Taylorism 20, 29, 160–1
Ternovszky, F. 188
Textiles enterprise 69–70;
    counterplanning 99; elections
    137–7, 141; introduction of brigade
    organisation 77; organic
    mechanisms 150, 153–4, absence
    of 155; party members in the
    brigade 168
theorising xiv–xv, 64–5
Thirkell, J. E. M. i, 1, 40, 134, 136,
    155, 197
Thompson, P., on the labour process
    161
Tilkidzhiev, N. 147
Tito, J. B. 175–6
Tomov, A. 59
Toth, F. 188
trade unions in Bulgaria: agency of
    organisational redesign 85–6;
    counterplanning 96; elections 135,
    144; as organiser of the labour
    collective 43; post-revolutionary
    strategy formulation 212–16; and
    societal development 221–2; under
    centralised model 36–7
trade unions in Soviet Union:
    administrative command model
    23–4, 35–37; NEP. 19–20; War
    Communism 16–17
transfer of property *see* property
Tremblay, M. A. defining key
    informants 64
Trenchev, K. 211, 219, 222
tripartism 215, 216, 221–2
Trocsanyi, L., and individual labour
    relations 2
Trotsky, L. D., and brigades 18; and
    trade unions 17
tsekh 35, 37
Tsonev, N. 133–4

udarnichestvo see shock work
uravnilovka 117, 119–21, 205

Van Velsen, J., and situational
    analysis 64, 70
Varna Docks Brigade 151–2, 173
Vesenkha 17, 19
VGMKs 171, 187–8, 197, 219
Vitak, R. 182, 183
Volga automobile plant 192
Volkov, Yu. E, on self-management
    181–2
Vrtiak, V. 320
Vukmanović-Tempo, S. 176

wage ceiling 105
wage fund: brigade 111, 112, 125;
    enterprise 103, 106, 109, 117–18,
    121
War Communism 15–18, 31
Wolnicki, M. 191
worker proposals 90–102 *passim*;
    secondary mechanism 205, 207; in
    Soviet Union 26

workers' control: and Bolsheviks 16,
    18; in Bulgaria 32; and
    edinonachalie 24
Workers' Opposition 17

Yanchev, B. 46
Yugoslavia: basic organisation of
    associated labour 179–80; design
    sequence 180; political origin of
    self-management 174–6; political
    aktiv 178; strategy formulation 58,
    176, 179, 198–9
Zaslavskaya, T., and the human factor 2
Zdrovomyslav, A. G. 162
Zhivkov, T.: and appointment of
    managers 43; on labour collective
    as stopanin 43, 47; *New
    conception of labour and labour
    relations* 2, 42; and
    self-management 40; and status of
    policy statements 60n; and transfer
    of property 54, 127–8